LEADING TH
ORGANISATION
TO LEARN

LEADING THE ORGANISATION TO LEARN

The 10 levers for putting knowledge and learning to work

MICK COPE

FINANCIAL TIMES
PITMAN PUBLISHING

FINANCIAL TIMES

MANAGEMENT

LONDON · SAN FRANCISCO
KUALA LUMPUR · JOHANNESBURG

*Financial Times Management delivers the knowledge,
skills and understanding that enable students,
managers and organisations to achieve their ambitions,
whatever their needs, wherever they are.*

London Office:
128 Long Acre, London WC2E 9AN
Tel: +44 (0)171 447 2000
Fax: +44 (0)171 240 5771
Website: www.ftmanagement.com

A Division of Financial Times Professional Limited

First published in Great Britain 1998

© Financial Times Professional Limited 1998

The right of Mike Cope to be identified as
Author of this Work has been asserted by him in accordance
with the Copyright, Designs, and Patents Act 1988.

ISBN 0 273 63524 7

British Library Cataloguing in Publication Data
A CIP catalogue record for this book can be obtained
from the British Library.

1 3 5 7 9 10 8 6 4 2

Typeset by Northern Phototypesetting Co. Ltd, Bolton
Printed and bound in Great Britain by
Redwood Books Ltd, Trowbridge, Wilts.

*The Publishers' policy is to use paper manufactured
from sustainable forests.*

About the Author

Mick Cope is an organisational development consultant with 15 years of experience in the field of business transformation. As a consultant, he has had practical experience in managing both the back and front office activities across a range of OD programmes. This experience includes project management, change management, total quality, ISO 9000, process management, Investors in People, European Quality Award, Stephen Covey seven habits, and a wide range of personal development programmes. He has published widely in the fields of organisational learning, knowledge management, workshop design, change management and personal development and is a regular speaker at international conferences.

He can be contacted by e-mail at MickCope@BTInternet.com, and actively welcomes feedback on the concepts offered in this book.

First of all, to someone that truly embodies the spirit of life-long learning, the authoress Janet Kite.

Most of all to Linda, Michael, Joe and Lucy – without your help we could never have got this far.

Contents

Part 3 · Interaction

Part 4 · Infrastructure

Part 5 · Intent

Preface

Of all the ideas offered in this book, the most cherished is that effective organisational learning cannot be realised without enhancing the individual's capability to learn and interact with other people. Unless companies can unleash the power and potential that resides within and between its people, then the notion of company-wide learning and knowledge creation might remain as a vague but inspirational goal in the corporate objectives.

As an experiment, the reader might consider their organisation and answer the question, on a score of one to ten: to what extent has the company released the full and untapped potential of all its people? The arrogant proposition might be that in the vast majority of cases, companies aspire for eight, reach seven (in some areas), and generally average around five or six. This is a shame, because when individuals are considered in totality, it suddenly turns out that in their spare time they climb mountains, dive the oceans for buried treasure, play the stock market or lead charity convoys to war zones – demonstrating capability and motivation that is unseen by the employer. What then if this capability and potential is harnessed at work, and the score is increased by just one or two points? How would this affect the effectiveness of the individual, the productiveness of the team and the performance of the business? Any reluctance to address this issue means that the organisation continues to pay out for vast amounts of untapped resources and talent, and is committing a cardinal commercial sin by under-utilising one of its key assets. Like buying a kilo of apples from the green-grocer and arriving home to find that the bag only contains 500g.

A second mind experiment might be carried out, to ask to what extent do people have the capability or desire to interact effectively – to learn and create knowledge through the use of synthesis? This point is succinctly set out by Covey (1992) when he talks about the importance of interdependence – the collective view that 'we can', rather than 'I can', thus operating in a collaborative rather than competitive mode. However, this isn't the soft and fluffy view of collaboration, where group and tree hugging are the de-facto standard: this is collaboration where a balance of courage and consideration is required.

Hence the bedrock of the learning model offered in this book stresses the importance of the individual and interaction. If these two aspects are not understood and considered by an organisation, then no amount of measurement, marketing, or management effort will bring about change in how the business learns and shares its knowledge.

This book is aimed primarily at those people who are interested in the idea of organisational learning and knowledge management, but have been unable to find any tangible models that will help them to investigate the phenomena in their own organisation. The core benefits will be to:

- offer a bridge that links the ideas of personal development and individual learning with the corporate perspective of organisational learning;
- offer a simple diagnostic framework that can be applied across all levels and divisions within a business;
- introduce a range of new analytical models that can be used to understand learning within the organisation;
- offer a bridge between the fields of knowledge management and organisational learning;
- develop a methodology that can help organisations investigate the use of possibility space as a way to consider new and unique ways of learning.

The idea for this book originated while the author was undertaking a literature review as part of a research programme on organisational knowledge flow. One of the primary conclusions to emerge from the review was the apparent fragmentation and confusion that exists in this field. The wide range of authors' viewpoints, consultancy models, and business experiences has created a management topic that people are excited about but often struggle to integrate and enact. Although most people appreciate that knowledge will be the key currency in the twenty-first century, fewer can get a firm grasp of the specific impact on their organisation, and how they and their people can become involved in enhancing the capability to learn.

In attempting to resolve this situation, this book seeks to deliver the following:

Consistency

To offer a framework that can fashion a degree of consistency and alignment across the field of organisational learning and knowledge management. Importantly, to build a harmonious model that clearly indicates how the various authors' works complement each other while developing a number of new diagnostic frameworks.

Clarity

The Integrated Learning Model offered in this book tries to create a sense of crispness around the idea of organisational learning and to do so in such a way that allows it to be understood by a wide range of people. Although the model has many component parts, it has been constructed in such a way that makes it easy for the reader to gain a solid and practical appreciation of organisational learning and knowledge management, and more importantly, what it might look or feel like in the reader's organisation.

Communication

As organisations embark on the learning journey, it can be difficult to communicate core ideals and desired outcomes. Often, *'those in the know'* have the dream of influencing a change in the culture, but trying to communicate this to everyone in the business can be difficult because learning is inherently such a subjective activity. As the message is cascaded and disseminated across the organisation, the learning objectives can become diluted, distorted and wrapped up in political intrigue. The resulting message can end up being presented as a series of sweeping corporate statements, built around platitudes and non-specific actions that don't give people a real feel for the end goal.

The book has been written as a 'guide book' to help people develop a personal interpretation of the roots and benefits of organisational learning and knowledge management. Crucially, a guide book doesn't tell people where to go or what to do, but it does help them to get a flavour of the terrain and what journeys might be taken. In the same way, this book doesn't attempt to tell people what to do; rather, it guides them to areas that might be of interest and offers a basic framework that will help people to build a view of how learning might be improved in their area.

Change ethos

Of all the disciplines that a manager has to master, change is probably the most difficult and frustrating. Importantly, this book does not seek to offer the definitive wisdom on how to 'implement learning', as this is a false god to which too many people and organisations aspire. However, it does offer a framework by which organisations can start to understand the potential relationships between change and learning.

There are possibly too many business books on the market that are prepared to offer miracle cures for the price of a Chinese meal. If it is really that simple to realise significant cultural change, then all management ills would have been cured years ago, and the UK's productivity would be climbing through the roof. The simple fact is that one company's organisational success cannot be readily transplanted into others; they operate in different contexts, have different people, and dream different dreams. Hence, this book does not advocate what people should do to enhance their learning processes. It simply offers people the chance to understand an idea of organisational learning from a pragmatic point of view. Once people understand a basic framework, then the hard work starts and they have to look inside their own team or business to understand what actions they can take to develop a more adaptive and reflective style of working.

One thing that will become apparent is the deliberate avoidance of case studies. Although this might be seen as acting counter to the style that currently pervades the business book market, there are four compelling reasons for taking this approach:

Cloning

Imagine it is Christmas and a child is given a brand new set of Lego bricks. In the box is a guide on the different type of buildings and instructions on how they should be constructed. On Boxing Day morning, across the country, there are likely to be thousands of neat little Lego houses, all looking remarkably similar in shape and design. Now consider the child that was given a set of bricks without any instructions. The end result is likely to be unique. Hence, this offers a simple view of the in-built tendency to use a clone and copy-cat mentality that reduces the level of diversity and variety in the creative process.

This cloning mentality can often be seen in management as the bow-wave that trails the launch of a new management model. Consider what happened as total quality, process re-engineering, and Investors in People increased in popularity and penetration. A bow wave effect could be seen in the Sunday papers as companies scrabbled to climb on the change bandwagon and recruit people who could do 'it' for them as well. Hence, the aim of this book is not to offer neat tricks or approaches that other people have used in 'distinguished' case studies. The assumption is that organisations actually want, and need to be unique, and not just clones of other companies.

Time

One of the classic problems with any book, is how to give it both currency and longevity. People want to read about something that is current and in-vogue, but the author's goal is to offer a piece of work that can retain value over time. Unfortunately, as the book discusses later, the rampant pace of change makes it very difficult to find case studies that will pass the test of time. Consider some of the major case studies that have been used by management authors over the past decades. Within two or three years, many of the companies held up as paragons of virtue had collapsed, been taken over, or just faded into obscurity. The approach taken here is to strive for longevity rather than short-term stimulation. The content is focused on the underlying theories and principles of organisational learning and knowledge creation. The hope is that people will then use this to interpret and re-form the models as appropriate in their own context.

Social construction

It is amazing to look at so many business books, and to find the same organisations constantly being offered as the supreme experts in a particular area. Now, it might be that these companies are gods in the field of quality, customer service, or whatever, but the problem is that 'good' is a social construction, not an absolute. So whilst one person might believe that one brand of whisky is excellent, another might find it revolting. In the same way, although a group of authors or academics might believe that a particular company excels in a certain area, it might well be that some employees of the company would vigorously disagree with the idea, because they have first-hand experience of something totally different. As such, the essence in the book is not to argue or present a case for what is good or bad, just for what might be interesting or possible.

Principle not product

Often there is a great deal of confusion in the business world over the emergence of new management ideas. Consider the history of management theory, and it can be seen that almost every decade, a gripping new idea has emerged that people want to investigate:

- *Taylor* – Scientific management (1910s)
- *Mayo* – Hawthorne studies (1930s)
- *Weber* – Bureaucratic organisation (1940s)
- *Fiedler* – Contingency leadership (1950s)
- *Simon* – Decision-making (1950s)
- *Herzberg* – Job satisfaction (1950s)
- *Blake and Mouton* – Managerial grid (1960s)
- *Berne* – Transactional analysis (1960s)
- *Janis* – Groupthink (1970s)
- *Porter* – Five forces (1980s)
- *Schein* – Culture (1980s)
- *Juran, etc.* – Quality (1980s)
- *Senge* – Organisational learning (1990s)
- *Stewart* – Intellectual capital (1990s)

However, what often happens is that the principle offered by the author becomes clogged up and confused with the products that are used to deliver the change. Take, for example, the quality movement of the 1980s. As a base line principle, it is almost impossible to disagree with the view that enhanced quality will lead to improved customer satisfaction and hence improve financial performance. So long as a sense of balance is maintained, quality as a business objective is valid and long lasting. However, ask many people about quality, and they might talk about their problems with the ISO 9000 audit process, the total quality programme that failed, or the company that won the Malcolm Baldrige award and then had major problems. The difficulty is that the principle and product have been confused.

For this reason, this book attempts to concentrate on the underlying principles that can help an organisation to stimulate its ability to learn. It avoids taking the prescriptive view, and advocating certain milestones and practices that organisations should follow in order to become a 'learning organisation'. The way that any organisation enhances its ability to learn and manage knowledge will be particular to the business itself, the industry and the context in which it operates. It is not just a product that can be bolted on to the back of a current management system.

When the notion of knowledge management is debated, much of the discussion can centre around the social-technical issues covering the balance of people's desire to learn and the extent to which the organisation provides the appropriate platforms for them to satisfy the need. In this book, the decision has been taken to focus primarily on the social aspects and to consider how learning and knowledge management work from the perspective of individuals and their interaction with other people. This is not in any way because technical issues are not important, simply that any debate on the way that technology affects the learning process warrants a piece of work in its own right. This point is clearly made by Davenport and Prusak (1998) when they suggest that excessive focus on technology is the most common pitfall in knowledge management. People default to technology because it's easier to buy, implement and measure. However, the final chapter uses the Integrated Learning Model as a framework to understand the implications of IT on the learning process, and to consider what steps an organisation can take to avoid some of the common pitfalls.

Finally, upon completing the book, the reader may feel that something is missing, a topic area that is always included in the best organisational theory guides, that of measurement. This omission is deliberate. The purpose of the book is to focus upon the individual rather than the corporate view. Clearly measurement of the organisation's intellectual capital is important, and a process that needs to be undertaken. However, the proposition is that often companies can take the short-term view and focus on the measurement system before understanding how the activity can be improved. This tendency to focus on measurement can in the long run be detrimental because people are pressured into providing numbers for a process that is not truly embedded. As such 'pseudo change' becomes the norm, and a short-term, fadism mentality comes into play. Measuring the intellectual capital of the business is important, but not as important as actually increasing the value of the business by releasing the potential within all of its people. The aim is to move towards the idea of becoming a possibility-searching company where people with rich and diversified individual knowledge bases can create new wisdom through the streams of interconnecting networks (Nonaka and Takeuchi, 1995, 115).

In conclusion, the hope is that this book is accepted with the purity of heart and humility in which it is offered. Although the intention is always to offer ways and means, rather than musts and shoulds, this can be difficult when certain ideals and beliefs are felt with passion. So although parts of the book might appear to be directive in nature, if the reader ever feels that the style or content is offering the 'right solution', then it should be consigned to the waste bin, and flaming messages sent to MickCope@BTinternet.com.

To prepare yourself for the world that is coming you must understand why it will be different from what most experts tell you.

Rees-Mogg and Davidson (1997)

Acknowledgements

I am quite sure that many authors have the wonderful ability to sit down and create something that is coherent, concise and captivating with the greatest of ease – unfortunately I don't. Writing this book has been a torturous but rewarding experience; one where I have learnt about new theory, and myself, along the way.

To help this happen, many people have been around to help me, and many of them possibly don't realise the part they have played in helping the book to emerge. I would like to thank especially Paul Oliver for his never-ending wisdom, support and humour; Dr Lizzie Beesley for helping me to realise the importance of focused and succinct writing (not that I have achieved it yet); Dr Peter Smith, my MBA mentor, and John Watts (for making finance fun) from Anglia University; Professor Colin Carnall and the DBA team at Henley who helped open my eyes to a new way of thinking; Ed Percival, who gave me the energy and focus to write the book in the first place. Finally to two men, who, in Dr Stephen Covey's words, were transition figures in my years as a 'pole and holes' man in BT; Peter Madder-Smith and Bob Henstridge. Without their encouragement and coaching, I would never have started the learning journey. I would like to thank Trevor Baylis for helping me to appreciate the importance of invention within a learning environment.

Secondly, I would like to thank those people who made the time to review and comment on the early version of the material. These include my wife Linda Cope; Paul Burns, Dave Reid and John Davies (BT); Greg Davis and Sarah Rowe (Catalyst Development); Jon Thedham (TDM); and Karen Faires my initial proofreader who undertook the painful task of correcting my passionate desire to put a comma after every third word.

When undertaking anything like this, the emotional support provided by people who bear the brunt of the author's irritation, constant absence and propensity to wake up at three in the morning with 'another great idea that needs to be included' is crucial. I thank my wife Linda, and my children (Michael, Joe and Lucy) for their endearing and patient support. Also my in-laws Jan and Fred for understanding why I ignored them every Sunday morning when they came over to visit; and Gary Porter for letting me have time off from recording the next CD (copies available at discount from the author). However, the bad news is that I am about to start on the next book!

Finally, to the Financial Times Management team: especially Amelia for helping me to understand the publishing maze; Linda Dhondy for the project management; Tony Quinn for the editing; and most of all Pradeep Jethi, my editor, who had confidence in my ability to deliver when I didn't have it myself.

Part 1

Introduction

Chapter 1

Building the argument for learning

Just consider how hard it is to convince a 12-year-old boy of the benefit he would get from doing his homework, rather than doing a part-time job at the local green-grocer. The job gives him cash today, the homework only gives the potential promise of greater earning power a long way off. He sees only the current benefits, and is unable to comprehend what value understanding the rules of trigonometry will bring to him in later life. If this is the case, how is it possible to convince an individual, team or organisation of the benefits of taking a more adaptive approach to life now, rather than focusing just on the task and meeting this year's targets?

There is often a wide range of arguments used to advocate and stimulate a greater focus on the issue of organisational learning and knowledge management. These arguments might be grouped under three headings: practical, panic, or pseudo-religious. Imagine a consultancy firm trying to convince a company to think about the benefits associated with organisational learning. The firm's first approach might be based on the practical aspects, where it advocates the cost savings that can be realised from product enhancements, increased competitive advantage and improved morale. However, one risk with this approach is that organisations have often heard it so many times, that it can be received with a wall of scepticism. The next response might be to hook into the panic argument, whereby people are told that since the competitors are doing it, they will lose a competitive edge if they don't adopt the same approach. Lastly, if this doesn't work, the pseudo-religious mode comes into play as the presenter assumes the look of a supreme being, steps into *guru-pee* mode, (Percival 1997), and commands the group to 'spiritually transform' themselves because Mr or Mrs X (the leading author this year) said it is the right thing to do.

In adopting one of these approaches, the danger is that the proposition can become viewed as a product or project that the organisation can bolt on to achieve short-term gains. The moment this starts to happen, the idea is regarded as a finite initiative and will be seen as something that can be installed, implemented or indoctrinated into the organisation. The base proposition is that such a mind set can be counter-productive, and may result in short term pseudo-change rather than a long-term, cultural and commercial shift within the business.

In developing an argument for enhancing learning across the organisation, the stance taken in this book is to 'not' build one. In trying to make a case for change within the organisation, the actual process of developing the business case, growing senior management commitment, and building some grand transformation programme can be a destructive one. Learning is something that individuals and organisations do every minute of the day. Like breathing, eating, or drinking, learning is not a separate activity that needs to be sold, managed and budgeted for as part of the yearly review process. In the same way that individuals are being encouraged to adopt the philosophy of life-long learning, so organisations must see learning as a core business process, rather than something to focus on this year. It is something that organisations do constantly to survive and prosper in the market. However, although they might do it constantly, it doesn't mean they do it effectively.

In the same way that fish are the last ones to see the water, organisations can often be the final ones to recognise their learning disabilities. Just look at the examples of organisations and industries that have failed to adapt and respond to changes in the market-place. Compare a stock market listing for ten years ago with today's and see which companies have failed to stay in the race. To the outsider, it is often blatantly clear that a company is not learning to adapt to changes. To the organisation, a sense of learning blindness sets in where it is unable or unwilling to accept the external stimuli that indicates where things are wrong.

The base line proposition then is not to make a case for people to 'install' new learning systems, procedures and processes into the organisation, because this tends to drive a project or product mentally. If organisations are serious about learning as a competitive issue, then the first step might be to look inwards and ask three simple questions:

- *How do we learn?*
- *How do we share our learning or knowledge?*
- *How effective are we at using the resulting knowledge?*

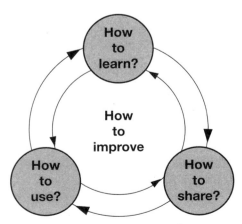

Fig. 1.1 Ask three simple questions as a first step to improving

4

Once considered, the next step is for the organisation to ask itself in each of these areas: how can we improve. Crucially, the emphasis is often on tuning something that already exists, not selling something new that can be applied like a plaster patch.

Therefore, at the end of each chapter is a review section that uses the model outlined in Fig. 1.1 and matches it against some of the dynamics that underpin each of the components. The suggestion is that the reader can use this as a simple process to take the book's concepts and recognise how they might be applied in a team or unit. So for example, at the end of the Soloist chapter, a matrix lists a number of dynamic themes that have emerged. Importantly, the list is not meant to be an exhaustive summary of all the topic area; it is simply an indication of some of the themes that have emerged. At each part of the matrix, the organisation can ask itself the question, for this particular aspect of the model: how do we learn, share and use knowledge? (See Table 1.1 on page 6.)

So for each of the components within the model, the organisation builds an understanding of:

- *How do we learn*, or in other words, how does this happen at present, what behaviour can be observed and how do people feel?
- *How do we share:* in what way is any positive learning outcome from this experience shared with other people in the organisation?
- *How do we use:* in what way is the learning being put to good use in the company, either as a commercial asset, or in enhancing the operational processes to develop future capability?

The review of each dynamic element is considered to understand what specific action might be taken to develop ways in which the organisation can be enhanced.

So, in answer to the conundrum posed at the start of the chapter, making a child go upstairs to do homework will not facilitate the long-term learning process. The boy might do it this once but as soon as the adult has left, he will probably revert to type. A better approach might be to help him to understand the nature of learning, and how it can enhance all aspects of life, including football, working at the green-grocer and school. Once understood, then there might be a greater chance that the child will respond to the idea of improving ability and willingness to learn, rather than being forced to improve in just one specific area. Consider this: does the school system teach children how to learn and share their knowledge, or does it focus purely on remembering a given set of facts without understanding what benefit they will offer? Even worse, does the school system foster a sharing or collaborate nature, or does it instigate and nurture a competitive spirit from an early age, one that promotes the idea of selfish learning?

Likewise, for an organisation, the focus might be on understanding that learning is a natural process. Hence it is important to take a holistic approach, and not

Table 1.1 Example responses to the questions

Soloist model dynamics	How do we learn?	How do we share?	How do we use?	How can we improve?
U-loop People talk openly about the tension and frustration of change	At present, emotions are generally dealt with in the manager review sessions, but they do seem to emerge in the informal groups	Problems with change are dealt with locally, and no sharing of mistakes or new ideas is transported across the organisation	When problems occur with change, it tends to be viewed as a problem, and must be fixed and forgotten. No learning is taken from the experience	Use focus groups, company publications and managerial review sessions to talk about how we manage change, and what can be done to make it easier to discuss
Continual learning People develop themselves in line with their goals and not just the company's	Although development is focused on business objectives, people are encouraged to change roles so as to broaden their knowledge	People are encouraged to share their experiences of changing jobs and developing new skills, but they tend to be quite insular	Individual growth is of benefit to the company, but possibly not maximised as much as it might be	Develop a greater understanding of the way in which individual growth can be harnessed by the organisation to develop its total capability
Etc ...				

6

to try to just install a new product or practice. If there is a true desire to enhance the organisation's collaborative ability to create and share knowledge, then the most effective way to achieve this might be by making the implicit learning process explicit, and not by launching into a mass programme that is designed to install new working methods.

So, in presenting the Integrated Learning Model (ILM), the idea is not to propose a new way of working, or to suggest that there is one right way for an organisation to learn and create knowledge. The model's primary purpose is to give people an integrated framework that can help them to understand their learning and knowledge systems, and from this to develop ways in which they might be improved.

Chapter 2

··

The learning– knowledge link

Davenport and Prusak (1998) argue that without an approach to managing structured knowledge, organisational learning is too conceptual and abstract to make a long-term difference to organisations. This book aims to offer just what people interested in organisational learning might need – a structured and simple model that will help make sense of the learning processes within their organisation. However, it is important to conceptually understand where the model fits within the current literature on organisational learning and knowledge management. In essence, it attempts to build a bridge between the ideas and concepts offered in these two schools of thought as seen in Fig. 2.1.

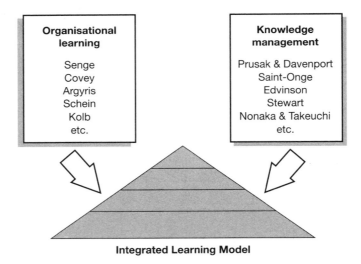

Integrated Learning Model

Fig. 2.1 The Integrated Learning Model: a bridge

Particular reference should be made to Peter Senge, whose book *The Fifth Discipline* woke the world up to the idea of organisational learning as a commercial issue, and Dr Stephen Covey who brings out the emphasis that must be placed on the individual rather than the corporate body. Second, the work of a range of authors must be highlighted (Prusak, Saint-Onge, Edvinson and Stewart, etc.), who were some of the early advocates for the power of knowledge management and intellectual capital. Although they use a model that offers a connection between the value of human, customer and structural capital, it is the idea of human capital that is focused on in this book. A key ethos is that people are the source of innovation and renewal within an organisation, and if this asset base is abused, or ignored, then the long-term future of the organisation may well be damaged (Stewart, 1997).

However, if an organisation is serious about enhancing its capability to learn and share knowledge, then these two factors alone might not be sufficient to really understand all the key levers. The proposition is that other organisational and management theories need to be considered so that a true holistic picture of learning and knowledge management can be developed. These would include ideas from authors who cover the fields of complexity theory, innovation, change management, people development, strategy development, organisational psychology and sociology as shown in Fig. 2.2.

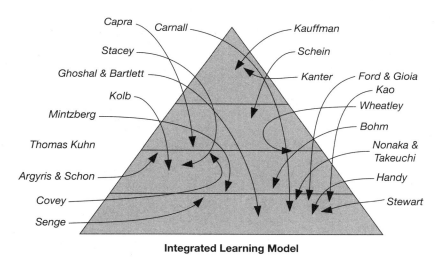

Integrated Learning Model

Fig. 2.2 Integrated Learning Model: source drivers

In developing such a model, the idea is not to give 'the right answer', but to create a framework for people and organisations to start the process of finding their own questions and answers; to understand how they learn, how they share and how they use their knowledge.

Chapter 3

Integrated Learning Model

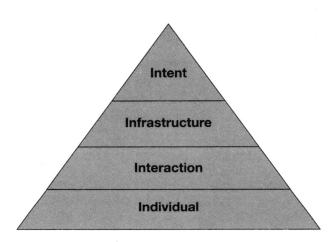

Fig. 3.1 The Integrated Learning Model

The Integrated Learning Model is constructed along two dimensions. First are the four core themes that provide the basic structure. These outline the principles that underlie the model and also provide the link point to the next layers. The four core principles are:

Individual

The key to maintaining a competitive presence in future markets will be through the generation, generalisation and embodiment of knowledge as intellectual capital. This value is derived from the knowledge-based intangibles that people add, such as technological know-how, product design, and close customer relationships. Hence, in an industry and society that is based upon learning and knowledge, the knowledge worker is the organisation's single greatest asset (Nonaka and Takeuchi, 1995).

Interaction

In seeing the organisation as a system, emphasis should not be placed on the component parts, but on the nature of the connectivity between the people. In considering this point of view, the Integrated Learning Model considers three areas of interaction that affect the process of knowledge creation and diffusion: the hidden or shadow features; the nature of self-organisation; and the importance of the socialisation process.

Infrastructure

This describes the process by which knowledge is transported through the organisation. Two areas are considered: the knowledge structure that underpins the transfer and embodiment; and the diffusion process that knowledge follows when being socialised.

Intent

If an organisation makes a declaration that learning and knowledge creation are important, then the strategy it chooses to facilitate its delivery is of critical importance. Simply dictating what people should do, building systems, and constructing intricate measures will not achieve the desired outcome. Any resulting strategy might need to focus on the principles of emergence, non-linearity and open-ended change, rather than deterministic outcomes, rigid milestones, and a centralist, driven approach.

In taking a closer look at the granularity of the Integrated Learning Model, each core principle has a series of supporting components that help describe it in more detail. This forms into the ten-component Integrated Learning Model that unfolds throughout the book.

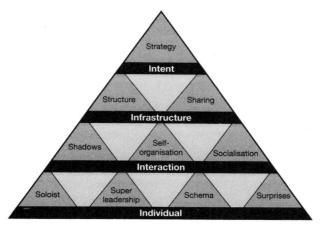

Fig. 3.2 The total Integrated Model

The Integrated Model in total (Fig. 3.2) consists of the following components.

11

Soloist

Quite simply, improvement in organisational performance will come through releasing the inert and latent potential that resides within all people. Ask any management team to score out of ten how much potential they have released in their people, and the answer is often around the half way point. By releasing this potential and creating a team of organisational soloists, the business can create a fountain of innovation and capability that can help it to outperform the competition.

Super-leader

For effective long-term learning, organisations need to develop effective long-term leaders, people who can move beyond the charismatic and directional model, and understand the prerequisites for effective knowledge management. To ease the process of learning, super-leaders should understand the role played by trust, values and the nature of internal networks.

Schema

People who only see the world from their own perspective are effectively imprisoning themselves in a jail of their own making. People who have broken free from this cell, and are able to understand how others view the world are better equipped to donate and receive knowledge.

Surprises

The creation of knowledge will become reliant upon the individualised nature of the structure, rather than the structured organisation of the individuals. Any company that does not have the capacity to either originate or import new ideas, innovations or surprises is creating its own long-term demise.

Shadows

There will often be a significant difference between what people and organisations say they do and what they actually do. The identification of this hidden area is of significant importance to the idea of organisational learning, because it can disrupt any plans that an organisation has with respect to improving its capacity to learn and create knowledge.

Self-organisation

Beneath the polished veneer that organisations present to the world, there exists the potential for spontaneous self-organisation. Within the stable mechanistic business processes that organisations typically adopt, there exists a living force that drives and supports the business, but in ways that are not always obvious.

To ensure the free flow of knowledge through the organisation, companies need to understand how both models operate, interact and possibly conflict with each other.

Socialisation

One of the key themes that emerges from the Integrated Learning Model is the role that socialisation plays in the knowledge creation and diffusion process. Consider the team that originates a radical, new idea. The likelihood is that they will be unable to progress it any further until it has been socialised and accepted by the organisation. This social network is something that is rarely defined but everyone intuitively recognises the role it plays in getting knowledge accepted.

Structure

If a business is to harness its learning capacity to create new knowledge, it should first develop an appreciation of how knowledge is transported into, through and out of the organisation. This is encapsulated in the five stages of the knowledge infrastructure as discovery, diffusion, delivery, delay and disposal.

Sharing

This might be seen as the final link in the organisation's capability to learn. The creation of organisational knowledge is about people, their interaction, and the synthesis that arises from the sharing process. To make the shift from individual learning to organisational learning, the company should understand how to rapidly and effectively move the lessons learned from personal experience and spread these into mainstream processes and products.

Strategy

Learning strategy is concerned with developing an action-based framework that can help to deliver the outcomes and behaviours that the organisation desires. The ILM offers a number of points that can help the organisation to create an open-ended approach around its learning initiatives. The five key factors that are offered for discussion include the themes of declaration, diagnosis, dialogue, design and deployment.

The Integrated Learning Model is not offered as a paradigm for success. Organisations should determine their own recipe for prosperity and cannot just adopt a strategic template that someone else has developed. However, the ILM can help people to develop a cognitive structure and diagnostic framework that will help them to understand how they learn.

Part 2

Individual

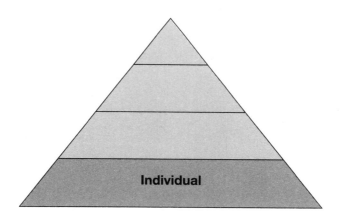

Chapter 4

....

An 'inside-out' framework

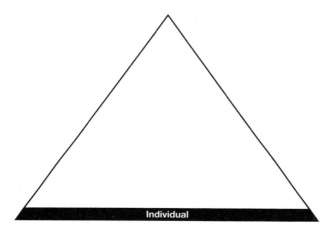

Fig. 4.1 Building on the individual

Peter Senge (1990) cites Kazuo Inamori when he suggests that 'the active force for any business is its people. These people will have their own will, mind and way of thinking'. Hence, if individuals are not motivated to acquire knowledge, then little learning can or will take place at an organisational level. The first step in creating this motivation should be to recognise the significance of the individual's role and value in enhancing the learning processes within the business. The second, and possibly more significant action, is to help and encourage people to recognise this value themselves.

One of the first steps in this process might be to help people maintain an equitable balance in life and erode the dependency on the organisation and the hierarchy. The goal is to move away from a style where 'I am my position', to one where people have a realistic sense of purpose of their value to themselves and the business (Senge, 1990).

In helping people to take on board a more adaptive and positive stance about themselves and the organisation, the Integrated Learning Model suggests that four key areas might be considered:

- soloist;
- super-leader;
- schema;
- surprises.

Quite simply, if the people in the organisation are not energised and in-tune with the idea of learning and knowledge creation, then little is likely to happen. However, developing people who are able and happy to embrace this view of life is not something that can be mandated or casually rolled out in a corporate programme.

Often organisations will undertake sophisticated organisational development programmes that are implemented with the highest possible integrity and intent. However, the problem is that they often seek to transform the organisation in totality. They try to work 'outside-in', defining how the entire organisation should look in the future, and then attempting to 'lever' the organisation into the new state. In contrast, the underlying approach advocated by this book is that since learning is a subjective activity, any change process that seeks to enhance learning should start from the purpose of the individual, not the organisation. The Integrated Learning Model is built on the axiom that effective learning processes should operate on a deployment ethos that follows an 'inside-out' framework. Then, change in the learning process resides with the individual and not the organisation. In basing any change process from the perspective of the individual, it views a company's competitive advantage as flowing not from the grand wisdom of top management, but from the initiative, creativity, and advanced skills of all employees (Ghoshal and Bartlett, 1998).

Chapter 5

Soloist

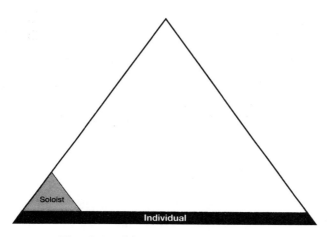

Soloist

Individual

Fig. 5.1 The individual as soloist

The age of the individual has arrived with a vengeance. No longer can organisations stay competitive if they simply rely on strategy, structure and processes to provide the market-edge. Human capital will be the factor that differentiates the organisation, and this will be stimulated by the growth of the individual, rather than the team, unit or division. Ultimately, learning and knowledge will be discovered and created by individuals, not faceless corporate bodies.

A clear analogy for this might be seen with the relationship between musicians in a band. Consider the musical soloist, the individual who is able to seamlessly switch between the role of team member and featured player in a band. Soloists, have to operate on a number of levels at any one time:

- Have the appropriate knowledge, skills and competencies to stand out from the band or orchestra, and be prepared to put their talent on public view.
- Be able to adapt to constantly changing patterns and themes in the music.
- Have the curiosity and desire to challenge themselves and possibly the composer who wrote the original score.
- Be prepared to reflect on, and learn from, each solo performance.
- Have a strong relationship with the band; one built on trust, respect and freedom.

- Care about their performance and the way other people contribute to their ability to perform.

In the same way that the soloist in a band needs to develop these attributes, so the energised individual within an organisation might wish to enhance their ability in these areas. In an organisational setting, the soloist traits might be described as:

- **Compelling future** – Develop clear personal goals and understand what learning will help them to achieve.
- **Change mastery** – Move from a position where change is feared to one where it is regarded as an invigorating and opportunistic process, to the extent that change can be regarded as a type of personal long-term security.
- **Challenging ethos** – Recognise that change and learning will always be about modifying paradigms and perceptions. To do this, individuals will need to challenge the existing status quo and feel comfortable breaking with past conventions and habits.
- **Continual learning** – Understand that the individual needs to continually re-invent themselves and their capability to learn.
- **Contract alignment** – Understand how change in the psychological contract has impacted upon their relationship with the organisation.
- **Caring** – Recognise how the interdependent relationship with others affects their ability to deliver a thrilling and effective performance.

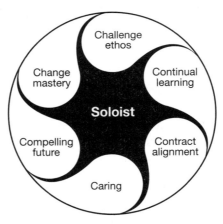

Fig. 5.2 Traits of the soloist

By no means are these six traits exclusive to the idea of creating individuals who are able to play a solo role. However, in focusing on these areas, the process of creating people who have a sense of mastery over their lives might be easier and structured in its approach.

Trait 1: Compelling future

Often people can spend time and energy learning new skills, growing capabilities and developing new pools of knowledge, only to find that they are of little value to either themselves or the organisation. If change or learning is to be effective, then people often need a goal or purpose to appreciate what education should take place. People can be helped to create a compelling future for themselves by setting out a personal map or metaphor that describes what the desired future might be. Importantly, this future will be flexible and adaptable, not set in concrete. It is interesting how children are encouraged to use their imagination powers to build fantasy worlds and dreams for the future, but once the teenage years are reached, then the doldrums of middle age are already approaching, and this type of behaviour is discouraged and viewed as immature. The supposition to be created is that people need to visualise and occasionally float into the future so they can start to realise what they need to learn today.

One way to do this is by use of a time line (James and Woodsmall, 1988). This where an individual considers life in the form of time-line, and reflects on all the accumulated memories, beliefs, ideas and experience to understand how they interpret and form a picture of the world. The next stage for the individual might be to project the time line forward to a point in the future, and to build a picture of where they would like to be.

This is a powerful tool that helps people to understand how they view the world. Some people look at their time line from an historic perspective, always reflecting on things that have, or might have, happened. Others tend to sit in the present, just focusing on today's issues, without thinking about where they might be heading. To develop the sense of a compelling destiny, the suggestion is that people need to orientate themselves to a future state. They need to move themselves along the time line and temporarily dwell at a specific point in the future. This can help people to programme their personal future; to create a goal that is so vivid and real that it becomes undeniable to the brain.

Questions that can be considered by individuals when developing their own compelling futures include:

- *What specifically is wanted?*
- *Where am I now?*
- *What will the future look and feel like?*
- *How will I know when I have it?*
- *What does achieving the outcome give me?*
- *What resources do I have now, and what do I need in the future to achieve the outcome?*
- *What do I lose by achieving this future state?*

By going through this questioning process, the individual can develop a clear picture of what the next stage of the time line looks like. Even more, there is a tactile sense of what it feels, sounds and smells like – the objective being to create a sense of association between the current and future state, thus moving the time line from a theoretical picture to something that is real and internalised.

In developing a personal and real sense of the future, the individual is able to use this as a reference point when taking important learning decisions. Although learning is often positioned as relatively easy or a soft option, the deep personal processes that an individual has to go through can be traumatic and stretching. The mechanic who is struggling to learn how to operate a new piece of machinery; the student who is in the final year of a Masters programme, or the manager who is trying to come to terms with a new organisational theory – for all of these people, the learning processes can be arduous, and often the individual has to be able to focus on a personal goal to sustain the energy to reach the end. One of the most pragmatic advocates of this idea is Covey (1992), who suggests that people should begin with the end in mind, where all things are created twice. First, there is the mental or first creation, like composers who hear the song in their heads before they play it, or footballers who can see themselves holding the winning cup even before the game has started. Following this is the second creation, which is the physical realisation of the idea, just like the composer finally performing a song in front of a live audience or the footballer taking the cup home to put in the trophy cupboard.

Ultimately, by encouraging people to have a focus on a personal end goal, the organisation is helping itself to have a clear focus on its end goal. If someone is not excited about their future, they are unlikely to be thrilled about the organisation's. Only by helping each and every individual to develop a passion for their future, might an animated sense of expectancy for the organisation's goals be realised.

Trait 2: Change mastery

The effective organisation is one that encourages and supports learning from change (Carnall, 1995, 13). The fact that an individual has learnt a new management technique, that an organisation has introduced a radical new process, or that a team is working to a new specification means that change has taken place. In fact, the supposition is that the two are inseparable. If this is the case, for individuals to be effective, as well as learning how to learn, they must learn how to master change.

Consider many of the management books, job adverts, and training programmes that can be seen in the market. One common feature is the requirement to find or train people who are able to manage change. This is now seen as a core competency for many firms, and will continue to be so as the pace of change intensifies. However, the proposition is that the ability to 'manage' change will in itself be superseded and be replaced by the requirement to master change. To shift from taking a reactive stance to one that is more proactive. The difference might be compared with the distinction between a proficient pianist and one who is regarded as a virtuoso. The underlying competencies might be broadly similar but the contrast is often around the performance and the sense of authority over the instrument.

To become a master of change, one should first know its nature. There should be an acceptance that control, conformity and consistency are things of the past, and turbulence, trauma and transition are in effect the new normalised state. In understanding this nature of change, it is important that people understand how this shift from equilibrium to turbulence will affect people; to have a clear picture of how individuals are likely to react when faced with something different or unexpected.

Responses to change

The U-loop is a powerful and effective change model that clearly maps many of the feelings associated with change and learning (Carnall, 1995). People will especially feel these emotions where the change process affects their self-esteem or position in the organisation. The suggestion is that there are five major stages in the process of change, as shown in Fig. 5.3.

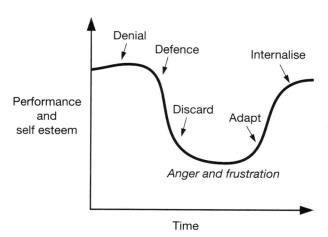

Fig. 5.3 U-loop shows five stages of change

- **Denial** – Many people feel uncomfortable with change. Often the typical response to any shift in the environment is to believe that it can be ignored. People either do not believe that it will affect them, or are resigned to the idea that there is nothing they can do, so it is best to ignore the threat.

23

- **Defence** – This is where people might take action to try and prevent the change from taking place. It might be simply withdrawing from the process, or in some extremes, taking premeditated guerrilla action to stop the change from happening.
- **Discard** – All change is about shifting people's schema or view of the world. To move forward, one has to discard past behaviours, feelings and consequences; to let go and be happy with what has gone.
- **Adapt** – At this point the past has been left behind so people can begin to explore the new ways of working. This can be a confusing time, as the old and new are still likely to be in conflict with each other. However, with the correct support processes in place, the individual can quickly shift to the next stage of commitment.
- **Internalise** – Once the change has been accepted, the individual can adopt it as the norm and internalise it as the current way of operating. At this point the energy returns, the process is owned, and the individual will, in many cases, try to convince others of its benefits.

As the rate of organisational change increases, there is a greater possibility that key people will be at the position of discard or adapt. In this position, the individual might become less effective and subsequently the process of organisational learning is likely to be impaired.

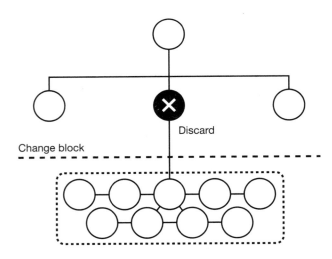

Fig. 5.4 One manager can block change

Consider the team manager in Fig. 5.4. While the whole team is energised and keen to bring about new ways of working, he has been informed that as part of an internal change, his post will be moved to another region. How does he react? In an ideal world, he will still be supportive of the change process, but in reality he might understandably move to the discard stage of the U-loop. In sitting at this stage in the change cycle, there is every chance that he will act as a significant attenuator to the transformation process, effectively blocking the flow of learning and knowledge within the team.

Hence, an effective organisation will ensure that it has processes in place that will respond to, and counter any potential damage for the learning process. The options include:

- Raise the U-loop model: make it 'OK' for people to feel anxious and unhappy about change.
- Create space in the organisation where people can talk about their feelings and concerns.
- Help people to go through the U-loop at a speed that is right for them and effective for the organisation.
- Raise any hidden and unspoken issues that help fuel the grapevine; in making things public they will seem to be less of a problem.

If an organisation accepts that people need to go through such a transformation, then helping it to flow in an open and visible way will help ensure that learning blockages don't occur within the organisation.

Becoming a change agent

Once an individual has attained a sense of change mastery, the shift might be to use this productively by becoming a change agent for the business. The definition of an agent for change might be seen as becoming an individual who can bring about new flows of knowledge across the organisation. The characterisation of this type of approach will depend upon a multitude of factors. However, the key things to consider are:

Break-with view

Being able to take a new perspective on issues and to do so by reframing any personal viewpoints. In many cases individuals may have an established set of personal styles, behaviours, and operational schemas that have served them well over a long time. The need to break with these personal views will often be painful and traumatic. However, in flexing the 'break with' muscle, it will get stronger over time and reach a point where individuals will regularly question and reflect on their existing thoughts and maps of the world.

However, this behaviour should be clearly understood in terms of the context and situation where it needs to occur. In most cases, the break-with style is not simply a case of reframing one's own view of the world. To stimulate learning across the organisation, the individual should be prepared to help others break-with their view of the world. Such a step means that the change agent will have

25

to overcome the resisting forces of tradition, social pressure and political reaction. This resisting pressure is often regarded as the cultural immune system. These are the unclear and shadow forces that combine to prevent a change of practice from being accepted and implemented.

Loving the turbulence

To effectively facilitate learning and change, an individual should also be able to adapt to internal forces that drive the organisation and it is important to recognise that these forces do not conform to the more traditional idea of predictability and stability. Most organisations tend to contain elements of unpredictability, complex relationships and organic structures. Hence, the key attribute for any individual who seeks to share their knowledge and wisdom throughout the organisation, is to be gloriously happy when working with uncertainty. Every step that the change agent takes should be with the absolute knowledge that they operate in a world that is strange and bizarre. As such, when taking action that is designed to produce a specific outcome, unexpected responses are to be anticipated and actively welcomed.

Using positics

The ability to help knowledge flow through an organisation is likely to depend on the individual's ability to take new ideas and sell them throughout the organisation. The individual should approach the internal sell with as much cunning and vigour as might be invested in selling a product to an external customer. The core element that underpins this idea is the notion of 'backstaging' (Buchanan and Body, 1992, 75).

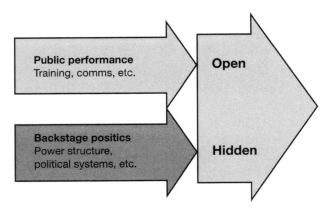

Fig. 5.5 'Backstage activity'

Along with the more overt and public actions associated with managing change (project management, communication, training, etc.), there is a need to understand the 'backstage activity' as seen in Fig. 5.5. This is typically the use of power skills to make interventions in the political and social systems. Learning and change are not always formal processes that can be managed simply and efficiently. They are often untidy, interrelated and overlapping processes that operate with shifting goals and team membership. As such, the processes that need to be used to underpin any adoption should also be unrestricted and adaptable in nature. Hence the need to use backstage techniques that complement the formal systems in the organisation. Although this might be viewed as machiavellian in nature, this is not so: it just requires a positive and open reframing of the understanding of politics; to consciously reframe the action and think of 'poistics', the 'positive application of politics'.

The goal behind organisational learning is the idea of enabling, creating and socialising learning beyond the range of the individual. Sometimes this will not happen on its own, hence a degree of influencing and collaboration might be required to facilitate its progress. Individuals cannot just sit back and say, 'well I have learned something new, so the rest of the business should come knocking at my door'. Organisational learning is an active sport, not one suited to a couch potato.

In being proactive, a sense of change mastery can be achieved – with this comes a new type of comfort and protection. Kanter (1984) suggests that rather than being a threatening and disrupting process, change can be regarded as a new form of security. In the more traditional organisation, security is based upon the acquisition of power: the power to hold resources, discipline people, control the finances and build personal empires. In organisations that value knowledge, people's ability to synthesise the energy of change and learning will ultimately offer a greater degree of influence and control than the ability to accumulate hierarchical power.

Trait 3: Continual learning

There are often two approaches associated with the idea of organisational learning: adaptive and generative (Schein, 1994). Adaptive learning is known as 'single loop' (Argyris and Schon, 1996), and focuses on the delivery of a short-term response (knee jerk) to an emergent problem. The generative path is known as 'double loop' learning, and focuses on developing a deeper appreciation of the problem. The generative style is effectively seen as 'learning how to learn', and can be seen as the primary method that helps to drive the development of learning within an organisation.

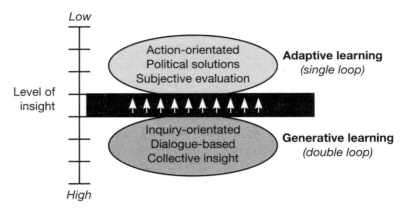

Fig. 5.6 Depth of learning

With adaptive or single-loop learning, any change in the process or system is perceived at a superficial level as in Fig. 5.6. The underlying norms, values and assumptions are not questioned or reflected upon in any way. For example, if sales of a product are falling, the response might be to alter the promotional discount, increase the number of outlets, or in extreme cases, sack the product manager. Alternatively, where a team member is failing to meet the expected goals, the response might be to increase the level of monitoring, reduce their pay rating, or in many cases, take steps to discipline them. In neither of these cases has any of the deep underlying issues been considered.

In taking a generative approach, deeper questions might be asked regarding the falling sales of a product. To what extent is there conflict in the marketplace with other products that the company sells? Are cross-portfolio problems emerging? Has research and development lagged so that the product is becoming dated? Are the sales performance targets at odds with the needs of the product turnover levels? For the individual who is under-performing, is there a problem at home causing concern? Does the individual need a change in roles to make the work more interesting, or is there any conflict in the relationship with the manager?

The key to double-loop learning is in the art of turning the question back on the questioner. To ask what underlying assumptions are being made: what are the values of the questioner in suggesting that a problem exists in the first place? For example, instead of the manager asking why the performance of a team member has fallen, they might ask why it took so long to notice, or what steps have been taken to develop the individuals in their team.

In helping an individual to move from an adaptive to a generative style of learning, the need is to migrate towards a style of self-reflection, inquiry and dialogue (see Chapter 14). In questioning the values and assumptions that underpin a situation, the first step is for the individual to have a clear and objective appreciation of their personal drivers and barriers; next, to appreciate why he or she might feel that something is a problem in the first place; and then to be able to consider the situation from an objective perspective.

Generative learning will often happen when different options have been tried but failed to bring about any long-term significant change. For example, where a product promotion or re-design failed to increase sales, or sending a team member on a number of courses failed to result in a change in personal performance. The enlightenment that can occur as a result of this exercise can be both rewarding and daunting. The rewarding parts are clear in that any change that causes a deep level of inquiry can be of benefit to the organisation. The daunting part starts when one considers some of the discomfort that should be encountered to bring about the alteration. Of all the most difficult things to do, moving down the level of insight requires that the question 'why?' is asked repeatedly, as in Fig. 5.7.

Product sales are dropping.

Why?

The sales force are not convincing the customer of the product benefits.

Why?

All the sales team did not attend the product launch programme.

Why?

They felt that it was not worthwhile wasting time on a course when they could be out with the customers.

Why?

The feedback from the sales people who went on the early course was that it was of little benefit.

Why?

The programme design was not piloted properly.

Why?

Because of a last minute re-allocation of product development funds from training to the sales bonus plan.

Action: Review product development budgeting process.

Fig. 5.7 Keep asking 'why?'

In addition to creating a long-term solution to the problem, undergoing such a deep level of inquiry opens up a clearer insight into the working of the organisation. If people are prepared to accept the opportunities to develop collective self-knowledge, such a process can help to pull many of the old skeletons out of the cupboard. This leads to the third, but least used, form of inquiry called 'triple-loop learning'.

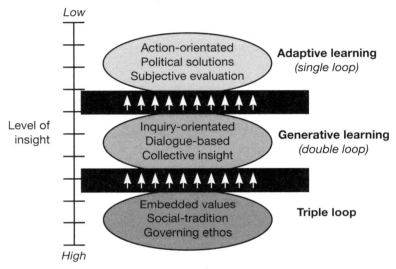

Fig. 5.8 Triple-loop learning

In triple-loop learning (Fig. 5.8), the embedded customs, ethos and behaviours are held up for scrutiny. The organisation will consider the bedrock that it has been built upon, and its appropriateness. This approach forces the organisation to ask: 'What type of company do we want to be; do we wish to exist in this market; and who are the key stakeholders for the business?'. This questions why they behave in certain ways, what has happened to make them develop certain views and beliefs, and how might they change their life to a greater degree of alignment and balance. However, taking learning to this degree means that people and the organisation must be able to take a challenging approach to life.

Trait 4: Challenge ethos

The challenge ethos becomes necessary because learning or change can fail unless existing world views or schemas are tested – where individuals consciously confront the existing status quo. In taking this approach, the organisation needs to allow people the necessary time to experiment and space to make mistakes.

Experimentation

The ability of an organisation to survive and prosper in the future is not defined and measured by the current level of knowledge: it is a function of its potential to create knowledge in the future. Ultimately this will be driven by the individual's ability to 'learn how to learn', to question how people have assimilated what they know already, and what processes were used to generate the knowledge.

Once understood, this experience can be used to increase the organisation's speed of learning. The goal of the organisation should be to ensure that personal experimentation is encouraged and that this is rapidly converted into concrete learning concepts and generalisations for the future.

Two key actions can be considered. First, that people should allow time to create learning opportunities and learn from their experiences, for example time set aside at the end of meetings to reflect upon, and learn from things that have happened. Second, the learning process is often improved by drawing on the ideas of variety and diversity to ensure that a range of experiences and outlooks are considered, so that just one schema does not end up dominating the process. The domination by one schematic view can reduce the long-term effectiveness of the learning experience as only one person's world view is being used to drive the outcome from the group.

Allow things to go wrong

The 1990s saw a shift towards greater levels of control and measurement within organisations. It was not untypical to find a manager who might have 20 to 30 different measurement criteria that should be reported against, often daily. The resulting shift in mindset has often been to reduce the acceptable level of risk, and so create a bias against the acceptance of mistakes. Here emerges a contradiction: the need to reduce failure cost while having to increase the levels of innovation.

John Cleese tells a wonderful story about 'Gordon the Guided Missile'. He suggests that, when a missile is first launched it has a broad idea of where it is heading but the absolute route is not known. It does, however, continually take a fix on where it is, the current trajectory, distance from the intended goal, and then modifies the flight path accordingly. In essence, its progress is constructed around making lots of 'acceptable mistakes'. These short-term deviations are of little concern as they are known to contribute to the end goal.

For the organisation, it is these short-term, minor deviations that can act as the fountain for knowledge and learning. Creative and innovative people often stumble, trip and make horrible mistakes. However, their highest and most acclaimed successes are often constructed on the rubble of humiliating failures.

Consider how many inventions have been created from the idea of serendipity: Archimedes' discovery of the principle of water displacement in the bath; or Fleming's accidental discovery of penicillin. These originated because someone happened to be in the right place at the right time and was observant enough to notice something out of the ordinary. (See Chapter 8 on serendipity.)

In moving to this mindset, people should be able to fail creatively and have the resilience to persist in the face of failure. The end result is that creative mistakes can be treated as learning opportunities rather than mistakes or a personal embarrassment (Gioia, 1995, 317).

Trait 5: Contract alignment

It is important to appreciate that the six components in the soloist part of the model are all interrelated. In particular, the first four areas (compelling future, change mastery, continual learning and challenge ethos) depend on the fact that the individual has a sense of personal security. For many people this sense of security arises from the contract with their organisation; the basic agreement that guarantees people the income and resources to satisfy their needs.

However, recent changes in the make-up of many industries has modified the nature of the contract. The old picture of a stable market with ever-increasing wage cycles and guaranteed jobs has gone. The first, and most obvious change, is the alteration to the legal side of the contract. The increase in part-time work, changing demographics, short-term contracts and the growth in self-employed people, has made the legal process of contracting more important for the individual. However, it is the second, and softer area, that proves to be most important for the idea of organisational learning. This is the psychological contract, an unwritten and emotional bond that ties people and the organisation together.

During the 1990s, the psychological contract was subtly modified. Company after company pursued efficiencies through re-engineering, downsizing, quality programmes and outsourcing, and these have effectively ended the idea of life-long employment (Ghoshal and Bartlett, 1998). This has broken many of the shared beliefs that existed between the individual and the organisation. As such, the nature of the long-term employee has undergone a radical restructuring, moving from predictability to turbulence, and from long- to short-term.

The question is, how to use this transformation to the advantage of the organisation and the individual. How can a new type of relationship be created that has the appropriate flexibility, but with the deeper psychological support that is essential to enable cross-organisation learning?

Rethinking the relationship

Organisations might need to shift from a position where they have a moral responsibility to provide life-long job security to one where they guarantee to provide learning opportunities, but in doing this, there is a reversal in role for the senior managers. From assuring that the company's competitiveness will be there to pay the wages, to ensuring that the employee's entrepreneurial initiative will safeguard their employability.

In considering this approach, Ghoshal and Bartlett (1998) raise a number of key points:

- The goal is for the employer to provide employees with continuous skill updating and to protect and enhance their personal flexibility, both inside and outside the company.
- People will move from being an asset that is exploited to one where value is infused to enhance the competitiveness of the company.
- It requires the individual to move from a position of 'I am my Job' to one where they take a personal responsibility for their learning.
- The shift towards empowerment means that people at the front line will make and take decisions without waiting for top-level approval. Hence a process of internal 'letting go' will have to take place.
- The new contract is not a carte blanch for the individual to demand training and development at will. There should still be criteria to assure business benefit.

The aim is to create a sense of 'shared success'; a future where both parties knowingly add value to the relationship so that joint benefits are accrued (Fig. 5.9).

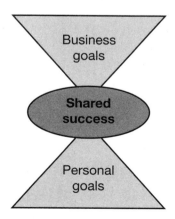

Fig. 5.9 Benefits for individual and company

33

The core objective of the process is to make the implicit explicit. To take the issues that were once unspoken, and move them to a position where they can be discussed in an open and honest relationship.

The new, open contract

In moving the implicit issues into the explicit arena, the primary focus is in raising awareness of personal development as a factor within the contract. An example of the type of things that might be covered include:

- learning balance;
- portfolio of opportunities;
- explicit trust description;
- motivation drivers;
- violation clause.

This is not meant to be a definitive list of things to include in the new open contract. It does, however, raise some of the shadow issues that are avoided within the contracting process. The ultimate idea is to bring into place a sense of alignment, helping the organisation, and its people, to realise that prosperity is built upon the notion of shared, rather than selfish success. A relationship where the individual and organisation can raise and realise their shared goals with a greater sense of honesty, commitment and effort on the part of both parties.

Learning balance

The suggestion is that both parties should always strive to gain from the individual's training and development. For example, someone might attend a training programme that is focused primarily on personal development but the business would explicitly consider what commercial benefits might accrue in the long term. Alternatively, the individual might focus on developing skills that are explicitly for the business to take advantage of, but there would still be a process by which the individual could leverage personal gain out of the experience. The proposition is not to take a selfish or short-term view, but to focus on the shared destiny and derive benefit from a synergistic relationship.

Portfolio of opportunities

One might, with some degree of confidence, assume that an individual will not do the same job, in the same place, with the same company for their whole career. Hence, it is important that opportunities are taken to build a breadth of experience and knowledge, as well as the depth that most people want. The contract might highlight what opportunities will be open to the individual and how they can be used to develop their personal career.

Explicit trust description

If one considers all the various activities, relationships and projects that occur within an organisation, they all depend upon the balance of trust between people. Trust provides the underlying strength to ensure that promises are kept, work is completed on time and knowledge is shared. Hence, there might be some benefit in developing a trust index within the contract that highlights the balance of faith in the relationship. The difficulty comes when considering what the criteria might be used to measure the degree of trust that exists because of the subjective nature of the topic area. However, certain core factors might be used:

- **Truthful:** the extent to which honesty and integrity are maintained.
- **Responsiveness:** Mental accessibility, or the willingness to share ideas and information freely.
- **Uniform:** the degree of reliability and predictability that is contained within the relationship.
- **Safe:** benevolence, loyalty or the willingness to protect, support and encourage each other.
- **Trained:** the technical knowledge and interpersonal skills of the individual.

Motivation drivers

So often massive assumptions are made about what motivates an individual. The classic example might be where the organisation wants to praise and energise a manager for something they have done at work. To do this, they arrange for the manager to have lunch with a director or senior manager. However, this might be stressful, so the end result might be a demotivated person. If motivational drivers are included as part of the contract, they can be reviewed regularly to consider their effectiveness.

Violation clause

Possibly the final element needs to be a description of how any violation of the contract might be managed. Clearly, for the legal side of the contract, violation is relatively simple (theft, redundancy, etc.), but for the softer elements, such clear-cut criteria might not be so simple. Contract violation can take place in one of three ways:

- **Inadvertently:** Both parties are able and willing, but an interruption takes place because of a misunderstanding.
- **Disruption:** Circumstances makes it impossible for either one of the parties to fulfil their end of the contract.
- **Reneging:** One side of the contract makes a conscious effort to break the agreement.

Although it might be possible to define exact ways and means by which the psychological contract will be violated, it becomes impractical to specify all possible infringements. It might be more valuable to spend time discussing and agreeing ways in which potential violations can be rectified before the idea of full separation occurs.

If people take the time to consider the psychological contract, they will realise that the most important idea is to make the 'un-discussible discussible'; taking those issues that are normally left to chance, and talking them through to a point where there is a more open relationship. This relationship is based on helping organisations and people to better understand their needs, and the options for meeting them. It is taking the often unspoken idea of 'What is in it for me' and turning it into 'What is in it for us'. When this collaborative style of relationship can be achieved, the process of learning and knowledge sharing will be eased.

Trait 6: Caring

As with any change process that is focused on enhancing the role of the individual, the danger is in making the pendulum swing too far. The goal is to give people the opportunity to gain a sense of empowerment, alignment and confidence, without pushing them into a position where they become selfish and insensitive. To do this they should understand how to map the balance of their relationship with others and know when the relationship is and isn't working.

Caring is about having consideration for the value that colleagues can offer in helping to deliver personal goals. As this book emphasises, the goal is not just to create a band of renegade individuals who are able to operate in an individualistic way. Organisational learning is about the stimulation of learning and knowledge creation through collaborative interaction between people. To achieve this, people have to interact with others on a practical and emotional level. More importantly, they need to have the sensitivity to know when to stand up and take a bow, and when to bring the band on for the final applause. A powerful soloist can make a band in the short term, but in the long term they can kill it with their selfish and insensitive attitude.

Conclusion

Learning starts with the individual. Without people who are committed, energised, competent, and happy in their workplace, little new knowledge will be generated. It is, therefore, important to ensure that processes are in place to facilitate a culture where people are encouraged to focus on creating the following personal traits:

- compelling future;
- change mastery;
- continual learning;
- challenging ethos;
- contract alignment;
- caring.

It is important to note that all six traits are achievable. There is nothing new or innovative. They are simply a distillation and representation of existing ideas and practices. The secret is in their unification and the resulting synergy that surfaces once they are in place as seen in Fig. 5.10.

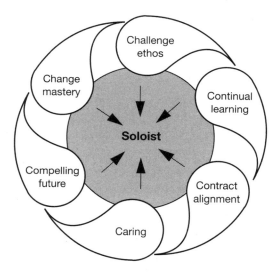

Fig. 5.10 The six traits of the soloist

So, why should an organisation seek to create the soloist nature within its people? What is in it for them? Ghoshal and Bartlett (1998) suggests that within every corporate hierarchy, there are numerous 'entrepreneurial hostages' striving to break free. These are people who have worked tirelessly for the benefit of the company, doing the things that they were supposed to do, but never quite putting their own personal stamp on activities. Once people realise the extent of the power, capability and influence they can attain, it is possible to use this to help turn a good company into one that is at the leading edge.

Once this latent power of the soloist is unleashed, then the organisation can start to understand the complex relationship that exists between individual learning and organisational learning. As Senge (1990) suggests:

'Organisations learn only through individuals who learn. Individual learning does not guarantee organisational learning, but without it, no organisational learning occurs.'

If a company employs people to work on indifferent tasks, senseless paperwork and childish infighting, then this is a negative capital asset. It might have people's bodies, but it doesn't have their minds. So for every person that is not reaching their true potential to be a soloist, the company is squandering its intellectual asset base, throwing money to the four winds and offering competitive advantage to its rivals.

Model dynamics

	How do we learn?	How do we share?	How do we use?	How can we improve?
Compelling future People have a clear outline of their goals as to what they want to achieve				
Change mastery People regard change as a source of excitement and security rather than a thing to be carefully managed				
U-loop People talk in an open and honest way about the tension and frustration of change				
Change agent People have the skill and motivation to drive learning and change across the organisation				

39

Model dynamics continued

	How do we learn?	How do we share?	How do we use?	How can we improve?
Generative learning People are encouraged to look in the deeper aspects of issues; to repeatedly ask why and question presupposition				
Challenging ethos Happy to confront traditional norms and assumptions that exist within the organisation				
Continual learning People develop themselves in line with their goals and not just the company's				
Contract alignment Contractual relationship with organisation is based on soft as well as hard factors				
Caring People recognise that effective interrelationships play as significant a role in learning as personal drive and innovation				

Chapter 6

Super leadership

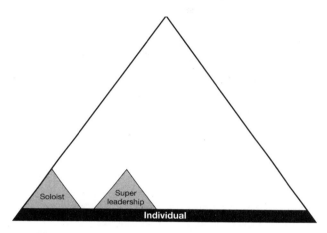

Fig. 6.1 The individual as super leader

Organisational leadership has undergone a dramatic phase-transformation but few people took any notice in the 1990s. No longer is a leader required to set the vision, values, mission, and then lead the charge from the front like General Custer. This style assumes that the leader has a moral, intellectual and spiritual dominance over other people, and they will automatically become followers, that people are reliant on the need to be directed and driven by someone else. An alternative view is that the leader will be the person that can use the power of interaction and connectivity to facilitate the creation, storage and embodiment of knowledge across the organisation.

If this is the case, then it suggests that a new set of leadership qualities might be required; those that focus more on releasing the potential of people, rather than setting boundaries and restrictive models of how the organisation should operate. In this sense, the role of the leader is not just to create the future, set the outcomes, or provide a controlled environment. It is also about understanding the intangible elements that exist within an organisation and helping these to prosper, synergise, and create futures that the leader might never have considered.

This is not to suggest that former leadership models are defunct or inappropriate, they just need to be expanded and enhanced. A new language should be encouraged, one that helps redefine and shape the leader's role. Words like

41

'knowledge amplification', 'value matching', 'trust indices' and 'constellation structures', could become part of everyday conversation. To achieve this, three aspects might be considered:

- **Trust:** As organisations reduce in size and grow in complexity, so the dependency on social interaction between the players becomes increasingly significant. Positive socialisation will only occur if people have the necessary level of trust within and across the various teams (Shapiro, 1996).

- **Relationships:** For an organisation (rather than an individual) to learn, there should be a flow of knowledge across the network. Therefore, the effective leader should be concerned with the creation and performance of the network. If this is the case, then it is worrying to consider how many organisations believe that their network is represented by the current organisation chart. The typical organisation chart is nothing more than a power diagram showing who controls the various people and resources. It does not indicate the true relationships between the people, where information flows, and how the shape of the network contributes to the creation of knowledge. The focus should move from seeing the business as one great 'organisation chart', to understanding the importance of the internal network and how it contributes to the creation of knowledge.

- **Values:** At the heart of an organisation are the deep values of individuals, the shared values of teams, and the underlying corporate values that emerge to make up the culture. It is these personal and shared beliefs that bind people together, push them apart, and generally make the world go round. Hence, the leader should be sure that the values of the people, teams and organisation are related in such a way as to facilitate effective social interaction, and the free flow of information.

The need for trust

Although trust is one of the unspoken essentials for a leader, it is often taken for granted, only surfacing as a topic for discussion once a violation occurs and the relationship starts to break down. When this happens, it is frequently too late to recover the situation, and if recovered, the employee–employer relationship can be seriously damaged. The problem is, how does one create a trusting relationship when the forces of change conspire to make it so difficult? Consider the following:

- The rate of internal change means that people will often have two or three managers a year.
- The shift towards electronic messaging means that face-to-face contact is diminishing.

- The use of audio and televisual links tends to reduce the amount of time for casual, getting-to-know-you conversations.
- The increasing use of part-time or portfolio workers reduces the manager's opportunity to spend time with the individual.

The end result is that low trust behaviours can be seen as common place in organisations, almost to the point where they become regarded as normalised behaviour. Typical low trust conduct can include:

- Revenge tactics: Taking business decisions just to get even with someone for past deeds.
- Authority paradox: Relatively senior managers that are able to take decisions on million-pound proposals, only to find that they are unable to buy a kettle for the office.
- Corrupt reward systems: The creation of bonus systems that offer a bias towards rewarding the favoured managers.

If a leader is to accept that trust is an essential part of the learning toolkit, then the first stage might be to understand those elements that contribute to its formation. As introduced in Chapter 5, any long-term, trust-based relationship will typically include the following (unspoken) elements:

- **Truthful:** the extent to which honesty and integrity are maintained.
- **Responsiveness:** Mental accessibility, or the willingness to share ideas and information freely.
- **Uniform:** the degree of reliability and predictability that is contained within the relationship.
- **Safe:** benevolence, loyalty or the willingness to protect, support and encourage each other.
- **Trained:** the technical knowledge and interpersonal skills of the individual.

If the super-leaders accept that trust is essential, the first step is to look inward, both at themselves and the organisation; specifically, to reflect on the normalised behaviours and how these are at odds with the trust criteria set out above. Clearly an individual cannot become a paragon of virtue overnight. However, it might be possible to identify certain overt behaviours that obviously corrupt the trust process which can be eliminated without any significant cost to the business.

Trust and relationships

Trust might be regarded as the oil that lubricates the flow of information through the organisation. With inter-relationships that are grounded in honesty and commitment, the free flow of knowledge will be fluid, wide ranging and often celebrated. In cases where relationships are grounded in distrust, power bases and backbiting, the information channels will lack the lubrication to facilitate the flow of knowledge. In low-trust relationships, there will be a greater emphasis on negative interpersonal relationships, where people focus on face saving, setting out boundaries, and creating power positions. This emphasis will often interfere with and distort the perceptions of the problem, causing it to seem insurmountable, or creating problems that do not exist.

So, is it possible to take a soft or woolly issue like trust and consider it from a bottom line position? Trust is the fulcrum that can effect different degrees of leverage in the organisation. In shifting the fulcrum towards the high-trust direction, one can almost quantify the reduction in time taken to solve problems and to create the facility to share knowledge. The transaction costs within the organisation will reduce as less money is expended on monitoring and control. If people do not have to worry about making mistakes and protecting their turf, they might be more willing to open up and share learning and knowledge that is created locally. Correspondingly, as the fulcrum shifts the other way, trust diminishes, power battles erupt, tribal camps form and the flow of knowledge become attenuated and in many cases blocked.

Trust and the flow of information

If the suggested purpose of a super-leader is to enhance the flow of information and knowledge, then in what way will the level of trust affect this process? The matrix in Fig. 6.2 considers four scenarios that can emerge when these two aspects are considered.

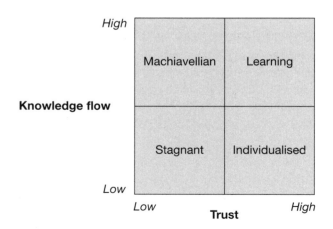

Fig. 6.2 Trust and knowledge matrix

The first scenario that emerges from this matrix is one of stagnation. In this type of organisation the problem is one of low trust and low information flow. This does not imply that the company is 'currently' performing poorly, as it might well be a blue chip organisation, perceived by external agents to be a growth option. However, the suggestion is that the stagnant organisation will not develop in the long run, as it has only limited capacity to create new knowledge.

In the Machiavellian quadrant, the organisation has high levels of knowledge flow but it exists in an ethos of mistrust. Here, people might use knowledge for personal gain, to grow empires and maintain personal power centres.

The third, individualised quadrant shows the level of trust is high, but the benefits are not being realised for the company as a whole. The low level of knowledge flow suggests that the organisation template is built around individuals and focused teams. The suggestion might be one of tribal units, each operating in a highly effective way but without the underlying structure and processes to share the learning. This might be an infrastructure barrier where people are physically distant from each other; a structural issue, where the organisation has been built around inwardly-focused profit centres, or a technological one, because people do not have the physical capability to share ideas and knowledge.

Finally, in the learning quadrant, balance is achieved where sufficient trust exists to facilitate the creation of knowledge, and the right systems and processes are in place to transport it across the organisation.

It is important to recognise that this matrix does not seek to indicate the effectiveness of the company at present. An organisation can sit in the stagnant, machiavellian or individualised quadrants, and can be extremely successful: the question is for how long? At some stage in the organisation's development, the absence of either trust or knowledge flow is likely to negate the business's ability to regenerate itself.

Trust and the super-leader

Super-leaders cannot simply rest on the laurels of acting and behaving in a trustworthy manner, they must be both trustworthy and trusted. Only by achieving both of these states can the leader be seen to help nurture the process of learning as in Fig. 6.3.

This idea can be framed in four different ways. First, in the instance of decay, the leader has failed to either act in a trustworthy way, or to convince others of his or her ability to be trusted. In this case the organisation should realise that the decay is interwoven into the social fabric of the organisation and as a result it is unlikely to be able to create generative learning across the organisation.

In the case of abuse, the leader has manipulated the system and the people to convince them that he or she can be trusted. However, since the leader is unlikely to act in a trustworthy way, this leads to a position where the trust might be abused.

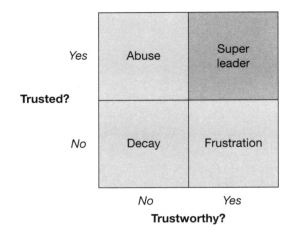

Fig. 6.3 Super leaders need to trust and be trustworthy

Frustration comes about when the leader has met the five trust criteria elements and continues to aspire to the role of a trusted leader. However, this behaviour has failed to result in a position of trust. This might be because of the person's inability to effectively communicate, or it might be due to previous bad behaviour. As Covey (1992) suggests, 'You can't talk your way out of something you behaved yourself into'. Whatever the reason, unless the leader can change this position, the ability to effect behavioural change across the organisation will be frustrated.

The super-leader is able to meet the five criteria (integrity, competence, consistency, loyalty and openness) and communicate this notion to other people. In doing this, the process of facilitating learning and change is oiled by the lubrication of trust.

However, trust is not a simple switch that can be turned on and off at will. The giving and taking of trust can vary considerably in its fragility and resilience, and can change quickly or slowly depending on circumstances. Trust associated with a close personal friendship is resilient and durable, and can be regarded as 'thick' trust. Once established, it is not easily disrupted, but when shattered, is not readily repaired or restored (Meyerson *et al.*, 1996).

Alternatively, a different type is the casual or short-term relationship, which is called 'thin' trust. This is often of the type seen on a project group or product team, and is conferred with some trepidation or withdrawn without notice. In this type of relationship people only tend to commit part of themselves to the other person. Examples of this can be seen when people put together a project team. Often managers will go for individuals that they know and have worked with before, simply because there is an established bond of thick trust as in Fig. 6.4. This saves time in having to negotiate new relationships, giving more time to resolve the task in hand. However, the disadvantage is that this can alienate other people, as they believe they are not being offered development opportunities. This can in turn result in a rise in the level of distrust within the organisation, thus restricting the sharing process.

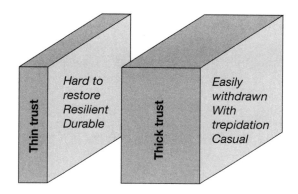

Fig. 6.4 Thick and thin trust

Understanding this level of trust might be aided by the use of a trust index. As part of the regular reviews with their team, people might be encouraged to review the topics raised in this section, in a sense, to create a dialogue that allows the individual to both share feelings about the relationship, and to identify areas where action might be taken to improve the degree of trust. This is like a meter that provides constant feedback on the trust level in the relationship, possibly varying between the thin and thick position, depending on the violations or builds that have taken place.

This topic is important for leaders who wish to enhance the organisation's ability to learn. They cannot simply rest upon their laurels once the trust index indicates that relationships are improving. The issue of trust needs to be constantly discussed and aired within the social setting, and not be allowed to remain unsurfaced until a violation takes place. Constant attention should be paid to:

- Raising the five learning factors (integrity, competence, consistency, loyalty and openness) for discussion.
- Being brave and facing behaviours (overt and hidden) that do not align with the espoused values.
- Considering the impact on the trust relationship when taking decisions.
- Encouraging people to map their trust index, and understanding how it might be improved.
- Understanding how the trust levels are attenuating or amplifying the flow of information and the creation of knowledge.

- Being aware that trustworthiness should be communicated to others if it is to add value to the organisation.
- Understand that it is not a black and white situation, and that trust can be taken and given at will by all people.

In essence two primary aspects may be considered. On a macro level, how can trust-based relationships be encouraged? On the micro level, how can 'I' behave in a manner that is trustworthy? Neither of these is easy, or will readily be achieved, but without any serious attempt to develop such an approach, the notion of stimulating learning across the organisation will be severely hindered.

Relationships

Put four intelligent people in isolated rooms in a building and little happens. The total sum of their output will be equal to the four people's individual effort. The barriers or walls constrain their ability to share resources, ideas, information or emotions. Although this barrier acts to protect the individual and allows them space in which to be themselves, it also acts as a self-imposed restrictor that maintains the status quo.

Consider then, when the walls are taken down or communications channels are established that will allow people to build relationships and work together. An amazing thing happens. Two plus two no longer equals four, it becomes five, six, seven or more. A synergistic multiplier effect comes into play, the value of which is only limited by the energy and imagination of the people. As individuals work together to share resources, ideas, information and emotions, so the benefits of the connectivity become apparent. It is the nature of such interaction that the super-leader should understand so it can be tuned to facilitate the flow of knowledge.

Super-leaders should accept that they cannot hope to influence or manage any situation without respect for the complex patterns of relationships that make an organisation function. In particular, they should be willing to view the inter-relationships as they really are, and not as the organisation chart suggests. The process of knowledge creation, and learning cannot be locked in and bounded by the arbitrary departmental structures that have been set by the business.

Nature of relationships

Many organisations make active use of the hierarchy chart to describe the structure and nature of relationships in the organisation, but what does it really indicate? In essence, it is about power and who has the (supposed) control over the resources of the organisation. For the leader in an organisation who is committed to learning, it fails to deliver what is really needed. It does not indicate where the knowledge is created, how information is transferred, who deals with whom, and where the links are with suppliers, customers, etc. It views the whole organisation as a simplistic bounded system, like a series of Russian dolls, where each compartment can be fitted neatly and separately into the other.

The hierarchy chart might be seen as a process of systematic dis-aggregation and re-aggregation of the organisation's tasks and responsibilities (Ghoshal and Bartlett, 1998, 204). It ignores the personal element that is so important in the creating of learning within the organisation. A box on a chart is a simple representation of one particular aspect of an individual's job. It does not in any way indicate the totality of the person, the potential they can offer, and how the individual relates to other people in the organisation. The reality then is that the typical chart shown in Fig. 6.5 is nothing like a true representation of the organisation and how it operates.

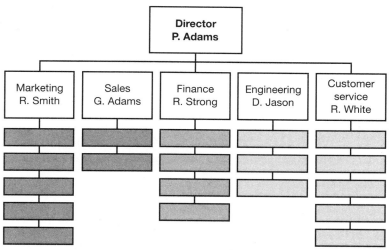

Fig. 6.5 Typical organisation chart

Take one person and ask them what they do. The answer will nearly always be that they make something for someone else, or work with someone else to produce a product. A single person might be considered as a soulless entity, unable to produce energy or a product until it meets another body. It sits in the organisation with the necessary potential and capability, but the actual realisation of a commercial value will only be released when the individual meets with someone else. It is often the formation of a relationship that produces the output, not the individual. If this is the case, then the purpose of any organisation map should be to indicate how the energy flows through the organisation, not where the people sit and to whom they report.

To truly understand how information flows within an organisation, the leader might have to rethink his or her views on the nature of organisational structure; to shift away from the view that the organisation is built around static and discrete blocks of people or teams. Instead, a leader might try and consider it as a constellation, a group of inter-dependent bodies that influence and relate to each other in real time (Fig. 6.6). The essence is to move from a focus on things and tasks, and to consider relationships and energy as a force that transports information and knowledge around the organisation.

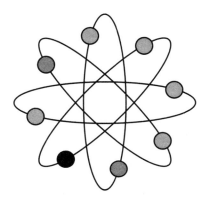

Fig. 6.6 An organisation as a constellation

If this is the case, the leader should understand how and why the patterns within the organisation change, and what factors influence their construction and destruction.

Relationship patterns

Underneath the rosy picture painted by the organisation chart, there is a shadow organisation where patterns shift and mutate like in a wind-swept desert. These patterns are formed as people leave, are promoted, or build political alliances. However, problems can arise when the structural pressure created by the formal chart conflicts with the natural relational patterns that emerge within the organisation. In the case where the formal structure of the organisation matches the natural patterns, there is likely to be a sense of harmony and alignment. Conversely, where the two are in conflict, negative tension can be created and may detract from the performance of the business.

So, it behoves the leader to look beyond the top level organisational chart and to understand the substructural relationships that operate within the organisation. To effectively map the terrain and to identify where knowledge is clustered, emerges, peaks and departs the business. For example, to understand that people naturally construct communities of interest which might be around social group-ings, shared histories, professional allegiance or simply drinking buddies. It is these relationships that in the past might have been seen as sub-optimal, and are often referred to as the 'old-pals network'. However, it is these social groups that often help the business to perform effectively. This is often where people draw the real maps of the organisation, share the true details of the profitability of the company, and learn who is in and out of favour. More importantly, it is also in these social groups that the real learning can take place. This is where people talk honestly about the product problems that need to be solved. They highlight people who are blocking the progress of a software upgrade, or borrow equip-ment from the squirrel stock to ensure that a customer order is completed. It is these social interactions that change almost daily and can dramatically amplify or attenuate the flow of information and knowledge through the organisation.

Even outside the informal social interactions, irrespective of the organisation chart, relationships will change. For example, when a project or product team is formed, the leader has to gather resources from within the organisation. He or she will generally have a degree of influence over who joins the team, and from where they come. The decisions taken at this time will shape the design of new relational patterns across the business, and will effectively set up *ad hoc* learning maps. It is through this network that information will flow, knowledge will be created, and new practices will be spread across the organisation, all bypassing the avenues laid down by the formal structure. Hence, the formation of this nat-ural network has a direct bearing on the way in which the organisation will gen-erate and store new intellectual capital.

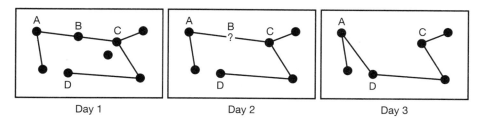

Fig. 6.7 Changing relationships

In Fig. 6.7, change in a relationship pattern is shown over a short period. In the space of three days, one person B has left, and the whole pattern of rela-tionships in the organisation has been transformed. Because A is in a power struggle with C, she decides to form links with D in order to build a new power structure. This changes the flow of information through the organisation, and has potentially slowed down the rate of knowledge diffusion.

51

This is likely to have happened without any formal directive and is unlikely to be shown on any organisational chart. What is interesting is that the new links are not necessarily made out of any business rationale. In this example, two people have linked with another because of a personal relationship, and the other has avoided a link with the person for political reasons. This highlights some of the intangible and hidden facets that drive relationships in an organisation. This change in the internal pattern will clearly affect the nature of the relationships and how the business manages the task elements. More importantly, it affects the flow of information, the creation of knowledge, and hence the ability of the organisation to learn.

The role of the leader in this situation is not to control directly or intervene in the process of patterning but to understand, influence and maximise the outcomes. This will be achieved by helping the people to develop a clearer appreciation of the issues that drive the formation of relationships.

Relationship formation

In truth, there are so many variables that drive the development of relationships that it would be impractical to work with them daily. However, there are seven key variables that the leader needs to be aware of so as to understand why and how patterns change over time (Fig. 6.8).

- Authority: Formal and informal power that people have to take responsibility for their actions.
- Effect: How the person feels about the relationship with another person.
- Dependence: The extent to which one person is dependent on another in the organisation in being able to meet objectives.
- Formal/informal: The nature of the relationship – is it formally sanctioned, or is it one based upon friendship, nepotism or a casual linkage?
- Intensity: The extent to which the parties interact with each other, both in frequency and duration.
- Information transfer: The extent to which information or knowledge is passed between the parties.
- Time shift: How the nature of the relationship changes over time. Does the content and form of the information change as time shifts, or is it fixed and independent of temporal changes?

These seven factors can have an impact on the relationship and the flow of information in a number of ways. For example, blockages can occur where one person incorrectly believes that the other has the necessary power to deliver a change. Alternatively, one person might require a lot of contact while the other is only looking for occasional meetings. Another example is where people fail to understand the implication of time shifts during the relationship. Objectives and goals agreed at the commencement of the relationship are often out of date by the time the first milestone is achieved. Unless both parties are mentally aligned across these seven areas, information transfer and knowledge creation can be seriously impaired.

In considering these factors, the leader has to undertake a mind experiment: to mentally think about people, the relationships, and the flow of information; to consider what relationships are crucial in the creation and mobilisation of knowledge; and think how he or she can influence or lubricate the process to ensure that maximum flow is obtained.

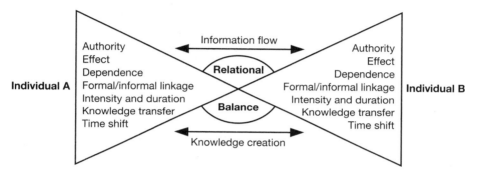

Fig. 6.8 Seven variables in relationships

For each relationship the leader should help the people to consider the seven factors and ask: what is the status for each individual or team? Is there a harmony between the two sides, or if there is an imbalance, how does it impact upon the flow of information?

Relationships and the leader

The leader can only set the framework in which people operate; it is not possible to control directly how people will behave with each other. Often, when change surfaces in an organisation, the leader might be tempted to intervene and try to fix the problems. One example of this is the way in which companies tend to constantly rebuild the formal structure in an attempt to fix internal problems. However, so often the deep problems continue as they are grounded in an inability of the people to collaborate and share learning, and are nothing to do with the structural design of the organisation.

In appreciating how the natural relationships can act as the knowledge carrier for the organisation, then the leader can appreciate what actions are necessary to ensure the free and effective flow of knowledge. Once the leader appreciates that the apparent random changes in the pattern of relationships are natural processes, he or she might be able to back off and leave the organisation to evolve naturally.

In accepting these ideas, super-leaders should be aware of the following:

- In many cases, it is the energy that arises from the relationships that creates learning in an organisation, not individuals working in isolation.
- The hierarchy chart used by many companies is an indicator of the power relationships, not how knowledge flows through the organisation.
- Individuals should be encouraged to map their personal relationship patterns, and understand how the map contributes to the flow of information and the creation of knowledge.
- There are many factors that drive new relationships. The super-leader will be aware of them and will constantly seek to encourage his or her people to be aware of them as well.
- It is through the pattern of relationships that information and knowledge are amplified and attended. People should be aware of the impact of change in the patterns and how it in turn impacts on the learning process.
- The process of developing knowledge maps can help people to understand where much of the current and future value exist within the business.

The issue of relationship management and connectivity in organisations is a woefully under-considered tool in the armoury of the leader. A common definition of management and leadership is the art of getting things done through others. Taking this viewpoint, the art of super-leadership might be seen as getting work done through effective relationships.

Values

The use of the word 'values', is (along with mission and vision) possibly one of the most over-used and least understood ideas in the manager's toolkit. Consider how many books, articles and training courses suggest that the manipulation and management of people's values is essential when creating a learning organisation. However, the danger is that (again like mission and vision) it is something that has crept into the leader's list of things to be 'done'. The suggestion is that people rarely take the time to appraise critically and understand its application and to take the time to really consider what they are, what they mean to the individual and how they relate to the commercial success of the organisation.

A working framework

One framework that helps to understand the idea of values and their linkage into organisational learning, is the Dilts neuro-logical model (1994, 35). It offers a systemic view of the relationship between personal values, people's behaviour and the environment in which they exist (Fig. 6.9).

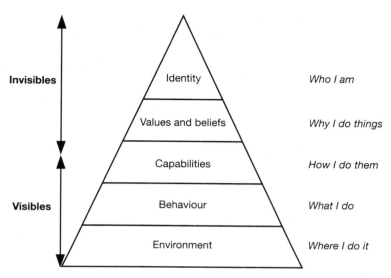

Fig. 6.9 The neuro-logical model (Dilts)

The neuro-logical model suggests that an individual may operate out of many planes at any one time. On a simple level, there are five places that an individual can respond from:

- Indentity/purpose: This is how the person thinks of a basic mission or purpose in life. This will be referenced by a statement of 'I am ...', such as 'I am a shy person', 'I am an optimist' or 'I am practical'.
- Values and beliefs: Values might be considered as the basis on which individuals form ideas about what is right and wrong. These drive the day-to-day decisions that an individual takes. They can both give an individual permission to take action, or restrict the ability to undertake something.
- Capabilities: These are the set of skills and strategies used in daily life. They are also termed as competencies and are the resources that people have as skills or qualities, for example, sensitivity, adaptability or flexibility.
- Behaviours: These are the specific actions that are carried out, regardless of the person's capability or beliefs. It is what people do and say, rather than what they feel or believe. The problem is that when change actions are set at this level, any deep or long-lasting transformation is unlikely to happen. To change the individual, the goal is to climb up the pyramid, to attack those areas that are deeper, personal and unseen.
- Environment: Environment refers to anything 'outside' the individual. It is the place where people work, live and socialise. Possibly how we behave in a casual social setting, or talking with people at work when having a coffee or lunch.

The benefit of using the Dilts model is that it provides a useful bridge between who people are at a deep level, what they do and how they can be mistakenly perceived by other people. Importantly, it also highlights that when considering people's values, there are visible clues that can be picked up to indicate how they feel. However, it should be recognised that there are also many hidden facets and issues that cannot be inferred from observation. This raises a number of important issues in relation to the use of values as an organisational factor:

- The values that people display may not be what they feel inside.
- The values that an organisation espouses might not be the ones that exist.
- The paradox of conforming to organisational values while aspiring to maintain one's own values can result in defence routines. This creates the falsification of behaviours and actions to simply satisfy the manager.
- In addition to focusing on values, it is also important to maintain an appreciation of 'who the person is' and how this affects their capability to learn.

In essence, it can be dangerous to introduce values into the organisational learning equation, since they can only ever be a subjective element. Any discussion about values at a cultural or organisational level can only ever be an approximation, and should not be taken as a prescriptive model that is applicable for everyone in the organisation.

Common organisational practice on values

It might help at this point to consider the views offered by a number of leading OL authors:

> 'The vision is an expression of basic values the company stands for, which all its members share enthusiastically and are unconditionally committed to realising' (Espejo et al., 1996).

> 'Core values describe how the company wants life to be on a day-to-day basis, whilst pursuing the vision' (Senge, 1990).

> 'When values are a central part of the organisation's shared vision and put out in full view, they become like a figure-head on a ship; a guiding symbol of the behaviour that will help people move towards the vision' (Senge et al., 1994).

> 'Values – the guiding principles that should help determine choice, decision policies, and behaviour which flow from the mission and vision of the organisation' (Peran et al., 1995).

> 'Core values provide the basic normative foundation of a business unit – they are the beliefs about what is good or right – the suggestion is that a clear set of core values helps to focus and motivate behaviour' (Tushman and Nadler, 1996).

Although this cannot be offered as the accepted view for all proponents of OL, there is enough similarity to infer that a number of core themes emerge:

- A set of centrally driven values will help to make the business more effective.
- These values should be set by the senior managers and link with the company vision.
- Hence, by implication, the senior managers have knowledge that is 'superior' to people in lower levels regarding what is best for the organisation.
- Also, by implication, there is some correlation between the delivery of the corporate values and the adoption of a required set of behaviours.
- A normalised organisation is preferred over a diverse one.

Here lies the paradox, the suggestion that cohesiveness, shared values and a common vision is essential, even when such processes may constrain the individual's ability to innovate and create new knowledge. On one hand, senior managers are pushed to offer 'the one and only way', a common set of lenses that everyone can wear to help them share a normalised view. On the other hand, there is the drive for people to create their own view of the world, become a soloist, experiment, and break the mould. It is this gap in the system, the space between the espoused values and the actual ones, that can create negative tension. This might be seen where chief executives espouse certain values for the organisation, only to implicitly support actions and behaviours that go against its meaning. This can help to create the idea that the publication of corporate values is a fad, and not something that has any deep long-term credibility (Argyris, 1990).

How then can the two views be reconciled to create a style of operating that offers the best of both worlds? There needs to be a process that allows the two views to co-exist and to offer a shared sense of purpose while allowing people to operate in an environment that does not offend their personal value system. The answer might be in using value mapping as a process to help align the needs of the individual and the organisation.

Value mapping

The assumption offered in this mapping process is that values are not black and white. They are likely to vary according to a range of different stimuli and circumstances. They can shift along two different continuums: the degree of rigidity; and the amount of focus.

First, values might range from generic to specific. Generic values might be referred to as the philosophical or ethical position that an individual holds. These are the deep beliefs that are routed in the individual's history, and drive many of their intuitive and instinctive decisions. Specific values are the things that people will give priority to and spend energy on pursuing in the short term or in a certain area of their life (Jacques and Clement, 1991). On a second

57

dimension, it might be possible to consider them in relation to the rigidity of the value set. Are the beliefs entrenched, and hence will never change, or is there a possibility that over time some modification will take place? Using these two variables, it is possible to develop a matrix that can identify the individual's value map and therefore, their propensity to exist within a culture of a differing value system.

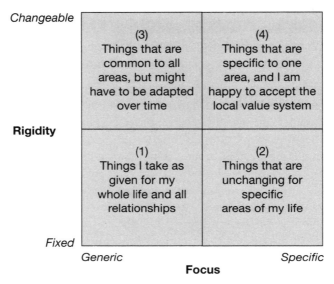

Fig. 6.10 Value mapping

Helping the individual to understand and map their value set is the first step that the leader can take towards aligning the relationship with the organisation. The next stage is to undertake a matching exercise where a comparative analysis is undertaken between the person's value and that of the organisation where he or she is working.

Value matching

Value matching takes the value that an individual has mapped and aligns them with the stated values of the manager or organisation. It is a comparative process whereby the values that the individual holds to be important are compared and reconciled with those the organisation holds to be of importance. This process means that the individual and their manager should go through a fairly deep and personal experience to allow them the chance to offer their schematic view of the world. To clearly understand what the other person's values are, and why they are held to be of importance.

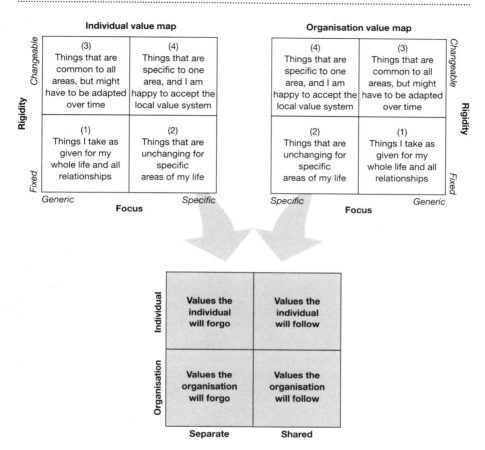

Fig. 6.11 Value matching

As value matching becomes more accepted and discussible, so it might make sense for it to be included as part of the contracting process. The proposition is that people who derive satisfaction from having values that are aligned with the organisation, will typically be more effective, happy, and willing to share learning with others in the team. If an individual feels that the organisation or colleagues do not operate from the same value set, there is every chance that the learning process will be slowed down or even blocked.

At the end of the contracting process there will be a clear view of four areas:

- The values that the organisation will reinforce.
- The values that the organisation is prepared to put aside for the individual.
- The values that the individual will follow which are over and above those offered by the organisation.

- The values that the individual is prepared to forgo while working with the organisation.

This process offers the benefit of raising and clarifying those issues that are often left unspoken. It might not directly resolve problems where there is a difference between the two, but at least in recognising this, sensitive action can be taken to resolve the differences. Clearly, this type of process will be difficult to manage, but in many ways, it is the process of dialogue – discussing and understanding each other's values that can be of more benefit that any final agreement on the matching process.

The role of the super-leader and values

The relationship between value matching and the creation of organisational knowledge should never be underestimated. In most cases it should be expected that people will put their best effort into doing something they care for. The more the activity is valued, the more they will express energy, imagination, initiative and proactivity (Jacques and Clement, 1991). Once the knowledge has been created by an individual, it will then be amplified through the process of socialisation as people connect with each other. If this process of interaction is corrupted or inhibited in any way, the idea of facilitating organisation-wide learning will be severely impinged. One of the primary forms of corruption is where the individual believes that either they, or the work they are undertaking, is not seen to be important by the organisation.

Hence the need for alignment between the individual's and the organisation's value set. The suggestion is that the leader cannot simply dictate what the values of the company are, as these will simply be a manifestation of what is important for the people at the top. It should be an overriding goal of any organisation to discover and capture as much as possible of the value that is held within its people. It is clearly not in its interest to slowly reduce the level of variety and diversity to a point where the business employs clones of the senior managers. So the need is to create a pincer movement, to offer direction from the top, where the senior managers share their beliefs in the values that are important and additionally, to gather reality from the bottom, using a bottom-up discovery process to identify what values the people believe are important.

The outcome of the value matching process can be a statement that embodies the needs of the organisation and the individual. This will then act as a major factor in creating an open flow of information through the organisation. No longer is it possible for the communication of company values to be a brainwashing process (Sims and Lorenzi, 1992). The objective is not to enforce a process of behavioural change. It is about creating a shared mindset, one that can help to create a common sense of resonance, even across a diverse and varied organisation.

60

Values are the things that move people together, push them apart and generally make the world go round (Jacques and Clement, 1991). One of the primary roles of the leader is to make sure that this is a positive process, and not one that distorts and corrupts the learning process.

Conclusion

The three aspects considered in this section are not offered as definitive solutions. They are simply aspects that leaders might consider to ensure that the process of knowledge creation and learning is facilitated throughout the organisation.

In doing this the super-leader might consider the interaction between the three areas and ask questions like:

- In what way is trust regarded as a key value by the organisation?
- To what extent is trust seen as important in building relationships by the people in the organisation?
- What is the rate of change for relationships in the organisation, and how does this affect the level of trust?

Although the role of the leader is sometimes overplayed, there is little doubt that a significant role can be played in helping to create and amplify the flow of knowledge. The key thing is for the leader to step out of the more traditional role and to consider the deeper, more intangible issues that can have an impact upon the learning process.

For effective long-term learning, organisations need to develop effective long-term leaders, not people who just have the buzz words and exciting capabilities to excel in 'today's' market-place. As Senge (1996, 311) suggests, learning is constrained by managers' inability to reflect with insight on their assumptions, and the inability to inquire effectively into others' assumptions. Only by reaching into these new levels of insight, will the flow of knowledge and learning be able to transcend the organisational boundaries.

Super leader model dynamics

	How do we learn?	How do we share?	How do we use?	How can we improve?
Trust Able to foster trusting relationships even when the forces of change make it difficult				
Trustworthy Behaving in a way that will help to develop a trusting relationship				
Thin and thick trust Recognise the difference between fragile and robust relationships and develop accordingly				
Trust index Able to define and manage a clear set of criteria for discussing trust within a relationship				

Knowledge flow Understand how trust lubricates the flow of knowledge within an organisation				
Relationships Understand how learning flows from the nature and patterns of connectivity rather than the normal hierarchy structure				
Neuro-logical levels Recognise how people operate and respond to stimuli from different levels in themselves				
Value mapping People understand their value set as mapped against the criteria of rigidity and focus				
Value matching People are able to match their values against that of their manager or the organisation				

Chapter 7

Schemata

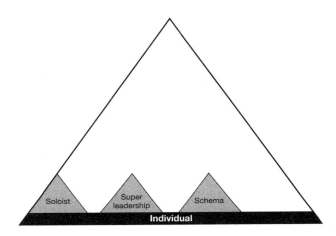

Fig. 7.1 Building in schemata

Imagine, a plane comes into land at Heathrow airport, and all of a sudden the pilot announces that the undercarriage is stuck and the plane will have to make an emergency landing. As the plane lands, the passengers are instructed to leave the plane rapidly, as a fire may break out. What will people do in this situation? The rational view is that they will quickly leave without waiting to unpack their luggage from the overhead locker. The reality is, in many crashes, people put their lives at risk by waiting to get their possessions out of the overhead rack.

The reason is that people still follow the mental map or schema programmed for a normal landing. They have not been able to release or quickly unlearn the process that exists in their head for ordinary departure of the aeroplane. The standard map is that upon landing, everyone stands up and waits to get their possessions, and that only once this task is achieved can they leave the plane. However, in an emergency, speed is of the essence, and the quickest person out of the plane stands the greatest chance of survival. The evidence is that the people who survive are those who ignore the existing schemata or self-imposed rules, and look for ways to circumvent the standard ways of exiting.

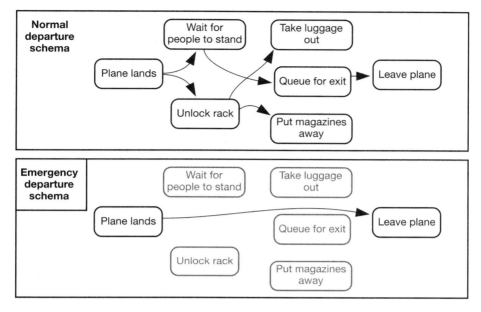

Fig. 7.2 Ignoring the rules

This story highlights the paradox that faces organisations. On one hand there is the supposed need to create a shared view or purpose so that people have a clear appreciation of the work they are undertaking and why the organisation exists. At the same time, if everyone is locked into the same mental view, the ability of the organisation to react to sudden change or unplanned opportunities can be limited.

The following aspects help expand upon the idea of schemata and their impact upon the learning process:

- **Schema description** – Introducing the notion of the schema as a mental map, and its relevance to the idea of organisational learning and knowledge management.
- **Schema types** – The various types of mental maps that people construct when making sense of the world.
- **Schema shift** – Explaining how learning and change are built upon the notion of breaking with the past, effectively shifting from one frame of reference to another in order to move forward.
- **Schema interaction** – Indicates how shared learning depends upon the synergy derived from the effective interaction between the individuals within the organisation.
- **Schema matching** – How the effective communicator within an organisation needs to master the ability to match and step inside another person's schema.

These five aspects of schema management form the underlying components that can act as a bottle-neck to the flow of knowledge through the organisation. If people are unable to talk, listen or share ideas, the channels through which knowledge flows will become congested. However, where schemata are open and shared, then the flow of knowledge can amplified as it moves from person to person.

Schema description

An individual's schema might be viewed as the mental map that guides their thoughts and behaviours. It acts like a window frame, letting some things through and screening others out. It helps to bring certain elements of the world into focus, while making others blurred and fuzzy so that they can be ignored or overlooked. The schema has a hard and soft element. The hard side emerges when it helps people to make decisions that are critical and potentially difficult to make. From the soft angle, they help people to take something that is abstract and vague, and make it a thing of pleasure or beauty for the individual.

Imagine a piece of music, be it jazz, rock, classical or blues. For the young musician, rock will be regarded with great reverence, and seen as a piece of art. However, to someone who has been schooled in the classics, this same piece of music might seem to be abhorrent, and to have no discernible quality or taste. This contrasting view is routed in each individual's schema that has been formed by the exposure to different experiences.

However, this disparity can result in more than separate tastes, it can act as blockage to learning and knowledge sharing. Consider two people who live in the country and work in the city. One has always travelled to work by train and the other has always travelled by car. Their start and destination points are exactly the same, but their routes are totally different.

Imagine each of the these people describing the best way to get from country to city. The answers will be different and potentially confusing to anyone who is listening. They will be using different words, patterns and experiences to describe the journey. Although the end result is the same, the way in which they view the experience is totally different. Imagine then the confusion when these two people try to agree on the best route. Their mental maps will be different, their language will be contrary, and it is unlikely that they will find it easy to reach a collaborative conclusion.

Until each can understand the other's view, they will find it difficult to learn or create knowledge that improves upon their personal schema. It may be that the only way that each of the commuters will be able to appreciate the other person's map is by experiencing the same journey. The question that organisations face is how can people in the same company get the sense of another's journey without experiencing it?

The experience of life helps people to build the lenses that they use to construct their map of the world. However, this lens will distort their view of the world, such that one shared experience can appear contrary to different people. As an example, consider the following text and create a mental picture as to what it is talking about:

> 'The procedure is actually quite simple. First you arrange things into different groups. Of course, one pile might be sufficient, depending on how much there is to do … It is important not to overdo things. That is, it is better to do too few things at one time rather than too many. In the short run this may not seem important, but complications can easily arise. A mistake can be expensive as well. At first the whole procedure will seem complicated. Soon, however, it will become just another facet of life.'
>
> Bransford and Johnson, 1972

In considering this passage, the reader is likely to have filtered it through their own schematic maps; to have used their personal blueprints, experiences and histories to draw a conclusion as to its purpose. The reader might draw a conclusion that the passage refers to the work needed to prepare the items prior to being placed into the washing machine. Another person might take the view that it pertains to the preparation of an end of year tax account or the steps to take when preparing a dinner party. Whatever the resulting viewpoint, the reader's own schematic map would have placed it into a specific pigeon hole, and any future thoughts about the passage might be influenced by this bounded view.

It is this restricted viewpoint that is so important when considering the idea of learning and knowledge management. Consider the issue of middle-aged, white-collar redundancy. To lose a career half way through one's life is a devastating and potentially destructive process. People can, and do, end up destroying themselves and those around them in their attempt to reconcile and understand why it has happened and why in particular to them. In many cases people will think themselves into a schema of 'I have had my time and am no longer required by the business world'. This is a limiting and bounded schema that creates a fatalistic sense of doubt. The way that this person views the world might well contribute to their inability to get a new job or start a new life. An alternative view is offered by someone who has an unbounded schema. There are cases of individuals who have become so frustrated at being unable to get a job, that they have stood next to the motorway with a sign saying they are looking for work. They have driven a shift in their own schema, to think of ways to get a job rather than reasons why they cannot get one. They have in effect created the world they wish to see. Therefore, the environment in which people operate is actually an enactment of people's schemata. So when looking at the behaviour of a group of people, an individual might consider and comment on the observed conduct of the people. However, this behaviour is a result of the way that people look at the world, and in particular the relational maps that they have constructed over time. This might simply be in the form of a picture as in Fig. 7.3 or it might be represented in the form of stories or metaphors that indicate how the individuals look upon the world. Whatever the framework, people who are able to understand how others feel and see the world from the inside-out, will have a significant advantage in creating effective long-term working relationships.

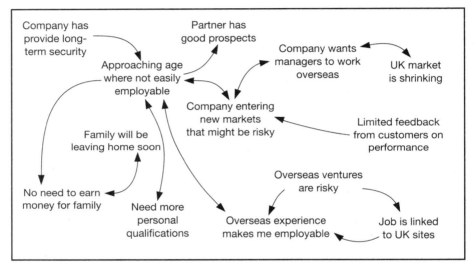

Fig. 7.3 **Reaction to redundancy varies**

The first step towards achieving this level of comprehension is to understand the different types of schematic frames that people construct and how they might interrelate and work with each other.

Schema types

The construction of an individual's schema is by its very nature extremely personal, since it is assembled entirely around their cognitive framework. It will have a range of variation and complexity that makes it difficult to map and structure. However, there are a number of schema types that might be considered to exist in people's minds. These might be viewed as the different labels or lenses that people use to make sense of the world as in Fig. 7.4.

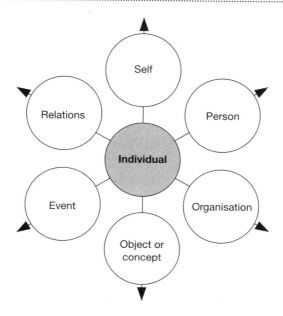

Fig. 7.4 Schema types

Of these seven types, the self schema refers to a picture that an individual will have of themselves. This might be based upon honest self-reflection or on social views that are offered as feedback from other people. Sometimes this self-view can help the individual to make choices when faced with difficult decisions. For example, people who believe themselves to be trustworthy are more likely to follow this map when faced with a situation that requires an ethical decision to be taken. However, there might be elements of self-delusion included in the self-schema map. On some occasions people will have a set of beliefs about themselves, only to find that they take alternative decisions when push comes to shove. Neither is right nor wrong, but having a clear view of one's schema is likely to enhance the individual's ability to work with other people in an effective way.

The person schema is formed by ideas, memories and feelings about other people. Examples might be how people build schemata about their manager, children or partner. On one hand this can be a positive factor, in that it stabilises a person's view of others in the group. On the other hand, it has the capacity to become destructive. Once a person is badged as a fool, administrator or home-maker, it can become difficult for the schema to be modified. Consider how a negative cycle can develop in relationships where each person's schematic view of the other can take them down a rigid and ultimately destructive path. This is often seen in the divorce, where both partners build schemata about their partner that can be based upon biased and subjective information. However, once the map is formed, they are often unable or unwilling to allow it to be modified.

An organisation schema might be regarded as a more generalised view of a group of people. This might be the individual's organisation, a client group, suppliers or nations. This can be seen in the way that different functional groups can view each other within a business. For example the way marketing people can view engineers as being too quality focused, and engineers view marketers as cavalier.

The object or concept schema relates to innate objects and how they affect the individual's view of the world. It might be a personal view of the office, how home feels, or the emotions associated with the smell of a baby after it has been bathed (Harris, 1994).

The event schema might be viewed as the way in which a person charts out events. This might be team meetings, weddings, or simply arriving home from work each evening. It may also expect certain behaviour by others. Imagine an individual who moves from a company where meetings are well-managed to one where they are regarded as gladiatorial contests by the incumbents. This sudden change in the expected schema is likely to create a great deal of dissonance for the new manager and might result in withdrawal from any interaction at the meeting.

Relational schema result from how causal links are built between independent units. For example, the relationship between a flat tyre and the poor performance of a car, or the belief that lower-paid people should not be valued as highly as well-paid executives. People use these links to make what they believe are rational jumps of cause and effect, that are in reality only subjective viewpoints based upon their schematic maps.

Although these schemata are shown as discrete units, they will not exist this way in someone's cognitive structure. There will be a complex fabrication of interaction and overlap between each of the areas that will in turn result in the creation of new schematic models. So although discussing these schemata in this way might be useful, in the sense of helping people to understand the nature and construction of schemata, it can be a dangerous over-simplification.

Interestingly, as the level of interaction increases, so the opportunity for dissonance and confusion can arise. As the separate elements are brought together in real time, they might present conflicting elements to the individual. This can happen when a person meets someone from work in an unusual situation. Imagine walking along the seashore, and unexpectedly finding one of the senior directors naked on a nudist beach. The apparent mismatch can potentially cause an embarrassing situation for both parties and one that they might try to avoid. Although such a mismatch is one that people often try to evade, it is often this type of situation that stimulates real learning and change to take place, as people are forced into a position where they have to confront their existing schematic maps. In accepting that such reflection and dissonance are positive processes, so a process of schematic shift can occur. It is this type of schema mismatch that is often seen in brainstorming or scenario planning sessions. When individuals or teams disagree with each other, the temptation can be to go for avoidance or compromise as the safe option. However, the stage at which learning will occur is when each side is encouraged to delve deeper into the point of confrontation, and to understand what drivers led to the construction of a particular viewpoint. Once the parties have been able to step inside the others' shoes, so their personal schemata will begin to shift. They might not necessarily agree, but they can at least appreciate why others think the way they do.

Schema shift

At the root of all learning is the idea of schema shift, where an individual has to be prepared to discard or throw away the current world view and accept an alternative frame of reference. This shift in process can be at a number of levels in the organisation. For the individual, it might be simply learning an improved way of operating a particular tool; for the team, it may be a series of processes that have been introduced to support the development of a new project. In the case of an organisational shift, there are examples of major change programmes like total quality, or business re-engineering modifying how entire businesses view their customers and suppliers.

In making this schema shift, the first thing is for the self-sustaining loop to be broken. This loop is a common process followed by everyone. People see the world in a particular way, and so expect it to behave according to the rules and criteria set out in their individual mental maps. One example might be the self-imposed beliefs that people apply to themselves. Typically, 'I am a loser', 'I can't drive' or 'I can become the head of the company'. Each of these schemata is imprinted in the brain, and so will influence how people see the world. For the 'loser' to change, the map should be realigned to see the world through the eyes of a successful person or for the person who cannot drive to actually visualise themselves driving (Fig. 7.5).

Once the world is seen in a new way, so the shift can be used to reinforce this new world position. However, this can soon drift into a negative position. If people decide to stop at that point, and do not use the change experience to energise further schema shifts, then the change or learning is only of limited value. Once the individual has created the personal ability to break with the past, then the idea of life-long learning can start to emerge. They have the chance to develop an iterative process in life, that they undertake as naturally as sleeping or drinking tea. Once this schema shift is locked in, so the action can become habitual. It is at the stage of habitual shift, that the idea of schemata becomes really powerful. In helping individuals and groups to take on board this type of personal action, so three of the traits presented in Chapter 5 come to life:

- **Change mastery** – Moving from a position where change is feared, to one where it is regarded as an invigorating and opportunistic process, even seeing change as a type of personal long-term security.
- **Challenging ethos** – Recognising that change and learning will always be about modifying paradigms and perceptions. To challenge the existing status quo and feel comfortable breaking with past conventions and habits.
- **Continual learning** – To understand that as an employee one has become a marketable commodity, and as such it is wise to continually re-invent and invest in one's self schema.

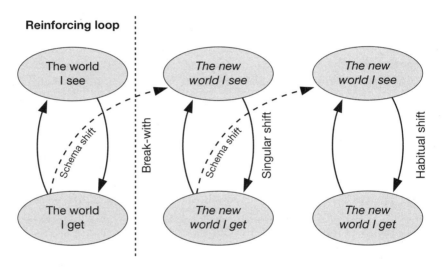

Fig. 7.5 Shifting schema

Each of these three traits is wholly dependent on the idea that schemata can, and do shift. In accepting the importance of the schema shift, it then becomes important to understand the factors that drive this process:

- To what extent the change is driven by intrinsic or extrinsic factors.
- The time taken to effect the change (short or long).
- The degree of transformation that occurs (small or large).

In considering these three dimensions, it is possible to identify eight different types of schemata displacements (Fig. 7.6).

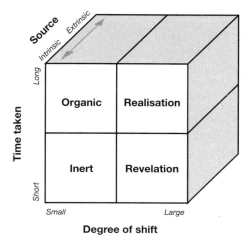

Fig. 7.6 Eight types of schemata displacement

Intrinsic inert

In this instance the schema shift is very small, happens quickly, and often unbeknown to the individual. It might be characterised by someone reading a daily paper. They have taken the intrinsic decision to update their view of the world, but changes to the mental map are small as they follow the shifting patterns of stories in the paper.

Extrinsic inert

Often a change in people's schemata can be driven by small and imperceptible factors. This might arise from feedback someone offers at work, or simply looking at a photograph of oneself and seeing the change in age or weight.

Intrinsic organic

A long-term but small shift can occur where people decide to take up a hobby. Taking up a pursuit such as pottery, car maintenance or drama will, over time, deliver a change in their schematic map, but the degree of shift is likely to be marginal.

Extrinsic organic

The long-term shift of a personal schema can also be driven by external factors. One example might be in the formation of a relationship. It is likely that over time the other person will change the individual's perception of the world, and so deliver a transformation in their schematic map.

Intrinsic revelation

In this position change over a very short space of time is driven by the individual and is of a large nature. This might be characterised by someone who has a sudden spiritual awakening, or the eureka effect that can arise when attempting to tackle a difficult problem.

Extrinsic revelation

Often there will be an immense change that happens instantaneously but is driven by someone else. This might happen where people are on a personal development programme, where the goal is to offer deep and intense feedback on someone's impact on other people. The sudden realisation by someone who believes they are perceived as friendly but are actually perceived to be arrogant, can be a major revelation, and is likely to change their world map in an instant.

Intrinsic realisation

The realisation process is one that happens over a long term and is of some magnitude. For the intrinsic model this might be characterised by someone who takes a decision to convert to a new religion or change their way of life.

Extrinsic realisation

Again, this schema shift is large and occurs over a long time but is driven by an external agent. This can be seen when someone acts as a mentor or tutor to someone during a development programme. While going through the change, the impact of the other person may not be apparent. However, on completion of the programme, the individual can look back and recognise how their view of the world has changed.

Each one of these schema shifts, although different in make up, has a common element. They all infer that a degree of change and learning has taken place; learning in the sense that the old ways are discarded and passed over, so that an individual can create or align with the new world view. However, it is this schema shift that is so often resisted in organisations. In Chapter 5, one of the key traits of the soloist to create a learning organisation is that of challenging; being prepared to reframe and offer counter views to those that exist at present. The pressure in many organisations is not to rock the boat, but to toe the party line. Who would dare proclaim that the emperor has no clothes if doing this will result in their dismissal, or being side-tracked when promotion opportunities arise. For schema shifts to occur in organisations, there is an underlying need for courage and trust. Courage to offer counter views, alternative theories and ground-breaking ideas. Trust to believe that when challenges are raised, no recriminations will be forthcoming.

Schema interaction

In Chapter 6 on super leadership, one of the key factors is the nature and effectiveness of relationships. For an organisation (rather than an individual) to learn, there should be a flow of knowledge across the networks that link people, and the flow should be seamless, speedy and synergistic. In going through this exchange process, single schema will become public, and shared schemata might develop into team visions. In many cases this will continue to iterate until a level of mutual understanding exists as to how the world is perceived by each individual.

The potential released from the sharing of personal schemata is dependent upon the extent to which exposure and feedback takes place. Exposure in the sense of people being prepared to share their personal maps with others in the group, and feedback as people share their perceptions of others' mental maps. In the cases where this process occurs, the organisation is able to take on a generative stance, where the sharing of schemata creates enhanced learning and new knowledge.

Although this sounds simple enough, when looking at how people interact and share ideas, there are at least five different characteristics (Fig. 7.7).

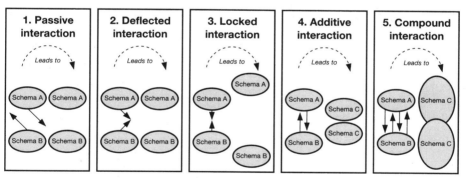

Fig. 7.7 Characteristics of interactions

Passive interaction

In this case the intercourse between two or more people is undertaken without any real sharing of the mindset. Each person might be talking at the other person and not taking the time to listen to their views and ideas. As such, each person retains their existing schema without increasing its depth or breadth in any form. Examples of this can often be seen in politics, where each person is there to simply put across a view, and not to listen to any opposing idea.

Deflected interaction

In some cases both parties can have a similar focus, but the idea under consideration is outside their personal schema, and emerging conversation can be seen as idle or superficial. Both individuals can be apparently engaged but there is little openness or debate around issues that are personal to the people. Examples of this will be seen in the gentle conversation that takes place in a bar, or at the start of parties. Polite articulation is taking place but no depth of exposure or feedback is apparent.

Locked interaction

This is where the people involved in the process are at odds with each other. The people are not just failing to listen to others, they are diametrically opposed to the other ideas and thoughts. As such, the process of sharing actually moves people further apart, rather than bringing the schemata together. Examples might be rival football team supporters. Their love of a team blinds them to the acceptance of anyone else's viewpoint, and they are unable to step inside another's shoes to experience a different point of view.

Additive interaction

A more positive viewpoint is where people are able to share their personal models and maps, and as a result each person is able to enhance their schema. In this case the process is one of a simple bi-directional exchange of ideas with little amplification taking place. This might be seen in the discussion at a team meeting where people share problems they have experienced and resolved them. Although knowledge is shared with the rest of the team there is little amplification of the ideas.

Compound interaction

The highest level of interaction might be where the communication between a group of people results in synergistic action, and the amplification of people's ideas. As people expose their thoughts, ideas and personal patterns, so the level of understanding and knowledge within the room will expand. Examples of this might be found in scenario planning workshops, where the interaction between people will create new ideas, themes and patterns that might not have existed prior to the event.

In considering these five options, it is possible to take an intuitive leap to suggest that option five might be the one that organisations should consistently aim to attain. However, this is not necessarily so.

In the first three options, each individual has their own view of the world, there is no real sharing between the people, and no collaboration in the development of a communal view. The next two, additive and compound, indicate that a similar schema is being shared or developed by two or more people, and this is commonly referred to as a paradigm. This proposition was offered by Kuhn (1970). He suggested that a paradigm is a constellation of concepts, values, perceptions and practices shared by a community that forms a particular vision of reality which is the basis of the way in which a community organises itself. Examples might be the original view that earth was the centre of the universe, or that man could never fly.

It is this pure form of a mutual paradigm to which so many authors aspire when they advocate the need for a 'shared sense of purpose', 'common mission', or 'collective values'. One example of where this seems to work is with Hewlett Packard and the HP way. The suggestion is that there is an underlying sense of the founder's ideals and ethos in all of the decisions and actions taken by the company, and this permeates throughout the enterprise.

However, this is not necessarily the model that all businesses should strive to follow. In some cases the development of a shared schematic view across the organisation can actually create internal barriers and attenuate the knowledge creation process. For example, imagine someone who creates a great new idea that can have tangible commercial value, but it doesn't align with the 'corporate' schematic view of the business's core operating areas. In this case the individual might either shy away from submitting the idea, or it might be immediately rejected as part of the socialisation process. The inability to accept variety and diversity within the corporate ethos has the potential to damage the long-term opportunities for the organisation. Attenuating the level of internal variety can inhibit the organisation's capacity to adjust to diversity in the market-place.

To counter this damping process, many organisations create spontaneity, excitement and energy, by deliberately encouraging people to follow option three (locked interaction) – to intentionally nourish the idea of head-to-head confrontation and make challenge and conflict a core behaviour within the corporate culture. This might be seen in organisations that create internal markets and competing internal product lines.

Clearly there are no right or best options for these five interaction types. The key message is that people should be aware of their schema, what style of interaction is taking place, and what style of interaction is common for the organisation. Most importantly, people should be encouraged to develop the ability to diagnose and accept other people's schemata, and in doing so, increase the ability to ease and amplify the flow of knowledge across the organisation.

Schematic matching

All too often, people assume that someone's behaviour is a direct replication of their schematic model. However, just because someone behaves in a certain way, this is not necessarily an indication of their personal beliefs or mental maps. In trying to understand someone's schematic map, it is important to climb beyond the outward displays and to really latch on to what is important for them at a deep personal level.

One example of this might be the notion of a leader who is attempting to impart his or her vision to the organisation. To be effective, the leader should be able to touch the hearts of a group of people with a single swipe. Through the use of stories, analogies and metaphors, he or she might be able to offer an idea of their goals for the future. From this people can start to assimilate the prospect of change and any future state into their personal schema.

The leader often needs to perform the magic trick of being all things to all people; pragmatic to those looking for facts and details; a dreamer to those who like to operate deep into the future; and an activist for those who need to get into the meat of ideas. In framing the right language, the leader will be able to create a shared schematic map that all people can understand. Although they might not agree with or accept the view, at least they can appreciate what the leader's schematic structure is and how it has been constructed.

Schematic matching is therefore one of the most powerful but underused tools in the manager's armoury. Its apparent failure to be used is most evident in the change programmes that many organisations embark upon. For learning to be successful in the long term, it is important that transformation is reinforced at the schematic level, rather than the behavioural one. Simply training people in a new customer process will have little effect, unless they understand why it is being introduced. Consider the shops where people respond with a supposedly heartfelt comment of 'can we help you?', or 'have a nice day', when clearly they have little belief in what they are saying. If the schematic maps of the individuals are aligned with the expected behaviours, the change process is more likely to produce the desired benefit and long-lasting gain.

One area where the idea of matching is of crucial importance is in understanding the effectiveness of meetings. It goes without saying that all organisations can be full of contradictions and confusion as at any one time and an individual is likely to have a number of conflicting personal and professional goals. The problem is that the majority of these goals can all emerge at the same time, in the same meeting, by different people.

Whatever the gathering, people will often take the opportunity to drop their view of the world (as filtered by their schema) onto the meeting. They are often incapable of seeing beyond their schema, and are only interested in offering their map to the world rather than listening to others. If one were to take a top-down perspective of the meeting, it might look like people lobbing ideas into a 'plop pot' (Fig. 7.8). This pot will gradually fill up during the course of the meeting until it overflows with people's lost ideas, suggestions and goals. It might be that a manager can measure the ineffectiveness of the meeting by counting the plops, as the ideas land in the pot.

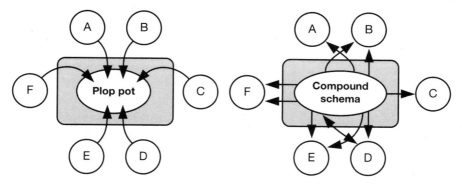

Fig. 7.8 Meetings: 'plop pot' and compound schema

The alternative view is where people are able and willing to match their schemata to others in the room. In working to offer their own schema to the group while actively building on and using the schemata of other people, the total map in the room will multiply and expand. This does not mean that people have to passively agree with each other, since challenging is a key part of the compound interaction process. It does mean that people should be prepared to understand other people's schemata before dropping their own onto the table.

Conclusions

The primary goal of this chapter is to indicate the importance of schema when developing effective organisational learning processes. If organisations are to deliver internal processes and people who can take the step into generative rather than adaptive learning, they might wish to understand some of the deeper issues surrounding learning and change.

In essence, the following aspects might be considered:

- Schemata are the lenses that people use to make sense of the world and as such directly affect their behaviours, attitudes and achievements of their personal objectives and the resulting business performance.
- They reflect the history, thoughts and experiences that individuals have accumulated over their life, and cannot be brushed aside as something that is too superficial for the organisation to be concerned with.
- They can be formed and changed without the person being aware of any modification. As such, it pays to ensure that people have the necessary time to reflect and understand what current schematic drivers are influencing their behaviours.
- Schemata are based upon deeply-ingrained and personal structures, hence the organisation should not assume that a schematic model for one person or team can easily be replicated in another area.

- The use of language is key to understanding people's schematic models. Although the words people use cannot always directly offer a view of their schematic maps, it may be a possible indicator as to how they cognitively map the world.
- Schemata can sometimes be more effectively understood through the use of metaphor and analogy. Asking an individual to describe how they feel can be difficult but asking them to relate it to an anecdotal story can make it somewhat easier.
- The key to creating a generative organisation is based upon enabling people to break with their current schemata, and in doing this, to use the 'break-with' process as an ongoing development tool.
- Accept that no matter how much one disagrees with another person's schema, to them it is the absolute truth and will be that way until they reorientate to an alternative viewpoint.
- Don't always strive for additive or compound interaction. The use of locked interaction can help to create the dissonance that is necessary to unlock rigid schematic structures.
- Schema matching can prove to be a powerful method for facilitating and easing the flow of knowledge across an organisation. As a skill it can be difficult to attain, but once people have the will to move outside their schema, so they gain the ability to interact at a deeper level.

Knowledge diffusion is about sharing schemata through the process of collaborative and challenging interactions. Hence, it is the social construction of knowledge that is potentially most valuable in creating intellectual capital within the business. The resulting synthesis that emerges following an interaction between two people, or groups, is where the real fruits of the future are embedded. In accepting this, the organisation must in turn accept the need for people to understand the importance of schemata at both an individual and organisational level.

People who are only able to see the world from their own perspective are effectively imprisoning themselves in a jail of their own making. People who have broken free from this cell and are able to draw on the schemata that have been influenced by others, are better equipped to understand and manage the complex everyday world of organisations (Bolman and Deal, 1991, 14).

Schema model dynamics

	How do we learn?	How do we share?	How do we use?	How can we improve?
Schematic maps The notion of the schemata as a mental map, and its relevance to the idea of organisational learning and knowledge management is understood				
Schema types People understand the different schematic maps that can be used when looking at the world				
Schema shift Broad appreciation of the fact that learning and change are built upon the notion of breaking with the past, effectively shifting from one frame of reference to another in order to move forward				

Schema model dynamics continued

	How do we learn?	How do we share?	How do we use?	How can we improve?
Schema interaction People recognise how shared learning depends upon the synergy derived from the effective interaction between individuals within the organisation				
Schematic matching Appreciation of the fact that the learning process can be aided by the use of effective communication framing				

Chapter 8

Surprises

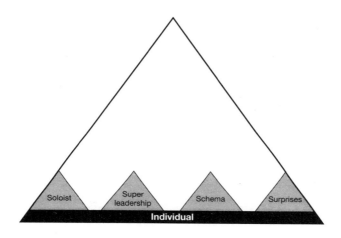

Fig. 8.1 Surprises complete the individual level

*I*magine, sitting watching the TV, possibly something relaxing that can help the *viewer to wind down and prepare for bed. All of a sudden a news programme comes on, one that raises the plight of people in Africa and the danger the Aids virus offers for them. The key issue highlighted by the show is the need to build an effective communication infrastructure so that people can be educated about the dangers associated with the virus. Radio is the logical answer but the lack of electricity in remote areas makes this impossible, since the cost of batteries is so high. Of all the viewers in the UK, one person sits and ponders this dilemma and starts to ask questions about how this might be resolved. He starts to daydream about other devices that have been used to produce sound in desert situations. He imagines the old generals sitting in the sun during the Boer War, listening to music on their wind-up gramophones, and wonders how this can be applied to the problem in Africa. All of a sudden he makes an intuitive link and realises that clockwork radios might be the solution for the problem of communication in Africa.*

From this idle daydream came the clockwork radio, an idea developed by the English inventor, Trevor Baylis. The radio is now being sold around the world, and is effectively helping to communicate the problems associated with the transmission of Aids in the poorer parts of Africa. It also provided a springboard for the development of a range of new products, such as clockwork lights, computers and a whole host of follow-me products by a number of large manufacturers.

So, what does this mean for the modern organisation? The proposition is that any company that does not have the capacity to either originate or import new ideas, innovations or surprises is effectively planting seeds for its own demise. Conversely, any organisation that aspires to improve its ability to learn and create knowledge, should foster the innate capacity to continually surprise itself and others with new ideas.

This chapter builds on this assumption and considers four key areas that need to be considered if they wish to develop this capability to create surprises, namely:

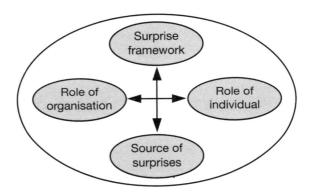

- **Surprise framework** – How different types of innovation and ideas might be categorised.
- **Role of the individual** – How the idea of the soloist, super-leader and schema change contribute to the idea of knowledge generation.
- **Source of surprises** – Key factors that contribute to the generation of surprises: intuition, experience, scanning, serendipity and relationships.
- **Role of the organisation** – What the organisation should do to ensure it is prepared to welcome surprises as they surface. Specifically to understand the idea of the diffusion process and the delta factors.

Surprise framework

A surprise in this context might be defined as a new action that happens over and above the normal activities undertaken by an individual, team or organisation. Clearly this can cover a range of existing organisational actions, such as innovation, invention, creativity or discovery. However, the aim in this section is not to become hung up on creating a strict definition, and possibly creating an erroneous boundary around the concept. The primary aim is to bring out the importance of releasing people's spirit of creativity, to ensure that a constant supply of ideas are generated to build the future organisation.

The idea is that all surprises can be considered in light of the extent to which they modify people's schematic view. Figure 8.2 attempts to capture the basic totality of all new ideas and innovation that might be offered within an organisation.

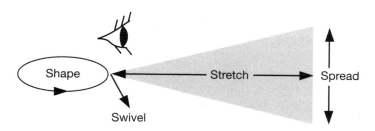

Fig. 8.2 Totality of innovation

Spread

This is the extent to which the idea broadens the application of the existing schema. One example might be how the idea of the clockwork radio has spread out to be used in other electrical appliances. The basic idea has been modified to use the concept to drive torches and back-up power for computers. So the expanded ideas are not paradigm-breaking or inventive, but take an existing idea and broaden its application.

Stretch

Stretch is the extent to which the existing schema might be pushed further or deeper. Examples might be the radical changes that one sees in the development of computer microprocessors. As Intel releases each development, the end application and customers are likely to be very similar, although the processing power has been improved.

Swivel

This is where an idea or surprise has been brokered that takes an existing practice or idea, and applies it in a new field. It might be something that forces people to look outside their current schema or frame of reference and build a new picture of the world. The acid test is that when someone first proposes the surprise, people might appear shocked but upon thinking it through can accept the idea as being practical.

Shape

The last notion of shape, is where basic assumptions are radically challenged. As outlined in Chapter 7 on schemata, people operate to personal maps and often these maps have combined to build a shared schema of the world that becomes entrenched and rigid. Occasionally, surprises will be offered that directly challenge this schema and will be resisted by many people, often for a long period of time. One example might be the notion that people could fly. The thought of such a thing happening was totally unacceptable until Wilbur and Orville Wright became the first humans to fly a controllable, powered aeroplane in 1903.

The proposition is that if an organisation is aspiring to increase the flow of surprises, then some type of shared descriptive model can help to ease the process. This makes it not only easier for people to understand each other but more importantly, it helps them plan how to sell the idea to their colleagues.

Clearly, walking in to see a manager and dropping an idea that fits the 'shape' description is likely to be received with some shock, concern and a possible rejection. Alternatively, if the general manager calls a conference to announce a radical new idea and then offers one that fits the 'spread' description, there might be some disappointment.

There is no magic formula for positioning any of the four models. However, it is important for the owner of the surprise to consider how the idea might be framed before launching it onto the world. Then, to think through and build a diffusion strategy that will ensure that the target audience is ready and prepared to consider the idea's merits.

Role of the individual

In considering how individuals can prepare and help themselves to create surprises, it pays first of all to consider how the first three components influence and support the development of the surprise component.

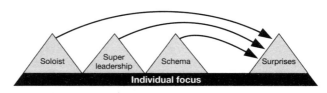

Fig. 8.3 Influences on the surprise component

Soloist (change mastery)

People will have to manage the change processes that are associated with the generation of surprises. The initiator of the surprise will possibly have to: act as a change agent to sell the innovation to the organisation; make use of 'positics' to mobilise the political forces to support the change; and help manage people through the U-model as they adapt to the change.

Soloist (challenge ethos)

Two key issues are paramount: The willingness to experiment and so innovate to create new schematic frameworks; and building on this, to create time and space for people to make mistakes, and to do things that might be considered as slightly off-beam.

Soloist (continual learning)

Often, the key skill used in creating surprises is the ability to look beyond the norm and to consider some of the deeper issues. As outlined earlier, surprises can come in many forms but the ones that really result in schema-breaking ideas, will often be those that look beyond the existing frames of reference. Hence, the double and triple loop learning emphasises the idea of digging deeper and asking 'why?' regularly.

Super-leader (relationships)

The map of connectivity acts as the river of opportunity across the organisation. Surprises will originate both from individuals taking personal action, and the sparring that takes place between people. This ability to spar, debate and create a dialogue is paramount for the process of learning. Hence, if the organisation creates communication channels that only flow according to the official charts, then the process of innovation will be stifled and hide-bound.

Super-leader (trust)

Clearly individuals are only likely to raise their heads above the parapet and offer new ways of working if there is a belief that they can do it with some degree of safety. If people have an experience of their ideas being subjected to overt criticism, or being stolen, this will limit their desire to open up to others. In the same way that the social interaction between players fuels the creation of surprises, so this will only occur if people have the necessary level of trust within and across the various teams (Shapiro, 1996).

Schema

Change underpins the whole idea of creating surprises. Unless people are able to stand back and reflect on their own schema, they will be unable to make the cognitive link to recognise how new ideas can be adopted by the organisation. They need to make the cognitive step of linking one schematic model to another, as James Watt did with steam from the kettle and the potential for creating a steam engine.

Source of surprises

The notion of creating new ideas is a complex and possibly contentious issue. Some people might consider it from a philosophical basis and question if people have *a priori* knowledge already embedded within them. Others might suggest that humans come into the world with a blank slate or *tabla rasa*, and hence all ideas come from experiential learning. Alternatively, another group might delve into the realms of psychology, to understand the processes around cognitive thinking and how ideas are originated. Others will consider some of the creative techniques proposed by authors such as Edward de Bono (1967), who investigated lateral thinking.

However, this book is not concerned with the deep processes that help the creation of ideas. The focus is more on helping people to understand some of the common creative factors and how organisations might experiment with new ways of creating knowledge. The following list offers a few of the more common factors that help to surface ideas within organisations:

- intuition;
- experience;
- scanning;
- serendipity;
- relations.

These five areas have been highlighted because they offer the opportunity to focus on some of the more practical things that people might consider when looking at the idea of learning and knowledge creation. To help give an example of each area, the clockwork radio story is considered as a running guide within each of the propositions.

Intuition (seeing with the heart)

In a recent study, 82 of the 93 winners of the Nobel peace prize over a 16-year period agreed that intuition played an important part in creative and scientific discoveries (Cooper and Sawaf, 1997). This suggests that what might normally be perceived as a structured scientific approach to life (hypothesis, forecast, experiment and analysis), is actually improved through the use of the softer or emotionally-based factors.

Intuition is driven by human emotion rather than any logical cause–effect analysis. It is the ability of the individual to have a hunch that something might work, even though everyone else says it will fail. Cooper and Sawaf (1997) take this theme, and offer a practical way in which this intangible emotional idea can be understood and harnessed. They suggest that there are three key components that can contribute towards developing an enhanced sense of practical intuition (PI):

- **Attentiveness:** Placing an increased emphasis on the inner voice and the gut feelings that people have but often ignore.
- **Questioning:** Placing greater importance on the idea of asking people what they mean, what they see and what they feel about things.
- **Curiosity:** Extending the ability to become interested in the boring and excited about the mundane.

The aim is not to try to codify something that is inherently a soft factor, but to make the point that people can choose to influence their ability to take intuitive decisions. For example, when in a meeting, a manager has the choice to frame a mind-set for each of these three factors. A manager can sit and actively listen, and really internalise the points that are being made rather than being outside the flow that takes place in the meeting (increased attentiveness). By using questions that are focused on people's feelings, ideas, thoughts and beliefs, the breadth and depth of inquiry can be enhanced (questioning). Finally, by looking at people's body language, listening to the words they use, and being closely aware of the environment, the individual can become excited by the surroundings (curiosity).

However, it is important to emphasise that the special focus on intuition does not mean that it precludes the notion of rationality. Although intuitive insights can appear not to make sense, and might seem to be the opposite of a rational response, when brought together they actually form a more powerful way in which to create new ideas. As Senge (1990) pointed out, Einstein never discovered anything with his rational mind – the principle of relativity came about after he imagined himself travelling on a beam of light. This intuitive idea, coupled with his brilliance as a physicist, allowed him to develop a scientific theory that helped change the world's view of itself.

Trevor Baylis would score high on the three areas listed above. First, he allowed his intuition to run free by ignoring his detractors and critiques and listening to his inner voice. Second, he related to the Aids problems at a deep personal level, and took the time to understand and ask questions about what he could do. Third, he took the apparently basic idea of a clockwork radio, and turned it into something that would take the world by storm.

Experience

One of the primary sources of surprises is from the deep experiences that people bring to work. Buyers for supermarkets do not live that role for 24 hours a day. They might also be parents, who experience the products on a personal as well as a professional level. This is just a simple example of the life experiences that an individual will bring to the workplace. The question is, to what extent does the organisation draw upon the fountain of knowledge and skills?

If an organisation is serious about learning, creating knowledge and generating surprises, it should offer the freedom for the individual to present their whole self to the organisation, to value the rich diversity that is innate within the workforce and to directly draw on the experiences that people have in their home life, handicaps, hobbies and holidays, doing this by making space for people to talk about personal issues, to create time and space where dialogue and openness are possible and encouraged.

Trevor Baylis might have had the dream of the clockwork radio, but without his practical experience, he might not have been able to build the original prototype. His home workshop is a mass of wires, machines and tools, a literal Aladdin's cave that allowed him to use his knowledge of electronics and engineering to build the prototype clockwork radio.

Scanning

The notion of creating surprises that are always totally new is impractical and unrealistic. The market is ever-changing and fickle, and as such, companies need to constantly monitor for new trends, products and services as they emerge. This offers the idea of active borrowing, scanning or searching the external world for ideas and inspiration.

Although the way in which this is undertaken will vary according to the organisation and the industry, there are a number of common approaches that can be identified. These are built around two key variables. First is the breadth of the search. Is the exploration based within the same industry grouping or does it move into an industry that is totally different? The second variable is the balance between a passive and active search. For passive, systems might be put in place and then left to indicate new ideas as they surface. Alternatively, does the individual or organisation actively go out to search for new ideas in a proactive way? The relationship between these two continua produces the matrix in Fig. 8.4.

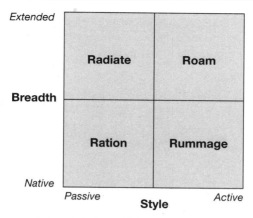

Fig. 8.4 Searching matrix

- **Ration** – In this case the organisation has only a limited interest in searching outside the organisation for new ideas. The passive systems used might be subscribing to industry journals or joining committees to help develop industry specifications and standards.
- **Radiate** – Here the company recognises that ideas from other industries might be of interest, but little positive action is taken to pick up on them. Examples might be subscribing to journals from other industries, attending trade shows, or attending conferences in different fields. Benchmarking might be one example of a positive process for identifying new ideas, although the extent to which other companies' ideas are actually adopted will indicate whether a reactive or proactive stance is being taken.
- **Rummage** – In this case the individual or organisation is taking the time to interact closely with other people from the same industry in order to identify new opportunities. When attending conferences people will be supported in the idea of presenting best practice from their area and inviting people to work on joint developments.
- **Roam** – For this quadrant, a positive decision has been taken to look aggressively for inspiration beyond the local domain. Companies might sponsor people to actively look for their counterpart in other companies, and to initiate dialogue. People will be supported in their desire to understand new skills and practices. One example might be supporting their personal development by attending cross-industry management programmes. Practices such as job swaps or sabbaticals might be encouraged to help develop people's capacity to think in a divergent way.

It is also possible to develop the model further by considering who actually initiates the scanning process (Fig. 8.5). Is it an individual who feels empowered to go out to make new contacts and so come up with surprises? Is it the team that takes the time to develop cross-border links with other companies to share emergent knowledge from the industry? It might be an organisational stance, where all employees are offered the backing to undertake cross-industry personal development.

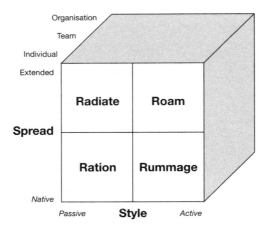

Fig. 8.5 An extended search matrix

Whatever the style, questions need to be considered around the investigating unit's ability to conduct the scanning process effectively. For example, do people have the freedom to do independent roams, or do they need to obtain permission from the business before they look outside the organisation for new ideas? Does the business trust teams to set up cross-industry relationships without worrying about the chance that some of the company's secrets might be released? No one style is right. The important thing is for an organisation to recognise the benefits that are accrued from the scanning process, and not just to assume that innovation will only come from within the business.

As a professional inventor, Trevor clearly operates in the roaming quadrant. All of his active energy is spent looking for options, inspiration, and ways to synthesize different ideas into something that is of commercial value.

Serendipity

In simple terms, this might be defined as the gift for making a fortunate discovery accidentally. Stories abound of the various inventions that have emerged from the process of serendipity: the legend of Newton's discovery of gravity; Goodyear's accidental discovery of the vulcanisation process for rubber; or Fleming's accidental discovery of penicillin. All of these originated because someone (apparently) happened to be in the right place at the right time, and was observant enough to notice something out of the ordinary.

However, simply being around when an accident happens is not enough to bring about new ideas and discoveries. The key is to be in a state of constant preparedness, and to recognise the difference between an accident and when fate has offered the chance to create something new. So a discovery based on serendipity might be seen as the fruit of a seed sown by chance in fertile ground. The idea of 'fertile ground' is an engaging one, and merits further discussion. How can an organisation create the fertile ground to allow for surprises that are based on serendipity? The list is probably endless but the importance rests in helping individuals to be in a state of readiness. All of the ideas discussed so far in the book contribute directly to the individual's capability and willingness to search for fortunate accidents. Consider how an eagerness to challenge, desire to learn, spread of relationships, and ability to reframe, all contribute directly to creating the fertile ground. In essence, to develop a total workforce that is enabled, energised and ready to snatch opportunities as they surface.

Trevor Baylis used the idea of serendipity to good advantage. The chance that Trevor would be sitting watching TV just when the programme came on about the Aids problem in Africa, coupled with a chance appearance on TV while an interested accountant was watching, must be too fantastic to consider. However, it happened and they both had the personal resources to put the process of serendipity to good end and to launch the clockwork radio onto the world.

Relational factors

The idea of surprises emerging as a result of interaction with other people is a key component in the knowledge creation process. There are times when something exciting happens between two people, a materialisation that would not have happened to individuals. This relational discovery process can take place in two forms, either at the tacit or explicit level. Tacit relational discovery might occur where people working together over a period of time improve their working methods but may not recognise the improvement. Alternatively, relational discovery can take place at the explicit level; for example, the surprises that can emerge as a team goes through a problem-solving process together. The dynamic interaction that takes place between tacit, explicit and relational creates the flow of energy that is necessary to stimulate the emergence of surprises.

The relational factor is of great importance with respect to the idea of serendipity. It is very rare that one could explicitly point to an idea that one person solely originated without help (known or unknown) from another human being. All people are subject to influence in their creative process, be it positively or negatively. The development of new ideas will be a buoyant process where one person's thoughts will trigger an idea in another, which in turn leads to a prototype by someone else. Hence, it is the social construction of knowledge that is potentially most valuable in creating intellectual capital within the business.

The crucial point in the development of the clockwork radio is that stage when it turned from a rough prototype into a full-blown demonstration model. Trevor was invited to show his prototype on BBC's Tomorrow's World, *and from this, an accountant saw the idea and recognised the potential that could be realised if the radio could be mass-produced. From this relationship between the two people, a synthesis of ideas and opportunities emerged that helped to launch the radio across the world.*

Role of the organisation

So far the main focus of this chapter has been on the role of the individual in the creative process. The next step is to consider how the organisation will respond when people start to submit new and innovative ideas. Most businesses will have a set of powerful restraining and enabling forces that can promote or kill any new innovations or ideas. It is crucial to understand how these will react when they are confronted by something that is new and different.

The organisational readiness to accept surprises might be considered using two concepts. The first is the diffusion profile, a method for mapping how the surprise grows and emerges across the organisation. The second idea is the delta factor – to understand how the internal factors within the organisation impact on the speed of diffusion.

Diffusion stages

For this model two assumptions are made. The first is that any surprise will go through five diffusion stages, from inception to capital payback.

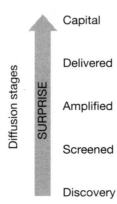

Fig. 8.6 Diffusion stages

Discovery

At the root of the entire process is the idea of creating new knowledge that sur-prises the organisation. This might be a suggestion as part of a new idea, the pro-posal for a product variation, or a new investment bid. On the basis that these are all new and not established as part of the current norms, they might have to battle with the existing products and processes to engage resources and political support.

Screening

This is the stage that determines if the idea is likely to live or die. It might be that the surprise has been originated by the chief executive, and as such might have sufficient leverage behind it to ensure that it moves forward without any resist-ance. Alternatively, it might be an idea put forward by an engineer on the pro-duction line, and so has to battle bureaucracy and hierarchy to fight for its survival. This stage is analogous to the justification phase offered by Nonaka and Takeuchi (1995, 86). Their view is that new concepts need to be justified as being truly worthwhile for the organisation and society. This screening process will include a range of factors, some of which are formally set out by the senior man-agers (finance committees, product review boards, etc.) and others which will be embedded into the unspoken shadow systems that drive the organisation (nat-ural teams or hierarchical status).

Amplification

At this stage the surprise has been formally accepted, resources are engaged, and a small group of people is working on the assumption that it will be progressed. It should now enter the amplification stage within the knowledge network (as covered in Chapter 12 on structure. The aim is to get the knowledge to a stage where it is accepted as being of value by all the primary stakeholders across the business. This amplification process might take many forms. It could be simply posting an idea on the notice-board in the tea-room, writing an article for the internal house journal, or presenting a formal submission to the management board. Whatever processes are applied, the idea is to socialise and grow the cir-cle of interest around the idea. In essence, to achieve as much political buy-in as required to ensure that the knowledge can become embodied in the appropriate area.

Delivery

This is the point where the idea has moved from a conceptual state and can be seen to exist in the organisation as something real, tangible and of commercial value. The embodiment process can be considered in three ways: fluid, fixed and firm (see Chapter 12). Although this offers a slightly simplistic view of the asset categories, it helps to understand the structure and location of the knowledge when trying to facilitate learning across the organisation.

Capitalisation

At this stage, investment in the surprise has paid a dividend and can be regarded as being of value to the business. This stage is deliberately separated from embodiment because an idea might go through the whole diffusion process, only to find that it fails to realise any commercial benefit for the business. Examples of this might be the Sinclair C5 car, the large number of small restaurants that fail to survive the high street, or the fact that many sweets that are launched fail to prosper.

Once these stages are understood it becomes possible to map the range against time; to produce a diffusion profile for the release of the different surprises (Fig. 8.7).

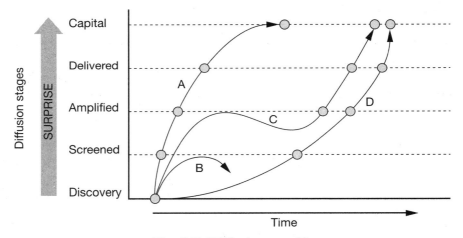

Fig. 8.7 Diffusion profile

Each of the curves in Fig. 8.7 indicates the potential diffusion process that can take place for a new idea:

- In curve **A**, the surprise has rapidly passed the screening phase, been amplified and delivered in an almost perfect diffusion process. Commercial pay-back has been achieved since the capital line has been reached.
- Curve **B** shows the surprise has been originated, but failed at the screening stage. For whatever reason, it did not meet the necessary formal or informal criteria for success.
- The surprise plotted by curve **C** was released, passed the screening phase, but failed to be successful in the amplification stage of the cycle. It might be that

96

a competing product line has raised an objection and tried to reverse the process. Alternatively, it may be that the idea owner moved on, so the initial sponsorship was lost. However, once the amplification stage goes into reversal, the idea is resurrected and progresses smoothly through the commercialisation stage.

- Curve **D** is very similar to **A** but the initial release has taken a lot longer. This might be because the owners of the idea decided to release it slowly, as they were uncertain about its potential or it might be that a series of reorganisations has made it difficult for the originator to submit it to the screening process. However, once locked in it rapidly progresses through to the capital stage.

The changes in the profile can be broadly attributed to the density of the organisation, i.e. how long it takes to move through the diffusion process from one stage to the next. This might be because of the formal commissioning procedures, dependency on sub-contractors, political resistance, etc. Whatever the reason, it will vary for each organisation as the structure and context of the organisation changes.

Delta factors

This leads into the next factor which is to develop the idea of delta, a function of the diffusion completion cycle, over the time taken to diffuse the surprise. Clearly, time to market (TTM) is a critical factor for all organisations, since having an idea lying dormant is of little value. In most cases the goal will be to move the surprise up through the five levels as quickly as possible, so that a return can be made on the intellectual capital. Hence, the organisation can use the delta model to understand its delta time for the movement of surprises from inception to pay-back. Table 8.1 offers examples of the various delta figures for a selection of possible ideas, where delta is calculated as the total diffusion process (taken as 1) divided by the number of days taken.

Table 8.1 Calculating the delta factor

Surprise	Time	Delta figure
New product enhancement	43 days	0.02
Proposition for change in work practice	15 days	0.07
Identification of new customer segment	20 days	0.05
Change to production line route	2 days	0.50

This table looks at the resulting delta figure for the completion of the total diffusion process. It might also make sense for the organisation to consider the delta rate for each of the five stages. For example, to compare the time taken for screening across a range of different innovations and surprises and in alternative divisions within the company.

The actual base line criteria and the process of calculating the delta figure should not be seen as the important issue in this process. Different organisations will use their own criteria and common time value, (day, week, year, etc.) as appropriate for their industry. The main idea is for rapid diffusion to be regarded as a core priority for the organisation.

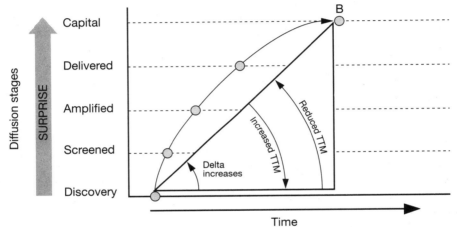

Fig. 8.8 Delta and the time to market (TTM)

Once this idea becomes appreciated, the organisation should be able to derive a greater understanding of the things that influence the delta figure. Delta is related to the angle of the slope. Factors which increase the angle of the slope reduce the time to market, and those that flatten the slope increase the length of time to market. Understanding these factors creates a shared language by which people can discuss the rate of diffusion (Fig. 8.8).

Conclusions

This chapter considers the idea that at the root of the learning process is people's ability to originate new ideas and constantly surprise the organisation. To achieve this, a number of key factors need to be considered:

- Understand the shape and structure that surprises take. In particular, to understand the difference between the spread, stretch, swivel and shape of the surprise.
- Appreciate how to sell the new surprise in relation to its fit within the framework model.
- The contribution that the traits of soloist, super-leader and schema change play in the generation of surprises.
- The factors that contribute to the generation of surprises, namely intuition, experience, scanning, serendipity and relations.
- The five stages that a surprise will follow in its diffusion process (discovery, screening, amplification, embodiment and capitalisation).
- The idea of diffusion profiles and the drag that an organisation's internal systems can put on the emergent process.
- The idea of the delta factor as an indicator that shows the effectiveness of the diffusion process, from discovery to pay-back.

The ability to create surprises should be an inclusive rather than exclusive activity. With deregulated markets, open structures, and the rapid rate of change, the idea of the organisational hero who will ride in on a white charger to save the day might become an obsolete allegory. Organisations will become increasingly reliant upon the individualised nature of the structure rather than the structured organisation of the individuals. Hence, people should be encouraged to realise that they too can take leaps into the dark, and so create surprises that will astound their colleagues as well as the competition.

Surprise model dynamics

	How do we learn?	How do we share?	How do we use?	How can we improve?
Surprise framework New ideas can be readily understood in relation to the surprise framework				
Intuition Intuition is encouraged as a practical form of learning				
Experience People are able to use their deep personal experiences to generate new ideas				
Scanning The use of active borrowing by scanning external markets for new ideas is encouraged				

	How do we learn?	How do we share?	How do we use?	How can we improve?
Serendipity The gift for making a fortunate discovery accidentally is seen as a positive factor and not a fluke				
Relational factors New ideas are encouraged through the use of widespread interaction				
Diffusion stages The stages that a surprise can go through from inception to commercial pay-back are understood				
Delta factor The organisation understands how internal blockages can attenuate the amplification and progress of ideas				

101

Part 3

Interaction

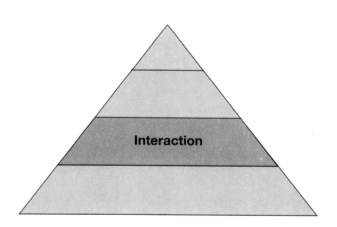

Interaction

Chapter 9

Quality of connectivity

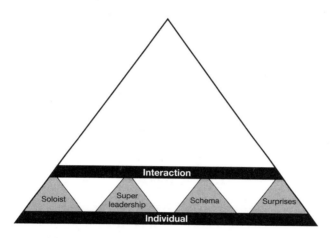

Fig. 9.1 Building interaction

In considering the organisation as an open system, value should not be placed just on the individual but also on the nature of the relationship or the quality of connectivity with the system. This raises an interesting point in relation to the way that organisations are built, and the underlying theory that pervades management literature. There is often a tendency to focus on teams and their construction as the backbone of organisation, suggesting that the ability to share learning is based upon the creation of a common purpose and vision. For the team, however, the danger with this approach is that it has a built-in self-limiting factor. One of the key elements that drives the sophistication of a system is its number of interconnections. In theory, as the number of components increases, so should the number of potential interconnections. However, by placing the emphasis on teams, the number of possible links can be reduced.

The potential limitation of the team approach, can be seen in the top part of Fig. 9.2. The free flow of information can be seen within each team, but the point of interconnection can act as a barrier to the flow of knowledge. In the bottom half, the number of possible connections is opened up as the team limitations are eliminated. The network has a greater degree of 'potential' connectivity, so enhancing the ability for knowledge creation and amplification.

Team configuration: 7 connections

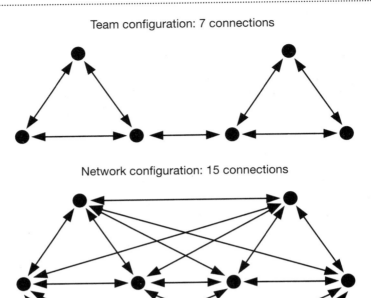

Network configuration: 15 connections

Fig. 9.2 Potential connections

However, this should not be read as a mandate for people to spend all their time on growing relationships and neglecting the primary goal of delivering an output. If too many connections are made and locked in place, then there is a danger that the network can actually freeze, like the potential for gridlock that exists in big cities. The goal is for people to understand that arbitrary organisational barriers should not be regarded as barriers to prevent the flow of information. That is why every person in the network should be seen regarded as a potential knowledge node, someone with whom knowledge can be created and shared.

This is not to suggest that teams and their corresponding structures should be dismantled since these are in essence the basic building block for many organisations. However, it is the underlying ethos that team membership can in many cases act as a barrier to the idea of stimulating learning across the organisation. People can consciously or unconsciously reinforce the false walls that power brokers erect around the functional, geographic or project teams.

Hence, greater emphasis should be placed on understanding the potential that resides in the expanded connectivity of the individual. However, so often this possibility is squandered because of the tacit acceptance of inactivity, even when the goal of interaction can be readily attained. Rather than jumping from inaction to interaction, it might be easier to map and manage the transition through a range of styles:

- **Inactive** – passive behaviour where little interest is shown in the idea of knowledge creation and socialisation.
- **Reactive** – where learning occurs as something that is 'done to' rather than 'done by' an individual.
- **Active** – a desire to interact, but within the limited boundaries set by the individual, team or organisation.
- **Proactive** – a desire to learn and to achieve this by moving outside of the more traditional boundaries and relationships.
- **Interactive** – confident and capable individuals that have the ability to discover, diffuse and deliver knowledge through their chosen network of connections. Such people view the network as part of the knowledge creation process and not just a medium for its transfer.

To understand the factors that block this progression, the integrated learning model considers three key components:

- The way that people interact can create a *shadow* organisation where interactions take place in a more hidden and covert way.
- That the relationship between people in the organisation can be seen as a living force, and as such has the capability to *self-organise*.
- For learning to be transported and amplified within the business, ideas and knowledge must be effectively *socialised*.

The importance of connectivity in the organisation is one of the most underrated and misunderstood factors in management theory. If organisations are to enhance their capability to learn and create knowledge greater attention should be focused on this topic area. Just consider how so many organisation use the idea of 'span of control' as a design criteria whereas the ethos might need to be the 'span of connection'.

Chapter 10

Shadows

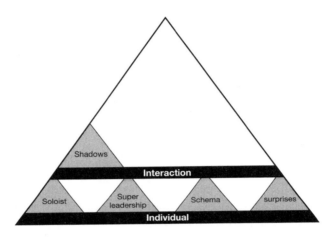

Fig. 10.1 Shadows on interaction

In his famous book, *Peter Pan*, J. M. Barrie tells the story of Peter Pan and offers the idea that people might have detachable shadows, parts of themselves that can be removed, only to be sewn back on at a later date. Similarly, in reality people and organisations tend to have two aspects to their personality, the open and the shadow side. The trouble is that since the shadow can't be detached, is has to work in conjunction with the open side. It is this tension that can create so many problems and blockages for the process of learning and knowledge sharing within organisations, such as power battles, political machinations and fruitless investment programmes.

In all forms of life, whenever people come together, there are two sides to the association. The open side, which relates to those things that people are comfortable with and are happy to share with others, and the shadow side which is the hidden or concealed area – those behaviours, thoughts and feelings that people are less comfortable about sharing. The shadow side deals with the covert, the undiscussed, the undiscussable and the unmentionable (Egan, 1994, 35). These sit in the shade of the person or organisation, and only appear when a light is deliberately shone upon them. Hence, this offers four separate areas that can be opened up for consideration, the open and hidden individual, and the open and hidden organisation (Fig. 10.2).

Open organisation	Open individual
Hidden organisation	Hidden individual

Fig. 10.2 Open and hidden

Table 10.1 builds on the four categories in Fig. 10.2 to offer examples of the behaviours that might be associated with each quadrant. The breakdown in Table 10.1 is not meant to be a bounded definition. It simply offers a general idea of the type of behaviour that might be seen emerging from each quadrant. Ultimately, individuals and organisations will have to identify what their own quadrant behaviours are and when they are likely to occur.

Table 10.1 Open and hidden factors

	Organisation	Individual
Open factors	Published reports and accounts Espoused ethos and ideals Company values Mission statement Personnel systems Formal communication channels Planned strategy	Personal objectives Team goals Personal plans Team briefs Monthly reports Casual conversations Yearly appraisal
Hidden factors	Internal politics Untapped potential Failed projects Local custom and practice Knee jerk reactions Race, gender or religious prejudice Decision-making Informal networks Emergent business strategies/plans Shadow structure	True personal goals Personal fears Unexplored potential Family problems Personal relationships Mistakes made Desire to change roles or company Feelings about manager or team Historic problems with company

Shadow diagnostic model

Taking the structure outlined in Table 10.1, a diagnostic model (Fig. 10.3) can be developed that considers each of the four quadrants and how they interact with each other. Although this model is a simplistic view of the shadow structure for an organisation, it offers a powerful tool for helping people to understand the nature of the shadow organisation. It contains three key elements:

- The four areas making up the hidden, open, individual and organisation components.
- The paths by which they might interact with each other.
- The idea of the shadow bar.

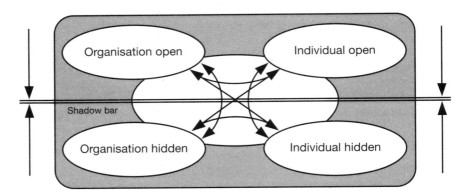

Fig. 10.3 Shadow diagnostic model

Each of the four areas can be described by looking at the elements within the four quadrants. The interaction between these areas produces some interesting facets. It raises questions about how people interact with each other, what underlying games are happening, and how they affect the organisation.

The shadow bar is representative of the way that openness is generated within an organisation. In considering the model, pressure can be placed on the bar, forcing it down, so the hidden facets become exposed to the open world and the undiscussible becomes discussible. Alternatively, in some organisations there is a pressure to reverse the thrust and to force the shadow bar upward. This has the effect of repressing people's feelings, and creating an organisation that is functional but operating out of a game-playing schema. The underlying assumption with this model is that the process of effective learning, creating surprises, and managing knowledge will increase as the shadow bar is repressed.

In considering the four primary components, it is possible to formulate a selection of archetypes that describe the process of interaction between the individual and the organisation. Each of the six models is described in Fig. 10.4 with a corresponding commentary on its likely operation within the organisation.

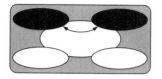

Model A: *Happy talk* considers the open way the people can interact with other people in the organisation.

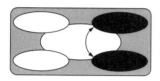

Model B: *If I was* turns the model inwards to look at the internal balance between an individual open and shadow side.

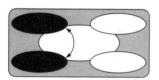

Model C: *Two tribes* explores the idea that an organisation will have two schemata – the one the people say they do, and the one that they actually do.

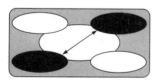

Model D: *Looking for clues* considers the difficulties that individuals have when operating in an organisation that is behaving in an apparently irrational way.

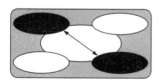

Model E: *It's all in the game* looks at the problems that arise when individuals use their shadow side to influence and drive an organisation's open systems.

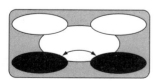

Model F: *Going underground* considers how the organisation's and individual's shadow sides can conspire together to bring about decay.

Fig. 10.4 Six models of interaction

Model A: Happy talk

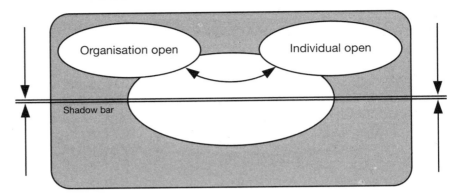

Fig. 10.5 Happy talk

Model A (Fig. 10.5) is the relationship where both the individual and the organisation are being honest with each other. Both parties are aspiring to operate on a trust-based relationship, where problems and concerns can be raised and discussed without any ulterior message or motivation. Both parties are happy to deal with the here and now and to act in an adult way about their behaviour and feelings. People are able to openly disclose their strengths and weaknesses without feeling threatened or subjugated by the organisation. The only tensions likely to surface are those that both groups know can be easily resolved, and hence are more about exploration and expansion rather than negative conflict.

Model B: If I was

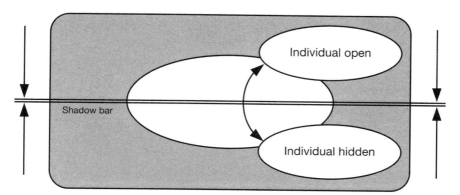

Fig. 10.6 If I was

Model B (Fig. 10.6) takes the first look at the hidden side, in particular to consider the shadow that all individuals take with them. It considers the interaction between the known and unknown parts of an individual and, in particular, how many people can actually be out of touch with their shadow side, and hence who they really are.

Often people can drift along in an organisation, appearing to be blissfully happy, only to find that all of a sudden an unexpected crisis will surface that they struggle to resolve. This is because people often hide parts of themselves from the organisation, from their colleagues, and from themselves. This idea is neatly encapsulated by the Johari window (Luft and Ingham, 1955), a model that offers four simple views of people's personality and behaviour. The proposition is that people can be considered through four different windows: the self we share with others; the self others see but which may not be known to the individual; the private self that others don't see; and the self hidden from both the individual and others. This is represented in Fig. 10.7.

This diagram offers a simple overview of the model and helps to identify the four quadrants that need to be carefully thought about when considering the balance between the open and hidden self.

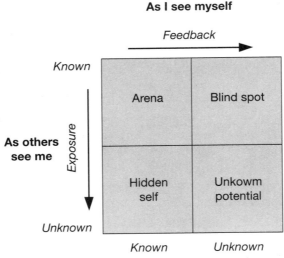

Fig. 10.7 The Johari window

Arena

The arena is the person that both the individual knows and all of his or her colleagues will recognise. Examples might be the hobbies a person has, the number of children, the type of food they prefer or their feelings on a particular topic. This is the quadrant where ideas can flow, learning occurs naturally, and the organisation holds on to the ability to grow its capacity to initiate surprises.

Blind spot

This is what other people know about the individual, but the individual is not aware of it. This might be the irritating habits that people have, or the way they look. Whatever, the attitudes or behaviours that sit in this quadrant have the potential to cause conflict with others, and to block the process of knowledge and knowledge creation in an organisation. Consider a colleague trying to share an idea who has such irritating habits that there is a tendency to avoid spending time with the individual. This will cause a breakdown in the sharing of knowledge, and a subsequent loss for the business.

Facade

This might be seen as the hidden self. It is those areas of the personal life and personality that the individual does not want to share with others. This might be the fact that they have recently been divorced or are having problems dealing with a dilemma at work. Again, this area does not help to generate a spirit of creativity and learning. If individuals are unable to share themselves with others, there is less chance that learning or surprises will emerge in the interaction with others.

114

Unknown

This is the undiscovered self, the area that no one knows about. It is this area that Carl Jung talks about as the unconscious area that might not be seen, but acts in such a way as to influence the behaviour of the individual. This can be seen in a positive and negative light. It might be that the unconscious 'other in us' can suddenly emerge in times of stress. For example, shouting at the children after coming home from a hard day's work, or walking out on the job when things get rough. Alternatively, it might be where a person has the latent and innate ability to play an instrument but time and fate have prevented them from ever taking the opportunity to find this out.

One key point to note in Johari window is that the four quadrants are not static. They will vary depending upon who the individual is with at the time. Consider the first time an individual meets a new director, the arena is likely to be more closed down than when they meet a manager who is known to them.

This process of changing the size of the quadrant is driven primarily by two actions. As the individual starts to expose themselves, so the arena and hidden self-boxes will enlarge. In doing this, there is more chance that others will give feedback on their perception of the person, and hence the arena and blind spot will again enlarge. In doing this, there will be an automatic reduction in the size of the unknown potential box. However, in getting this feedback, there is every chance that individuals will invoke a series of defensive routines so as to protect themselves from being damaged by other people's unfavourable comments.

Model C: Two tribes

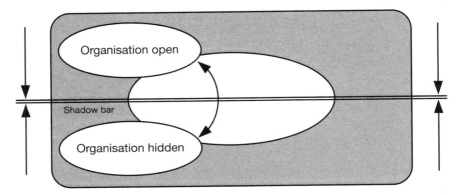

Fig. 10.8 Two tribes

In the same way that two people can interpret a piece of art in different ways, so two people can see an organisation differently. In asking one individual to describe a business, he or she might talk about the pay, procedures, polices and products that it has. Another individual might talk about the power battles, the covert actions against the competition and the way it disposes of unwanted people. Although they are talking about the same organisation, one is looking at the overt or espoused factors; the other is viewing the hidden or shadow elements that operate at a subterranean level.

For example, consider how many businesses manage their formal promotion process. In most organisations there will be some type of personnel procedure that outlines the method by which vacant posts will be advertised. Using this, people are screened, interviewed, and the final selection takes place. Formal processes are typically used to ensure that the organisation can be seen to operate its internal selection in a fair way. In many cases the driver for this is the need to satisfy the legal requirement that no racial or gender discrimination takes place.

However, the gap between the stated and actual process can in some cases be as wide as the Grand Canyon. Often a post will be advertised and people will apply in the belief that it is a vacant position that is open to anyone who meets the criteria. However, in some cases the post is clearly not open, and will not be filled by one of the legitimate applications. The advertisement is simply a smoke screen to satisfy the legal system within the organisation, and the position will actually be filled by a friend or relative of the recruiting manager. In this case, the organisation is tacitly accepting that there are two rules, 'one for us, and one for them'. This example indicates a fundamental flaw that can exist within organisations, namely, the difference that exists between those actions that sit in the open part of the business, and those that sit in the shadow side. In essence, it highlights the difference between the espoused theories and the 'in-use' behaviours that are being used.

116

This topic is considered in some depth by Argyris (Argyris and Schon, 1996), when he suggests that an organisation is likely to have a dichotomy within its system. There will be the espoused theories, the things that it says it will do, and there are the theories in use, which can be seen as the actual behaviours. Although the organisation might believe that these two are aligned, in many cases there will be a gap between the desired and actual outcomes. As an example, he suggests that formal business documents, such as organisation charts, policy statements, or job descriptions, not infrequently contain espoused theories of action incongruent with the organisation's true patterns of activity.

Table 10.2 offers an example of the type of espoused and in-use behaviours that might be seen in organisations.

Table 10.2 Espoused behaviour and theories in use

Espoused	Theories in use
Individual needs taken into account when geographic moves are planned	Anyone who refuses an assignment is off the promotion list
Drive for creativity and innovation	People fired for taking risks
Rational decision-making techniques used to select projects	Resource allocation based on political contacts
Value of team work trumpeted by organisation	Reward systems focus on normal distribution curve thus biased towards lead performers
Safety stated as key factor	Cost reductions force unsafe practices to take place

The important thing to recognise is that this is not a judgemental issue where the espoused theories are viewed as 'good', and theories-in-use are deemed to be 'bad'. Consider many of the large organisations that have been around for some time. It is very likely that many of the overt policies and practices have changed but much of the day-to-day behaviours will remain the same. Often it is the theory-in-use behaviours that give the organisation its sense of permanence and longevity.

Argyris offers the army as a good example of an organisation that has changed in many ways over the past 50 years, but has also remained the same. Although the people, uniforms, and weapons might have changed, many of its core values and practices are unchanged. It is these seemingly abstract theories-in-use that have given it the sense of longevity and in many ways help it to retain a sense of reality.

Conversely, it can be that the theories in use are the very thing that prevents the organisation from creating knowledge and learning. If these unspoken and tacit behaviours are so entrenched, any significant culture change programmes are likely to be attenuated unless they are given adequate time, support and resources. Indeed, two of the most established organisations in the UK have had to tackle problems associated with theories-in-use. Both the army and the police were actively trying to overcome problems associated with racism in the 1990s. This is something that is often very deep and difficult to modify. Simply issuing a new set of instructions, or arranging a series of training courses is unlikely to make any short-term difference. The only time that a radical change in the espoused theory is likely to modify the theories-in-use, is when there is a clear and undeniable need for change. This is often why many companies have to go to the brink of bankruptcy before they are able to bring about a radical trans-formation in working practices.

Model D: Looking for clues

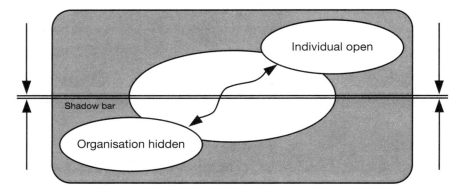

Fig. 10.9 Looking for clues

Model D (Fig. 10.9) explores the frustration that occurs when the open part of the individual attempts to work with the shadow cast by the organisation. Essen-tially, how do people deal with the imbalance that occurs when they are trying to deal in a rational way with an organisation that is behaving in a covert and superficial way?

While much of the organisation's time is spent in operating on an open and rational level, there are instances where the image of the organisation's shadow is presented to the people. The dominance of the shadow image is normally when the organisation is placed under stress. It might be:

● When the organisation has to downsize due to falling profits.
● If the business has grown too fast and major changes are required in the infra-structure.
● An impending merger with another company.

118

For all of these situations, it is likely to adopt a non-standard response, doing things that it might have thought unthinkable before. Examples might be the imposition of stringent budgetary controls on senior managers, such that they can sign off million dollar projects but cannot order a kettle. Conversely, if the business is expanding but does not have the experience to deal with compound growth, it might resort to a more autocratic and dictatorial style of management. Another shadow behaviour might be the increased use of the grapevine and social network to spread ideas rather than using the formal communication channels.

So, how does the average individual feel when forced to deal with these shadow behaviours? In many cases the effectiveness of the average manager can be halved during times of turmoil and chaos (Litwin *et al.*, 1996). The reduction emerges because people can resort to a bunker mentality when they have to deal with the uncertainty offered by operating in the shadow world: 'If all the world around you is in chaos, keep your head down and wait for the bad times to pass by'. This in turn results in a set of behaviours that are not conducive to the learning process.

The problem the individual faces is a daunting one. A lone person can do little against an organisation that is operating out of the negative shadow arena. Dealing in a rational way with irrational behaviour is not necessarily successful. The end result is often a weakened culture, one that is driven more by fear and repression rather than creativity and generative learning.

Model E: It's all in the game

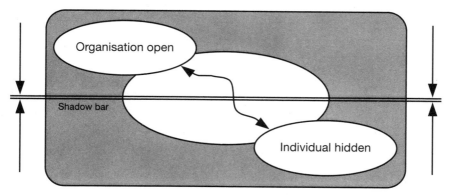

Fig. 10.10 It's all in the game

Model E (Fig. 10.10) considers the relationship between the formal and visible aspects of the organisation and its interaction with people's shadow side. This often manifests itself as game playing with people trying to manipulate the formal systems to meet their own ends.

119

Examples of this type of behaviour often abound within an organisation, typically where people either knowingly or unconsciously decided to circumvent the systems to satisfy their personal needs. Of all the formal control systems that exist within an organisation, the use of budgets and their linkage with corporate plans and strategies is potentially one of the most abused. In a typical organisation, the budget is used to convert the long-term strategy into a set of short-term action plans. In theory, it helps to decide the allocation of resources, and to monitor spend against planned expenditure so as to understand the financial consequences of any actions. Hence, a manager without a decent budget will be relatively ineffective within the business, and is unlikely to be able to deliver any of their objectives.

Taking this scenario, since a manager will potentially live or die by the budget allocation, there can be a clear motivation to get as much budget funding as possible. Now, taking the view offered by model E, the organisation is operating on an open basis, and the individual is running in the hidden or shadow mode. The first thing an individual is likely to do is to develop a schematic model of the budget process – building a mental map that describes how the process operates. Once this is done, the manager can use the process to achieve self-seeking ends.

So what are the hidden assumptions that drive many budgeting systems?

- Budget holders who stay within agreed limits are rewarded.
- Reward is based upon recorded output rather than honesty.
- Tendency to focus on headline costs and not causes of costs.
- Budgets are driven by formal hierarchy rather than value-added work.
- Budget games can take time away from the value-added activities.
- The easiest cost reductions are those that deliver long-term benefits (training, research, etc.).
- The process of effective budget management is highly visible and valued by senior managers.

Taking these drivers as common to many budgeting systems, an insightful individual can soon develop a powerful shadow framework. One of the first behaviours to be encouraged might be dishonesty. If the reward system is based upon meeting forecast deadlines, what benefit does the manager gain from offering a saving against the deadline? Even more, what recognition will there be in producing an overspend, even if it has been on something that will deliver long-term commercial benefit? The second reinforcement is around the idea of concealment. If funds happen to be squandered on a pet project, it does not matter as long as the total budget expenditure does not increase. Third, there is little reconciliation between money spent this year and the subsequent financial years. The best corporate contract in the world is one where the payment is deferred for 12 months because both signatories will probably have moved on to pastures new. Finally, developing the skill to 'present' budgets, is far more valuable than actually delivering reconciled ones. People who are looking to climb the corporate ladder will always seek exposure to senior managers. The skilful presentation of a budget will normally guarantee senior managers' utmost attention and subsequent chance for promotion.

Model F: Going underground

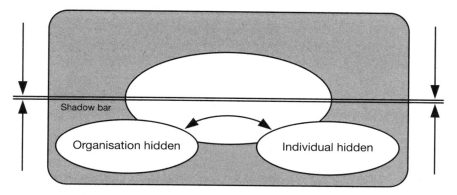

Fig. 10.11 Going underground

In model F (Fig. 10.11), both the individual and the organisation have a tacit and unspoken contract to avoid those issues that might prove potentially damaging to their well-being. This phenomenon is referred to as defensive routines, and has been extensively covered by Argyris since the 1970s. They might be defined as routines used by both the people and the organisation to keep themselves deliberately in the dark so as to avoid unpleasant surprises, threats or anything that might be construed as uncomfortable (Egan, 1994, 35).

As an example, consider a manager who joins a new company and is slowly being introduced to the local systems and practices. In reading the in-house company papers, she is pleased to notice that the company is registered to a formal quality system and all the notice boards and paperwork support its use. This is further reinforced by the files that exist in everyone's office on quality standards and local procedures. However, the files are never used, and people do not follow the system. Even worse, when she tries to adhere to the processes laid out in the files, she gets gently ribbed by her colleagues, and fails to make any head-way with progressing her work. After a while, she starts to watch what other people are doing, and decides to follow the local practices rather than what is laid down in the book. All seems fine until she is asked to attend a team quality review meeting with the local auditor, then she worries that her team will be penalised for failing to follow the processes. However, at the meeting she is shocked to find that all of the team members tell the auditor how good the quality processes are, and how much more efficient the business is with them in place. She is left with some confusion over the gap between what people are doing and what they say they do.

In this case people have established a shared defence routine to protect themselves from any embarrassment or surprise. The avoidance of the quality procedures is wide-spread and systematic, and is accepted throughout the organisation as acceptable behaviour. If challenged on this, the directors will say that the organisation is adhering to the standard, although they might have a suspicion that they are not really being followed. However, as the operations are running well, they are loath to lift any rocks to find out what is really happening. The team believes it is OK to ignore the standards because they assume that the directors do not really want them to be followed as it will slow down the production rate. A gentle stalemate is reached where neither side raises the issue on the tacit assumption that it is acceptable to let sleeping dogs lie.

The interesting point is that under these conditions, people are likely to have good and bad feelings about the situation. The positive factor is that both the directors and the team are pleased at not having to follow procedures that might be constraining. On the downside, there might be a sense of frustration in both camps. The directors might well feel that the team should follow the quality procedures, since they are part of the overall company management system. The team may be dissatisfied that the directors do not care enough about quality to ensure that the standards are enforced. Through these shared defensive routines, the people are using great skill to carefully avoid the issue of quality and adherence to the standards.

However, lies can only be lived for so long, one day the truth will out. As with so many organisations, value chains are being interlocked across companies as they become inter-dependant upon each other. In this situation there is every chance that a customer might well start to look more closely at the supplier's quality system. When the realisation comes that the company has been flouting the system for a long time, and the company is close to losing the contract, what will happen? Well, as in all good organisational stories, the witch hunt will probably begin. The search will be on to find the guilty party who failed to ensure that the systems were followed. The next response is likely to be that people will adopt their best defensive routines. They will convince themselves and others that they really were using the system, and that it must have been someone else who created the problem. The final stage will probably be to fire the auditor and to employ a team of external assessors to build a new quality system for the company!

This is a prime example of defensive routines kicking in, and also a good example of the failure to employ double loop learning as outlined in Chapter 5. The nature of the defensive routine is that it emerges once people feel that they might be getting to the root of the dilemma and starting to uncover some real problems and issues. Neither party has any real desire or motivation to go beneath the surface of superficiality. Defence routines exist but they are undiscussable. They proliferate and grow underground, and the social pollution is hard to identify until something occurs that blows up in people's faces, or the legacy of deceit is passed on to the team further down the value chain (Argyris, 1996, 82).

Argyris suggests that there is a fundamental set of behavioural rules that crosses all nations and cultures (Argyris, 1992, 134). People keep these rules in their head to help them deal with embarrassment or threat (Fig. 10.12).

Meeting (*shadow*) ground rules

1. Bypass embarrassment or threat whenever possible.

2. Act as if you are not bypassing them.

3. Do not discuss 1 or 2 while it is happening.

4. Do not discuss the undiscussability of the undiscussable.

Fig. 10.12 Dealing with embarrassment or threat

In tacitly following these four rules, people will inherently lock themselves into a 'I know it's true because I say so' style of behaviour. The problem surfaces if someone decides to tackle any of these four rules head-on by asking people to clarify what the problem is, trying to discuss some of the deeper issues in the office, or raising problems that people do not want to talk about. All of these are likely to trigger some form of defensive reaction. The problem for the organisation is how to avoid this defensive reply and the resulting strangulation of the social processes within the organisation.

This is difficult because people will typically have come to live with such behaviours and expect them to continue. Often suspicion surrounds the behaviours associated with defence routines, and this leads to cynicism and distrust. People are likely to ignore anyone who tries to delve deeper, and might respond with comments like:

'*It has always been this way.*'

'*The managers never listen, so why bother?*'

'*Here comes another fad.*'

'*Leave well alone or you will stir up a hornet's nest.*'

'*You're just a new girl, wait until you settle into the way of things.*'

In considering the models A to F, it is important to point out that these only offer a simplistic view of the way in which the open and shadow sides interact. The model can be developed further to indicate how other types of transactions can drive the business (parallel, complementary and crossed) but they are not covered in this book. The important thing is to accept that the shadow side does exist, and then to understand how to accentuate its positive aspects and discount the negative factors. These are considered in the next section where the focus is on developing managed responses to shadow behaviours.

Positive responses to shadow behaviours

When working in an organisation that operates out of a negative shadow framework, a number of reactions are possible. The first might be to go for fight or flight: to either challenge the other people directly, or to simply run away and search for other battles. However, if a long-term relationship is to be held with the organisation, then an individual needs to develop a set of personal strategies. They need to ensure that they are able to operate effectively, and not bang their head against a brick wall. The following ideas are listed to help the process of defining what the correct strategies might be. Clearly they will not be right for all organisations, since shadow behaviours will always be contextual, but they might help to offer a framework to start the process of developing a set of positive strategies.

Help to cultivate the idea of positics

Internal politics are traditionally viewed as a negative factor, something that people either avoid or use to their own personal end. In taking the power of the political system and turning it into a positive light, the individual and business can benefit.

Encourage individuals to find information that is valid and truthful, rather than based on rumour

In most organisations the grapevine and gossip factories tend to offer the most current and juicy pieces of information. However, they can also cause significant problems with the element of back-stabbing and disinformation that they contain. The best option is to be aware of, and tune into the grapevine systems, to act quickly if information is being disseminated that is incorrect, and respond by issuing formal communications that put out the correct message.

Use power to build long-term relationships rather than short-term empires

From the first day in a job, there is almost a social conditioning that drives people to sense out the power wielders and brokers. The intuitive sense that if these people are not locked into personal social circles, little output will be achieved. However, while it is useful to understand the nature and structure of power in the organisation, damage can arise when individuals seek to operate in a machiavellian way, and to harness this power for themselves. Clearly, as a management process, this cannot be eradicated but the organisation might make some effort to ensure that it does not shift from being a positive enabler to become a destructive force with the organisation.

For every question asked about a problem, ask one related to how people feel and how they view the issue

Often organisations have a tendency to focus on the production issues and forget about ensuring that people have the capability to deliver the production goals. One of the positive things that all managers might consider is the conscious use of the hamburger model whenever discussing a project or problems (Fig. 10.13).

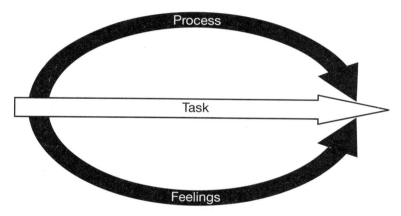

Fig. 10.13 The hamburger model

While the task is of major importance, failure to think about the process of achieving it, and the feelings of the people involved in the execution, will possibly fuel a sense of resentment. This in turn may lead to a situation where people are not willing to co-operate on later ideas.

Encourage exploration of different schemata

Shadow systems often develop because people have a tendency to view the world from their own schema, and find it difficult to accept other people's frames of reference as valid. Wherever possible, people should be encouraged to experience and understand others' viewpoints. They should be prepared to offer their mental models, and from this develop a synergistic view rather than one that is pluralised.

Shift to a higher level of working; move from compromise to collaboration

Often the pressure of aligning the shadow side with the open side of the organisation tends to bring about a mindset that says it's OK to reach a less than satisfactory agreement. If two parties are in conflict, pressure will be on to achieve a compromise, rather than to use the variety and diversity of views to collaborate and achieve something that is stronger and more creative than the original two ideas.

Map the terrain

If people wish to understand both the open and hidden facets of people and the organisation, it makes sense to map out the territory and understand who might affect their ability to realise a goal. When considering the players within a business, there will be people who have very open and clear agendas, and others who operate very much in the shadow arena, using negative politics and manipulative tactics to achieve their personal goals.

Consider a manager who is attempting to build support and find resources for the development of a new product. Egan (1994) suggests that this type of problem can be overcome by mapping the different people who can affect the decision-making process against a taxonomy of types:

- *Partners* are the people who are in alignment with the proposal and can be counted on to help drive it through.
- *Allies* are potential supporters but their actual support cannot be counted on until they have voiced their support.
- *Fellow travellers* will support the individual because of the relationship, not necessarily because of the merits of the product.
- *Fence-sitters* have yet to make a decision. Their final decision might be driven by a view of which party will win in the long run.
- *Loose cannons* can be powerful allies once on board with the project, but until they have a clear grasp of the details, are likely to shoot from the hip and be destructive.
- *Opponents* are against the idea but not against the individual. There is still a solid relationship, so the individual can try to convince them.
- *Adversaries* may view the project in a positive light, but are against the individual on a personal level. If they hold power, these people can operate in the deep shadow areas and cause problems.
- *Bedfellows* have some support for the project, but have yet to build a relationship with the individual and, until this happens, are unlikely to come out in favour.
- *Voiceless* are the silent majority, who on the outside might seem to have little power, but once they begin to organise, can hold influence over the proposal.

126

As Egan's list suggests, the range of people who might become involved with the proposal can range from the totally in favour, to those who are totally against. The thing to question and understand is where this energy comes from; is the support or resistance from the open side or shadow side of their personality? If the energy is from the open side, dealing with it can be relativity easy, since a simple process of dialogue might help to influence the person's views about the project. If the resistance is from the shadow side, or if there is a deep reason for any opposition that is unlikely to be disclosed, the strategy for collaborating with the person will have to be totally different.

Although there is no simple answer to building a relationship with someone who is operating out of a shadow perspective, there is one absolute that should happen. The individual should be able to mentally climb inside the body of the person who is operating against them, to forgo their own values, beliefs and goals and feel what the other person is feeling, no matter how alien or bizarre it might seem. In doing this, it becomes possible to understand what their personal needs are, and why they are operating out of the shadow side of their personality. Once understood, then it becomes possible to develop strategies for moving the relationship to an open level.

Conclusions

Although the shadow element is rarely spoken about, it can covertly destroy many of the good learning practices that originate within an organisation. Consider all of the initiatives that have surfaced over the recent ten years, such as ISO 9001, total quality or process engineering. All of these have been seriously affected by shadow culture. If people, or organisations, decide that an initiative is doomed to fail, the voiceless majority can erode its use in the business.

So, in considering any initiative that seeks to improve the learning or knowledge processes, the following should be considered:

- The organisation is made up of four interconnecting components: the open organisation, the hidden organisation, the open individual and the hidden individual.
- The relationship between these four areas will affect greatly the ability of the business to achieve its goals.
- People should understand the use of the shadow bar and how forces can be applied to drive the degree of open and hidden elements within the business.
- The six models shown in this chapter are not exhaustive but they do give an indication of how the interrelations between the open and hidden areas emerge.
- The idea of the organisation having both espoused and in-use behaviours

127

means that at any time, an individual is possibly using two independent schemata to drive their behaviours.

- The emergence of defensive routines in an organisation is entirely natural but can result in short-term, face-saving reactions that do little to enhance long-term performance.
- In time of crisis, the company's shadow behaviours might come to the fore, and cause long-term damage.
- Game playing is a key factor. Although it can appear to be productive in the short term, the long-term impact might not be so healthy.
- A common response when dealing with a shadow issue is to avoid discussing the undiscussable. Doing this only defers the problems; it does not solve them.
- Of all the possible responses to negative shadow behaviours, adopting positics is one of the most powerful actions.
- Before embarking on any project, people should be encouraged to go through a process of mapping the terrain, to understand and paint the political climate, to determine the people who will operate out of their open quadrant, and those that will operate from the hidden areas.

Trying to eliminate the shadow side would be as realistic and practical as trying to do away with world poverty. It scores ten out of ten in terms of the vision, but zero in terms of deployment. Instead, organisations might focus first of all on raising and understanding the issues and being truthful about their shadow side. Once this is underway (it will never be complete) people can start the process of choosing where they want to operate. In some cases there might be a valid reason for choosing to operate out of one's shadow side as there is often a latent and dormant power that sits in the shadow side that can be exposed in order to unearth the latent potential of the business. The danger is when organisations choose to ignore the shadow issue and then go blindly on wondering why things are not getting any better. A sure sign of this is when a business repeatedly introduces new management ideas and theories, only to see them all fade or fail after a few months.

Shadow model dynamics

	How do we learn?	How do we share?	How do we use?	How can we improve?
Open individual and organisation People understand the importance of stimulating the open side, those things that people are comfortable with and are happy to share with others				
Shadow individual and organisation People are encouraged to look into the hidden or concealed area – those behaviours, thoughts and feelings that people are less comfortable about sharing				
Shadow bar There is encouragement to use the idea of the shadow bar to help hidden facets become exposed and the undiscussable becomes discussable				

Shadow model dynamics continued

	How do we learn?	How do we share?	How do we use?	How can we improve?
Shadow models People understand the selection of archetypes that describe the process of interaction between the individual and the organisation				
Johari window People appreciate how personality and behaviour can affect the learning process				
Espoused v theories in use The impact of espoused and in-use behaviours on the learning process is understood				

	How do we learn?	How do we share?	How do we use?	How can we improve?
Defensive routines The use of defensive routines – the behaviours used by the people and the organisation to keep themselves deliberately in the dark so as to avoid unpleasant surprises or threats – is discouraged				
Positics People are able to take the power of the political system and turn it into a positive force				
Terrain mapping Mapping the different people who can affect the decision-making against a taxonomy of types is common				

Chapter 11

Self-organisation

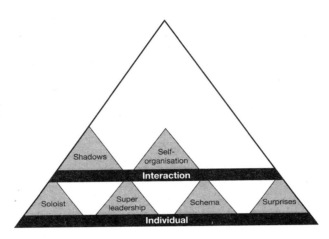

Fig. 11.1 Self-organisation

If a light were to be shone upon many of the existing management concepts, it can be seen that they are often built upon the common themes of predictability, stability, equilibrium and attenuated control. However, sitting in the shadow of the light would be a world that is complex, emergent and adaptable – this is the domain of self-organisation. This might be defined as the capability of a bounded group of agents to interact and spontaneously re-organise themselves in order to adapt and respond to changes. This can be seen as the ability of people within a business, to unexpectedly manage themselves without any intervention or control from an external agent. The impact of self-organisation can be seen in the sheer power and randomness of political systems, the pursuit of personal goals and the way that random problems emerge every month, day and hour. No one plans internal politics, no committees exist to chair the formation of informal social groups, no edicts are laid down for the creation of a bowling club, but they always exist, and in many instances actually drive and steer the organisation.

A clear indication of this tension between planned and self-organised action can be seen in the diary of Fig. 11.2. Consider the entries for a few pages and it might be seen as a mix of planned and unplanned events. It is a clear battle of order fighting the apparent disorder that emerges from somewhere within the organisation. However, it is the practised ability to manage unplanned and emergent interactions that allows an organisation to rapidly respond to changes in the market-place – like wild animals in the jungle that survive by a combination of planning and natural instinctive responses. Self-organisation demands that a system draw upon its own resources, not the hierarchy's, in order to meet the challenges that it faces (Goldstein, 1994, 3). Like birds flocking in the sky, children in the playground, people leaving a football stadium, or massed peace rallies, once the boundaries are set, and simple rules are offered, then harmony can emerge from a situation that is apparently chaotic, essentially 'order for free' (Kauffman, 1995, 71).

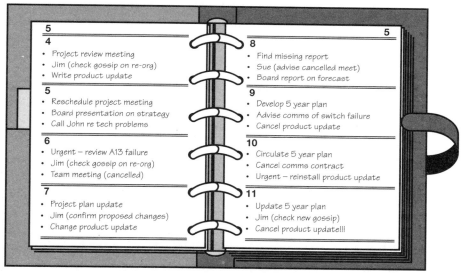

Fig. 11.2 Tension in the diary

So, like Jekyll and Hyde, organisations can be seen to operate out of two different schools of thought. The first, the mechanistic school, suggests that cause and effect can be traced; that the future can be determined and that the organisation can be made to follow certain rules. On the other hand, the idea of self-organisation suggests that people are free agents, and any attempt to predict or control what they might do can be counter-productive.

If this idea of two schools is accepted, then organisations can be operating on the boundary between stability and instability. They sit in the domain between the two, using the permanence of mechanistic systems to hold on to the common routines, and the dynamics of self-organisation to provide the energy and originality to stimulate the idea of learning and knowledge creation. However, this means that friction can arise as people are pulled apart by two conflicting systems, as in Fig. 11.3.

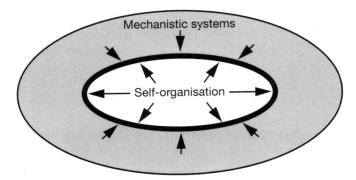

Fig. 11.3 Two conflicting systems

However, before considering this idea, it is important to understand in more depth the existing mechanistic or machine-based schemata that many organisations overtly use to control the business.

Underlying mechanistic assumptions

Consider the typical assumptions that drive the formation of an organisation's management system: The first supposition is that equilibrium, stability and control are the desired states; next, that organisations can be separated into discrete components (function, department, product groups, etc.), and these elements can operate independently of any other unit within the business; third, organisations should always allocate resources in trying to determine what the market will look like in one, three and five years' time; that cause and effect relationships can be traced through the business; and that when something goes wrong in one part of the business, it can be isolated and repaired without affecting other areas.

The suggestion is that these assumptions are driven by a set of deep, underlying constructs:

- deterministic presumptions;
- hierarchical 'chunking';
- negative feedback;
- unitary;
- singular view;
- variance intolerance;
- entropic assumptions;
- logic, not feelings.

134

The following eight points expand upon these and discuss the core themes that pervade many of the organisational constructs.

Deterministic presumptions

Consider how many people in an organisation will be employed in the role of soothsayer or prophet. Organisations are often awash with market forecasters, business planners, strategy builders and economists who advise the organisation of what is likely to happen in the future. The whole premise on which these positions exist, is that the future can be predicted. Clearly, while strategies themselves can be stable, the environment that they seek to predict will be dynamic. Stacey (1992, 158) suggests that the long-term future of a dynamic system is unknowable because cause and effect links are lost in the detail of what happens. Consequently, forecasting with accuracy is only possible in a closed system where the change processes are under someone's control. However, organisations do not have this type of control. This is not to decry the value of looking to the future; the danger is when the organisation believes the predictions. Organisations need people who are able to think ahead, plan for the future, and develop strategies, but these people should not be regarded as visionaries who are able to predict the unpredictable. Their value is in keeping the organisation supple and in a state where it is able to respond to the environment, not to shoehorn it into a particular structure or operating position.

Hierarchical 'chunking'

Within many organisations there is often a desire to divide the organisation into manageable chunks, on the assumption that things can be taken apart, dissected literally or representationally (as with business functions and academic disciplines). The conjecture is that by comprehending the workings of each piece, the whole can be managed (Wheatley, 1994). The chunking that might typically be seen in organisations is by function (marketing, engineering, finance, etc.), geography, hierarchy, product groups or project teams. The trouble is that in forcing arbitrary divisions onto an organisation, it automatically constructs internal barriers that can create learning blocks. One prime example might be the knee-jerk reactions often seen following a reorganisation – the race to issue the first revised organisation chart, a rash of team-building sessions, or the mugs and ties proclaiming the new team's name. While this might help the team to bond within themselves, it does not make communications easier. The danger is where the organisation legitimises this separatist ethos, and encourages the team to become an island within the business. When this happens, the team's ability to exchange and create knowledge with other teams becomes restricted, as natural barriers form between the tribal groups.

Negative feedback systems

Most systems operate on negative feedback. Control systems, such as objective setting, budgetary structures and resource allocations, are driven by a common approach. People are asked to forecast what is required, report any variance against the forecast, and then take action to rectify and limit the variance. Although in some cases this type of control is necessary, an alternative approach is to use positive feedback, where the output from any action is fed back into the system so that it builds into a virtuous loop. A clear example of this can be seen with the launch of rival electronic and computer systems, where one is able to get early dominance in terms of scale and can create a positive loop as people start to believe that one brand is more popular than the other (DOS over Macintosh, VHS over Betamax, etc.). The lesson might be that instead of automatically turning to negative feedback models, the use of positive feedback may generate more creative or productive results.

Unitary goals

Of all the words that have come to prominence in business, the most used and abused must be vision and mission. Rarely can a management book be opened without finding the author stressing a need for one common shared vision and a central mission statement. The dogma is that without such a centralised focus, the organisation will be doomed to wander in the wilderness for years. Such a doctrine suggests that people are unable to exist without some sign from above directing how they should behave. As an idealised model, this might be a positive working practice, and one that should be encouraged, but the danger is that it can create a state of paralysis through analysis, with everyone waiting for the senior manager to produce the new vision set out in tablets of stone. Often directors disappear into weekend huddles to produce the visionary commandments that predict where the company is heading, only to find that people didn't want to know in the first place; or over the weekend the company has been bought out; or that half of the top team has been head-hunted, so another workshop has to be held to rebuild the vision.

Singular view (*the manager knows best*)

Linked into the suggestion that there may be an over-emphasis of the need for vision and mission, is the thought that too many of the top-down edicts (mission, vision, values, ethos, etc.) might be driven by the thoughts of one small group of people. By their very distance from the organisation (functional, hierarchy and physical), senior managers' views are routed into the espoused rather than in the theories-in-use setting. If decrees are given out that only align with the espoused values, all that happens is a reinforcement of the incorrect management system. Although the manager might have the most up-to-date and strategic view of the business, it does not necessarily mean this is the most accurate view of the company's position in the market.

Variance intolerance

In considering the management ideas that have emerged since the 1970s, there is a common theme of installing greater levels of control to prevent variance. Consider ISO 9001, total quality, process management, investors in people, all of which can be used to reduce the space that people have to take risks and originate surprises. While this level of control is necessary in certain areas, there is possibly a degree of oversell, overload and overkill in some areas. Quality standards were originally designed for manufacturing. Great care should be taken when they are thoughtlessly transported for use in the human resource areas of the organisation. People that operate to fixed paradigms and rules may ensure that business is not lost today, but to what extent are they creating the business of tomorrow?

Entropic assumptions

Many management paradigms are based upon the implicit view that organisations are closed systems, that will run down and lose energy without any direct prompting or stimulus and that unless managers constantly take time to tinker and direct them, they will decay and die. There is often little belief in the idea that they can act as a living organism, able to adapt and prosper in a changing environment without external guidance. Organisations interact with the external environment daily, and receive masses of energy and insight from this process. Organisations or teams that are left to themselves might just be capable of growing and adapting without any direct intervention from an external agent.

Logic not feelings

The idea of espoused and in-use theory is a key factor in the way that systems operate. Organisations are typically (overtly) driven by tasks, business goals, corporate objectives and the assumptions that people come to work for the love of the business. Often there is a view that people's feelings are left at home. Many organisations can be built around the idea of a repressed model, where any mention of emotion or sentiment in a business meeting can be enough to cause apoplexy for the traditional manager. The base (espoused) assumption is that business decisions are based on logic and sensible decision-making processes. The reality is that they are often driven by personal ambition, greed and fear as much as for the good of the business.

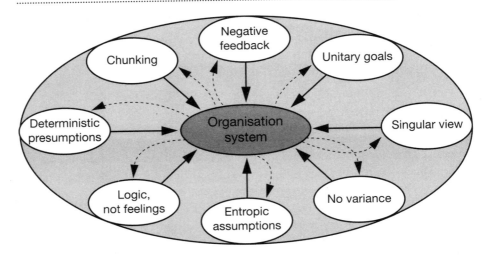

Fig. 11.4 Rationality prevails

The picture of the organisation offered so far (Fig. 11.4) is built upon the idea that rationality prevails, order is desired, and uncertainty is something that should be banished. However, how will such a style and structure fare in a world where change is discontinuous, random and complex? A world where unexpected market shifts occur at global rather than national level? It is beyond dispute that the notion of predictability and stability are false idols, and as such, organisations must re-adjust their operational schemata to understand how they can be more adaptive, and hence enhance their ability to learn.

Part of this change in the schema and style will come from understanding the principles of self-organisation. Through this process, companies can develop the capability to manage spontaneous and radical self-organisation without the need to be driven by formal strategies, structures or procedures. It is a way of operating that might work against the traditional view, and allow change to take place through a process of self-direction, self-regulation and self-regeneration.

Self-organising organisations

One of the significant factors with the mechanistic model is that emphasis is placed upon the cogs in the system, that is the people themselves, defining the roles, objectives, and their place in the hierarchy. With the self-organisation model, the emphasis is placed more upon the nature of connectivity with the system. The way in which the organisation behaves, its effectiveness and ability to deliver the end result, is based around the flow of information through the business. So importance is placed upon the interconnections, the configuration, and the map of the relationship between the components and its ability to adapt and respond to changes in the environment.

The following sections offer an overview of some of the characteristics that might be observed in a self-organising system.

Self-stability

There is a high degree of stability, not in the traditional sense of being fixed or unvarying, but in the capability to maintain the same overall structure in spite of any changes or replacement of component parts. The nature of the system means that it is able to remain stable, even when small disturbances occur. Since the inherent design of the system is based upon adaptability and self-regulation, it is able to contain any surprises which might occur that could have been disruptive. Alternatively, in a system that is mediated by external forces, wasteful energy is likely to be expended on restoration following a minor turbulence.

Self-sustaining

The proposition is that an organisation might have the ability to continually reproduce itself in order to meet its goals in two ways. First, while the overall structure of the organisation remains the same, the components or people in the network will continually change. In doing this, it modifies its internal elements but retains its overall identity or pattern of organisation. This might be analogous to the continual churn of people that happens within the organisation while it is able to retain a similar output and purpose.

An example of this can be seen in the way that people rebuild their pancreas every 24 hours, the stomach lining every three days, and blood every month. The body is able to do this because it continually regenerates and changes the cell structure within the body (Capra, 1997, 213). The second way in which the organisation rebuilds itself is by modifying the structure of the internal network. So it changes topological designs, creates new connections, breaks redundant links, and redefines the bonds with external agents. As these links are reformed, so the organisation absorbs internal and external information, and continually responds and adapts to environmental needs.

Self-regulation

Underpinning this idea of the self-sustaining organisation is the notion of self-regulation. Often, a regulatory system will be built around the idea of negative or positive feedback. Negative suggests a restraining process, like the governor on a steam engine, or the speed ramps on a narrow lane. Positive feedback can be seen as feedback from an audio system; whenever the microphone is too close to the speakers it re-amplifies the signal so that it goes out of control. Both types of regulation exist for organisations, and have already been discussed in this chapter.

However, the point to consider is the difference between intrinsic and extrinsic regulatory systems. Intrinsic regulation is where the system has its own capacity to regulate its operation and hence its output. Extrinsic regulation is where the control comes from outside the natural system. For example, imagine a team working on an important project, where the deadline is rapidly approaching but they still have critical milestones to meet. There might be a natural tendency for the team to work longer hours and put more of themselves into the project. Although this might help to resolve the problem, it might make them tired and irritable, and cause them to make silly mistakes. The question is, does the organisation allow them to self-regulate, and decide when enough is enough, or should a senior manager step in to suggest that they are taking on too much? There is no right answer, as dangers exist either way, but the question is, to what extent does the culture of the organisation tolerate self-regulation?

Nonlinear

The stable and conforming view offered by the mechanistic model assumes that life is a linear process, one that can be predicted, directed and controlled. However, a look in the newspapers, or a glance at the stock market will immediately highlight that this is not always so. The ideal of predicting one's future is a fairy-tale that human beings have always toyed with; only now is there a wider acceptance that this is a foolish and impractical desire. Life and organisations are built on a set of constructs that use chance, random disturbance, changing dynamics, turbulence and inter-connectedness as the base presuppositions. This view of the world has been famously characterised by the advance of chaos theory, and along with it the butterfly analogy. Here, the proposal is that a butterfly could beat its wings in America, and the combined system factors of positive feedback, amplification and interconnectedness would result in a hurricane in the UK. Clearly trying to realise this example in practice might be difficult, but it is possible to see examples of this type of behaviour across organisations. Small industrial disputes can build until they close the business down; the chance meeting in a bar between two directors can lead to a merger or take-over; the opportunity for an engineer to become involved in a quality team might lead to his personal invigoration and eventual progression through the ranks of management. Non-linear systems are nothing new and organisations should recognise that life is not an orderly system. They should learn to recognise nonlinear undercurrents, so as not to be surprised when things do not go as planned. In cases where the organisation is viewed using only linear systems, then a state of mind is created that forces people to hide mistakes, and avoid taking risks, thus restricting the learning process. In a nonlinear system there is a potential for transformation and growth; critically, change is not imposed, it is released.

Attractors

Self-organising systems have a tendency to be attracted to a natural style or pattern of working. This natural or stable state is often known as the attractor, areas where order arises out of disorder. For example, look at a group of school children playing at lunch time. There is apparent disorder and chaos, but if the picture is considered in terms of patterns and relationships, different shapes will emerge. It will be possible to see patterns in the guise of repeated games that instigate a set of behaviours. Football will set up one pattern while the game of 'It' will drive another pattern.

When any forms of apparent random activity are observed, several different types of attractor patterns can often be identified.

Point attractor

Is where the behaviour of a system is always drawn back to one particular point, like gravity pulling objects back to earth (Fig. 11.5). An example of this might be the draw that someone has to a particular brand of car, or a type of drink. No matter how much they are attracted by other brands, they still come back to the same type.

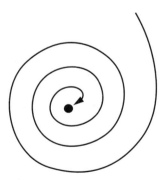

Fig. 11.5 Point attractor

Limit cycle attractor

In this case, the behaviours of the system are drawn towards two separate areas (Fig. 11.6). At any one time, either of the two states will be viewed as the prominent attractor. So first A, and then B will take prominence. This pulls the system in two directions at alternating times. This might be likened to the change that many organisations go through in the shift between a centralised and de-centralised structure.

141

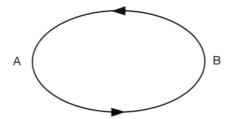

Fig. 11.6 Limit cycle attractor

Torus attractor

Where the system is pulled in many apparently complex directions at direct times, but there is still an underlying pattern within the framework. While the behaviour of the people in the system might be similar each day or month, the actions are never exactly the same (Fig. 11.7). Thus, variation takes place but it is still broadly predictable over a constant timeframe. So people might come into the same office each day to do broadly the same type of work. However, the actual minutia will generally vary according to the time of day and what projects are underway.

Fig. 11.7 Torus attractor

Strange attractor

With this model, the system will constantly act in a different way, and the exact position can never be predicted (Fig. 11.8). However, the movements are all contained inside a structured framework, so an apparent pattern seems to emerge from the behaviours. The pattern will jump all over the place, with no apparent structure, but then suddenly islands of related behaviour might emerge. The key thing with strange attractors is the linked dependency to the initial condition that sparked the action. A minor change to any of the initial parameters at the start of the action can radically change the whole pattern and structure of the resulting behaviour. This type of behaviour can be seen in the flow of water

142

through pipes. Consider how the turbulence has the look of confusion but is in fact built up as a number of different eddies that reoccur. After a while it becomes possible to notice an overall pattern or theme within the flow of water.

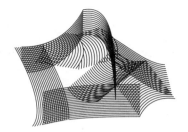

Fig. 11.8 Strange attractor

One of the problems that people have with the idea of attractors, is that in many ways they do not actually exist. They are simply a charted representation of how something behaves in a space–time continuum. Hence, mapping the shifts and turbulence within an organisation can be difficult. One important idea to understand is the way that people's ideas and beliefs can set up attractor states within an organisation. No matter how hard a company might try to shift the way that people operate, there is a chance that they will be attracted to their natural state. Once someone develops the intuitive ability to understand and recognise the various attractors, many of the apparently jumbled behaviours that the organisation exhibits can be understood.

Emergent properties

Emergence within a social system can be described at the creation of new sets of patterns through people interacting according to their own sets of behaviour. The end result is a global pattern or shape that would not have been predicated according to any existing local rules. This feature is one that exists in many organisation, but is more often than not ignored, or deemed to be due to people's mistakes or changes in the environment. As such, business can spend time and energy trying to counteract the forces of emergence rather than using it as a force to enhance its operations.

The challenge this offers managers and the organisation is how to create a learning culture that helps people to feel comfortable with the emergent style of working. To work within a framework where it is acceptable to not always know why something has happened, or what will happen tomorrow, but to trust in the skills and abilities of the people and organisation to deliver. Clearly, since the long term is unknowable in specific terms, managers have to adopt a form of control and style that enables new action and behaviours to emerge through a process of self-organisation, social interaction and real-time learning.

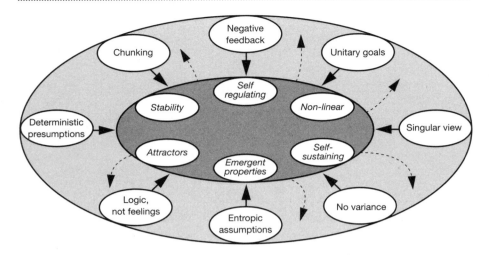

Fig. 11.9 Underlying forces drive a company

The end result is that these six factors all come together (Fig. 11.9) to give an indication of some of the underlying forces that drive and steer how learning occurs within an organisation. Simply believing that learning and knowledge creation will happen along the lines of a structured process is naïve and foolish. Organisations tend to operate on a balance between the mechanistic and self-organisation model, and as such are constantly pulled in both directions.

The key message about self-organising systems is that managers might need to lose some of the intense beliefs in the gods of direction, stability and consistency. Life is simply not like this and never has been. Hence, it is important to help the people and systems to become more adaptive by creating the ability to operate in a setting that is able to adapt to the mechanistic and self-organising principles.

Impact on learning and knowledge

So what implication does this have for an organisation that seeks to enhance its knowledge creating capability? How can the scientific and academic theory be translated into something that organisations and managers can operationalise and use?

Trying to map the cross implications of the elements covered so far with issues covered in this chapter would be impractical and probably take up a book in its own right. However, it is relatively easy to draw out three basic problems that might occur as a consequence of the mis-alignment.

144

Transporting knowledge across the network

The transportation of knowledge across the network is inherently dependent on interaction between the people. This flow depends on the creation of relationships that are open, flexible and adaptive. However, it might be that individuals who are in the path of the knowledge flow operate from different underlying assumptions.

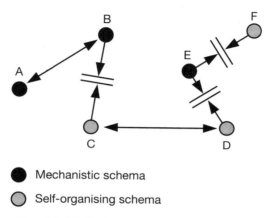

Mechanistic schema

Self-organising schema

Fig. 11.10 Behaviour network map

Consider the network map in Fig. 11.10. The people indicated as A, B and E all have a natural tendency to follow the mechanistic school. They have an implicit belief that formal systems drive an effective business. C, D and F take the alternative view, and have a bias towards the self-organisation model. They manage their work through informal groups, using the political systems and influencing people across the network.

In this model, person A has a piece of knowledge to socialise and pass through the business filter systems in order to gain approval. B accepts it in an enthusiastic way and is committed to progressing it through the business. However, when B talks to C, there is a schematic gap. B has received formal approval for the idea, but C has other information. Through social contacts, C is sure that there is going to be a change in policy regarding the product range. However, because it was told in confidence, C is not able to explain this to B, so just stalls the idea. This both corrupts the diffusion rate for the idea and can cause conflict between B and C. As the network is followed through, it can be seen that the process of amplification and attenuation can occur where the schematic differences occur. This is a classic example of passive interaction outlined in Chapter 7 where the two individuals were operating on separate levels, and so were unable to build any kind of shared relationship or cognitive link.

Contract and value alignment

In the same way that the schematic misalignment can cause a problem with people's view of the world, it can also occur in understanding and defining people's relationships with the business. Imagine an individual who operates out of the mechanistic model, working for someone who follows the self-organising approach. The subordinate might well be looking for feedback that confirms a long-term role within the organisation. However, the manager might be giving signals that this is not possible, and the individual should be prepared to move around and be more flexible. In other ways, the individual might be looking for a feedback style that is based upon error correction or negative feedback. The manager might be trying to focus on accentuating the positive areas, and helping the individual to find their personal strengths. Conversely, if the roles were reversed, it might be the case of a project manager who prefers the emergent schools of thought who is working for a manager who prefers the idea of chunking and deterministic milestones.

When they are talking about milestones achieved and yet to be completed, the subordinate will be talking around the things that are likely to be happening to complete the project, and how synergies might be derived that are not on the project plan. The manager might well feel uncomfortable that the agreed milestones have not been completed, and that there seems to be some deviation from the agreed schedule. Neither person is right. The problem is that they operate from a different schematic model. Unless they can accept the two different ideas about managing the system, there is a chance that the relationship will drift into conflict without either person understanding where it went wrong. As a result, the opportunity for them to share learning experiences or to create new knowledge together will be limited.

The moving target

So often, training and development is built and managed around the idea of a planned and stable business model. Courses are planned months, even years, in advance, development objectives are linked to business goals, people have a training development plans that stretch for years into the future and finally, the Investors in People standard introduces the notion of a highly-structured methodology that organisations should follow to ensure that training is aligned with business objectives. This is not to suggest that this approach is wrong, but clearly, if an organisation's activities are changing monthly or weekly, then it can be difficult for the training system to stay aligned within the business goals. This suggests that a degree of flexibility might need to be built into a company's training and development system, so that it can follow and match the changing dynamics that operate.

Conclusions

In summary, the following points might be drawn from this chapter:

- There is no one best way of working. This chapter does not seek to suggest that all organisations should throw all their formal systems out of the windows and let everyone do what they want. For some extraordinary organisations this might be effective. In the real world this would be a destructive process, as the inherent mechanistic systems would not be able to cope with the change. The proposition is that organisations should be prepared to accept that there are alternatives to equilibrium, stability and consistency.

- It is false to assume that stability and equilibrium are equal to control and effectiveness. A business can operate out of the self-organising model and still be stable. The difference is that the stability and power is based on the strength that comes from self-managed action and the connectivity within the network, rather than managerial imposed dictates.

- If the idea of non-linear systems is accepted, then it reinforces the notion that solutions that work in one business or industry cannot readily be transferred across to another organisation. If the transfer of a product or solution does work, there is more chance that it is because the self-organising systems have taken the idea and incorporated it into their system, rather than its ability to overlay and work with the formal systems. Maybe this is why so many total quality and re-engineering programmes seem to fail – the businesses possibly tried to overlay it onto the formal system rather than inculcating the change into the informal systems, practices and groups.

- The idea of system attractors offers a powerful weapon for helping people to see stability within a turbulent situation. Often people are used to looking at the short-term detail. If they can be encouraged to stand back and look at situations from a more objective or helicopter viewpoint, then it becomes easier to see how the shift in style and behaviour are being drawn by different attractors within the system. Hence, the apparent jolt to one style of operating will in all likelihood be reversed at a later date. Consider the familiar dichotomies and bi-polar shifts that operate within organisations:

Centralised v Decentralised

Downsizing v Recruiting

Functional working v Matrix structure

Segment by customer type v Segment by market size

- Often, when faced with conflict, there can be a tendency to take remedial action based on the 'apparent' cause of the problem. Schematic gaps are often at the root of communication problems, hence it might pay organisations to deal with conflict in an alternative way. Before trying to understand the problem that is driving the conflict, consider the underlying assumptions upon which people have built their personal and organisational systems. If it becomes apparent that they are operating out of two different management models, as in Fig. 11.11, then the issue should be addressed at this level.

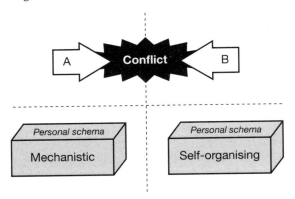

Fig. 11.11 Conflict from different styles

- The only way to bring about an alignment between the mechanistic and self-organising models is through open-ended dialogue. People should be given the time and space to understand how other people actually manage themselves, their time and their tasks.
- Do not view changes in the environment as a threat, instead build in adaptive systems that can actively respond with speed and efficiency, and so use environment shifts to create a competitive advantage. Once the organisation has acquired or developed the ability to adapt and respond to the external environment, then it has potentially achieved one of the most competitive strategies that can be used.
- Be aware of the delicate balance between the formal planning systems and the process of emergence. Mintzberg (1994, 284) highlights the point that only one in ten strategies is implemented successfully. If this is the case, what are the others doing? The supposition is that the strategy being followed is an emergent one, but may not be formally recognised by the business. It makes sense for organisations to understand and be open about the emergent elements of their behaviours, ideally to reduce these where they are less than effective but to also give them free rein where they prove to be working.

To bring any of these ideas to life, it is possible that people might need to operate in both camps at the same time. There should be an appreciation of the mechanistic system and its associated benefits, but with the willingness to adapt and adopt a style of management that is grounded in open-ended, spontaneous and divergent behaviours. Effective working possibly sits on a knife-edge, balanced between the area of bounded instability, where anything is possible, and the highly-controlled approach where stability and equilibrium are the norm. This is like a parent who must give the children sufficient structure and equilibrium to give them a sense of stability and balance. However, the parent also needs to offer them sufficient freedom and space to develop and grow their individual talents.

Self-organisation models dynamics

	How do we learn?	How do we share?	How do we use?	How can we improve?
Deterministic presuppositions The business is not locked into the belief that accurate long-term forecasting can be delivered				
Chunking The business is able to consider the organisation as a holistic whole, and does not always seek to chunk it up into discrete component				
Negative feedback systems The limiting impact of negative feedback within the organisation's management systems is understood				
Unitary goals The organisation is not locked into the idea that it must only focus on a fixed future goal				

	How do we learn?	How do we share?	How do we use?	How can we improve?
Singular views The idea that one person's or group's vision is superior to another is regarded as limiting				
Variance intolerance The organisation is willing to relax some levels of control in order to create more variety				
Entropic assumptions The organisation accepts that some units should be allowed to operate without external intervention				
Logic opposed to feelings Organisation can be built around a repressed model, where any mention of emotion or sentiment in a business meeting is seen as alien				

Self-organisation model dynamics continued

	How do we learn?	How do we share?	How do we use?	How can we improve?
Self-stability The capability to maintain the same overall structure in spite of any changes or replacement of its component parts				
Self-sustaining That an organisation has the ability to continue by reproducing itself				
Self-regulation The use of positive and negative feedback to maintain control of the organisational system				

	How do we learn?	How do we share?	How do we use?	How can we improve?
Non-linear An organisation's ability to use chance, random disturbance, changing dynamics, turbulence and inter-connectedness to good effect				
Attractors The tendency to be repeatedly attracted to a natural style or pattern of working				
Emergent properties To work within a framework where it is acceptable to not always know why something has happened, or what will happen tomorrow				

Chapter 12

Socialisation

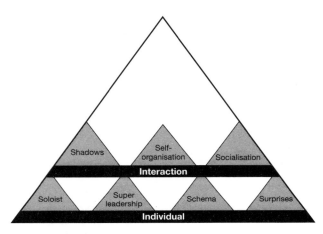

Fig. 12.1 Socialisation

Consider a country that has a series of fast interconnecting trains and roads; then consider another where the infrastructure is made up of single track lanes and a run-down, ill-equipped railway system. Both countries might have companies that are investing in new plant and training, but without a tight, fast and smooth infrastructure, little growth will happen. In the same way, an organisation can invest fortunes in its asset base, but if people are not able to talk, share ideas, and create knowledge through synthesis, only limited improvement will emerge from the capital investment.

This social network is something that is rarely defined, but everyone knows what it is, and the role it plays in getting a new idea accepted. In some cases it will be the formal committee and review bodies that formally sanction progress. In other cases, it will be the power brokers and stakeholders who hold the purse strings that need to be charmed. In most cases it is probably a combination of the two that come together to create the socialisation network.

The next step is to look deeper into this activity in order to understand how the flow of knowledge is amplified and attenuated within the socialisation network. However, developing a composite model that clearly explains and predicts how the socialisation process occurs would take until the end of time and be pretty foolish. Since no organisation can be replicated by another, there cannot be a single model that represents a common set of behaviours. However, it is possible to consider what key actions can occur in the socialisation phase, and what the important factors might be in relation to the creation and flow of knowledge. The areas seen in Fig. 12.2 are expanded on in the rest of the chapter.

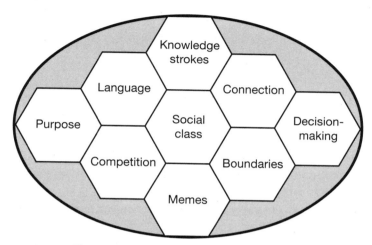

Fig. 12.2 Key areas in socialisation

Purpose

A core theme in organisational learning literature is the notion that to be effective, organisations need to have a shared vision or purpose. The supposition is that without this bond, the process of learning and knowledge creation will be fraught and difficult. Although this might be seen as plain common sense and difficult to argue, the problem comes not in the desire, but in the deployment.

The players in a football team, musicians in a band or actors in a travelling show, will generally have a shared sense of purpose because they made the choice to work with a group of colleagues that had an end goal. As such, the assumption is that the flow of knowledge and the facilitation of learning is relatively easy, because there is a shared outcome. However, can the same be said for organisations? Is it sensible to suggest that when people choose to make widgets, answer the phone to arrogant customers, or stand in the cold to erect a building, they do it for the love of the end product? Or are they at work quite simply for money, so they can provide for their family, pay the mortgage or satisfy other personal needs, such as hobbies or saving for their retirement?

This presents all organisations with a dilemma – how to build a shared sense of purpose when there is not one, and in addition, how to help people to care about the idea of learning and knowledge creation. In a climate of downsizing and transient workforces, how can people be encouraged to innovate, take risks and develop a soloist attitude if they do not expect to be around for long? Often the company response is to run the obligatory team building workshop, send out leaflets that proclaim the mission and vision of the company, and best of all, give everyone a personal mug with company vision imprinted on the side! Once this happens, the result is that the gap between the 'espoused', and 'in-use' behaviours widens, and people play at having a shared purpose and thus play at the idea of knowledge creation and learning.

Although it might not always be possible to create a shared sense of purpose, the organisation can discover what each individual's sense of purpose is, and use this to build a bridge with the company goals. It might be to say that it is OK to come to work for the money, acceptable not to have a deep sense of belief in the company values, but it is not agreeable to bluff or lie about it. Once the individual and the organisation have exposed their personal sense of purpose or values, then it is often easy to build a linked purpose, something that both parties can work towards as being of benefit.

This idea builds on the value alignment model (Fig. 12.3), where alignment of values and purpose does not mean that either party imposes them on the other. It assumes a collaborative approach, where both parties can live with each other's viewpoint and create a shared area that becomes a collective sense of purpose.

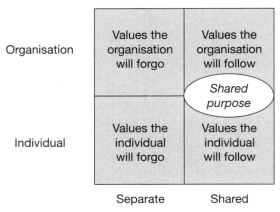

Fig. 12.3 Value alignment model

Boundaries

The erection and eradication of internal barriers is a key factor in the flow of knowledge within the social network. Boundaries help the organisation to create safety zones, tight management systems, and reduce elements of ambiguity. These boundaries are typically formed by the formal structure that the organisation designs for itself along the lines of functions, project team or product group. Whatever the formation, the moment a reorganisation takes place and the hierarchy chart emerges, the new boundaries are established and people have to re-align themselves within a new confine. However, this tendency for people to group themselves in discrete units can also lead to the tribalised view that drives negative behaviour. These boundaries can be precious to people because they offer power, safety, a sense of comfort, longevity and a badge to wear highlighting their role in the company, woe betide anyone who threatens to bypass or ignore them.

Consider Fig. 12.4. Team X has originated a new idea and wants to socialise it through the organisation to gain political support. However, the leader of team X doesn't get along with F who is the leader of team Y. The boundaries that are drawn around the team effectively prevent D from approaching F to either encourage or demand support, so apparently, the idea will be kicked out of the socialisation process and passed to the discard stage of the model. However, C is a member of team X and plays squash with B. C knows that B is a close friend of E who works in the Y team. Using this, C follows the informal boundaries to route the idea through a secondary path. So all of the people sit in the bounded area, and hence within their comfort zone, but the idea manages to be socialised outside the formal limits.

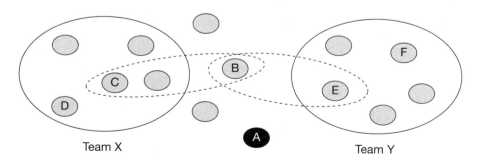

Fig. 12.4 Informal links may overcome boundaries

In understanding the idea of organisational boundaries and their impact on the learning process, organisational members can make a radical impact upon the diffusion rate of their idea (Fig. 12.5).

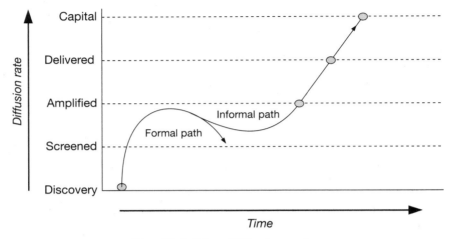

Fig. 12.5 Idea diffusion rates

This diffusion profile indicates the two paths that the idea put forward by team X might have taken. The formal route would have left the idea bounced out of the socialisation process into discard. The informal path, although slowed down by the initial rejection has bounced back and progressed into delivery.

The creation of boundaries is a natural psychological process, and one that all people will follow. However, to ensure that the socialisation network is kept oiled and flexible, the organisation needs to understand the issues that drive the formation of its boundaries. In particular, to appreciate what factors can slow the progress of the socialisation within the organisation. An idea that becomes blocked in the socialisation process is one more lost opportunity for the business.

Connection

Often people can work together for years without really understanding one another. They might sit at the same desk, share lunch together, but still not know the names of the other person's partner or children. Conversely, people can work together for a short while and build a relationship that is closer in many ways than they have in their home life. This might be characterised by the camaraderie and closeness that one associates with the emergency services – organisations where people spend large amounts of close intimate time together under stressful situations.

This issue was considered in Chapter 11 because the assumption is that the nature of the interaction is likely to affect the rate and depth of knowledge exchanged between people, so as people become closer, and more in tune with each other's schema, so the flow of knowledge will improve.

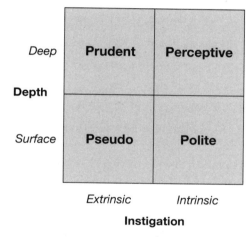

Fig. 12.6 The nature of relationship

The model shown in Fig. 12.6 suggests that two factors might be considered when mapping the nature of a relationship. The first point to consider is the depth of the interaction. Do the individuals' discussions, thoughts and feelings operate on a deep level, as between close friends, or are they at a surface level as one might correspond with a stranger in a bar? Second, does the drive for interaction originate from an extrinsic factor, or is it intrinsic as in something they choose to do? The combination of these two dimensions offers four potential interaction scenarios that might impact upon the learning process.

Pseudo

This type of interaction operates at a superficial level and is driven by an external agent. It might be the manager telling someone to go along to another department to learn some of their tricks, or being given a question to ask at a senior manager's presentation. Whatever the context, it is unlikely that any significant knowledge will be socialised or transferred. Critically, if a team of people is operating on this type of level, then the chance of the socialisation process being effective is likely to be limited.

Prudent

In this case the interaction is of a deeper level but is still driven by an external agent. The flow of open knowledge might be eased but there might be some suspicion about its adoption and use. This might be likened to a good friend offering someone unsolicited advice about how to fix a leaky tap. There is every possibility that the individual will carry on and do things their own way because the advice was unsolicited. Had they chosen to ask someone's advice, there would be more chance that the wisdom would have been received and acted upon.

Polite

This desire to share the knowledge and learning is driven by the individual without any external prompting, but the degree of openness and depth is limited. Hence, knowledge might be transferred, and some wisdom will be internalised, but there might be a question around the depth of experience that is being transferred. The learning might be focusing on tinkering and making small improvements, rather than delivering any really innovative ideas or changes.

Perspective

In this quadrant there is a greater chance that learning will be effectively socialised, and there is also a chance that it might be acted upon. This might be indicative of a product team member who has come up with a radical improvement and is sharing it with colleagues. The team is motivated to listen to the idea, and have a deep enough relationship to take the proposition seriously. Any decision from the team, be it move to embodiment, storage or discard, has a good chance of being accepted by the innovator as a worthwhile judgement.

The intention is not to offer a rigid model that directs how people to behave, more to highlight how changing the depth and direction of people's interaction might also change the content and flow of the learning process. Spending time socialising can be seen as a failure cost by companies, but often in developing closer ties between the individuals, the pay back can be in the speed with which information can flow through the socialisation network.

Competition

The idea of competition within an organisation can be viewed in different ways. Some organisations create internal competition to manufacture creative tension and mimic the external market by creating an internal market. Other companies believe that internal competition creates duplication, duplicity and an unnecessarily negative environment and it brings the aggression and tension of the market to people who should be working as colleagues and compatriots. The reality is that it is not a black or white situation, as there will always be some degree of competition between teams. Although separate groups will have their own goals and objectives, the structure of any organisation will be built around the demand for financial and manpower assets, and this will result in a competitive environment.

If this is the case, then how does it impact on the organisation's ability to effectively socialise knowledge? Schein (1998, 173) describes the way in which intergroup competitiveness can impact upon the teams. He considers what happens within each competing group, between the groups, to the winner, and the loser. In a competitive situation, the following might be observed:

- **Within each group** – The group creates closer ties between members and is prepared to ignore previous disputes or differences. There is a shift towards a more autocratic style of management, and the team emphasis shifts from friendly relationships, to more task-focused activities.
- **Between the group** – The group will regard the other team(s) as the enemy, and will reduce the amount of communication that it extends. There is a shift in perception, with each group seeing the other in negative stereotypical terms.
- **The winner** – The winning team may retain the sense of tightness and cohesion but can lose its sense of urgency and market awareness. The shift is from task back to personal relationships, and the positive outcome encourages people to retain the stereotype's schemata that they developed during the period of confrontation.
- **The loser** – The loser might attempt to distort the reality in order to see the loss in a favourable light, or find excuses. The shift stays on the task activities rather than the interpersonal aspects of the job, and there is an emphasis on working harder to win next time.

The net result in this case is that internal competition seems to provide active stimulation in certain areas, but there is some question over the total gain for the business. However, the focus here is not to consider whether or not competition is good or bad, but to understand the impact on the flow of knowledge.

The picture so far is that both during and after the competitive process, a split can be driven in the organisation. With both teams involved in the competition, and their allies being forced into separate tribal camps, a wall of confinement can be erected within the organisation. The suggestion is that the net result for the business is to hamper the knowledge creation and transfer process because:

- The walls created by the team have a negative impact on the ability of the groups and people to effectively interact.
- Reinforcement of the competitive style of management is at odds with the idea of developing synthesis through collaborative solutions.
- The inter-group tension takes the focus away from the long-term generative style of management to looking for short-term gains and single loop solutions.
- It drives a shift to task-based management rather than keeping a balanced perspective on the importance of managing relationships.

Competitiveness between groups is a natural part of life in a complex society. Any group of people will generally drift into social groups with a shared sense of purpose, and degrees of rivalry can emerge. The question that organisations need to consider is how far do they amplify the natural tendency to compete, and to what extent is there an overt desire to set groups against each other? If the organisation does take the decision to use competition as a way to enhance the learning processes, it should appreciate the potential negative factors that might be triggered.

Decision-making

At any stage in the socialisation of an idea, there comes a time when decisions need to be taken. Will the idea be progressed through the organisation, will it be passed through to embodiment, or possibly regarded as of little benefit, and so passed to discard? It is crucial for both the innovator and the business to understand how and why decisions are made as they pass through the socialisation process.

Critically, the task of decision-making can be viewed in terms of the espoused and in-use models described earlier. Research by Simon (1960) raised these key points about the decision-making process:

- People normally act on the basis of incomplete information about the sources of the data, and the choices they can make.
- People find it difficult to truly explore the potential solutions and options for a situation.
- The values that people attach to a decision will be limited and driven by their personal association and meaning.

162

Simon offers the view that at best organisations can only achieve a limited degree of rationality. So although people and teams might believe that they have taken decisions that are grounded in rationality and hard facts, the truth is that they have only taken a decision within a 'bounded rationality'. In essence, to have taken a decision that is good enough based upon the limited search and analysis options that were open to them (Morgan, 1986, 81). This conclusion was supported by Janis and Mann (1985), where they argue that people tend to take the easy way out and read only limited sources of information, particularly those that align with their personal views. One of the outcomes of this is that when taking decisions, there is a tendency to follow what the perceived 'expert' in a subject area proposes.

Coupled with this, many of the ideas put forward about the nature of self-organising systems raise further questions about the nature of decision-making. If one accepts that organisations are driven partially by the ideas of non-linear, spontaneous and random processes, then the following questions might be considered:

- If the long-term outcome is not known, by what criteria should a decision be taken?
- With a high degree of mobility, how can corporate responsibility be attached to a decision, so that accountability is established?
- If the future cannot be known, of what use are financial tools such as discounted cash flow, in the analysis phase?
- Given the role that political systems play, what emphasis should be given to political factors when trying to take a rational decision?
- Given that an organisation will use its feedback system as a regulating tool, what regulatory process will be triggered in response to a decision?

So, the socialisation process can be viewed according to two dimensions. The first is the extent to which decisions are taken according to the espoused or in-use process. For the espoused approach, decision-making will be clearly set out in the organisational procedures. For the 'in-use' approach, decision-making will be undertaken in a way that suits the people taking the decision and will not be grounded in rules and procedures. For the linear organisation, the decisions will be taken on the assumption that the forecast outcomes are achievable; if the non-linear outcomes are assumed as the natural operating style, the decision will be taken on a very short-term basis.

Drawing together these themes, four styles of decision-making might be observed (Fig. 12.7).

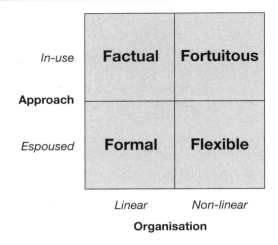

In-use

Approach

Espoused

Factual	Fortuitous
Formal	Flexible

Linear   Non-linear

Organisation

Fig. 12.7 Four styles of decision-making

Formal decision-making is very tight, controlled and clear regarding the process and anticipated outcomes. The expectation is that the process would be very well project managed and documented, but might be unable to cope with decisions that require a quick turn-around, or deal with something outside the main stream of work.

The factual approach is still very structured but there is a greater sense of reality about the approach. There is a willingness to deal with decisions in a pragmatic way rather than being hidebound by the tradition of rules. However, even though there is a greater degree of flexibility and openness, the assumption is still that any agreed outcome or plans are deliverable irrespective of changes in the environment.

The flexible approach is grounded in the idea that procedures and rules have been developed but they exist to help manage the process at hand, not to contain the decision against future goals. There is a sense that even if a decision is taken, it can be changed and improved at a later date, according to how the environment changes.

In the fortuitous domain, the assumption is that decision-making is both flexible and realistic. The decision will be taken based upon today's knowledge, and on the assumption that taking a decision does not mean that it is locked in stone. The decision process is adaptable and responsive to the people and environment needs, and is not in place to constrain the action in any way. It might, however, appear slightly chaotic and risky to people who are looking for a stable process, and might appear frightening to stakeholders who were not used to the turbulent style.

Although the four quadrants offer a view of some different approaches to decision-making, they are not offered as the decision-making options. Decision-making is a human process, and as such will be full of inconsistencies, confusion, power plays and problems. As such, it might be foolish to frame a model that can predict how the socialisation process might truly facilitate decision-making. However, it can help organisations to develop a view of the way that decisions are taken within the business.

Language

The world contains at least 4,500 natural languages, and this total ignores the variation between local dialects, and the changes in style and content between age groups (Honderich, 1995).

Often there can be a misconception that language is just used as a way of describing something to another person. Language is a magical process that takes the ideas and schematic models from one person's mind and creates them in someone else's. By the use of words, patterns, inflections and sounds, a person builds something new and original in someone else's mind every time they speak. So as an idea is socialised through an organisation, it is not just a case of an idea being passed from one person to another like a relay race. At each juncture, the idea is reborn and created in another person's mind. Each time this creation takes place, it will be subject to the factors of amplification, distortion and attenuation. Like the game of Chinese whispers, the language element of the socialisation process can have a significant impact on the way in which knowledge is received.

However, considering the total use of language as a communication medium in a short section of this chapter is impossible. Understanding the hows and whys of language is something that has consumed people's attention ever since humans uttered their first words. Hence, the focus here is just to consider how language might contribute to the socialisation process; primarily to think about the structural component of language as it facilitates the transportation of a new idea around the social group. In particular the factors that drive the nature and form on the social interaction will be considered. Is each interaction unique or is there some common theme that can be identified, so as to draw a clearer picture of the process?

In considering each time intercourse occurs, the depth and breadth of communication will be enormous, including body language, speech signals, visual signals or contextual factors. However, putting this to one side, there are a number of common steps that people might go through in the transaction process.

Consider the first point at which an idea is put to someone, be it using speech, mail, e-mail, hand signals or sign language. There are likely to be a number of logical steps that the proposer will go through to put forward an idea. There will also be a corresponding number of steps that the receiver will use to develop a response.

Fig. 12.8 Steps in intercourse

Offer

First, someone must develop a proposition as a tangible form or structure. For example, someone who works in a bookstore suggesting to the manager that it might be nice to offer free coffee to people as they come in the store. Next, they build concept. Once the basic idea is developed, the individual will put this into a conceptual model, possibly to picture the idea being implemented, considering how it might be enacted and what the problems might be. Effectively a schematic map is built that can be offered to other people.

Then, they must choose a frame. Once the overall map or picture of the idea is prepared, the individual will need to present it to someone else. At this stage a number of questions surface. To whom should they talk? What medium should be used? How do they approach them? Even down to the detail of what is the best time of day to suggest the idea. This is the frame that they build around the content of the message to make sense of it for the other people. Finally the offer is made, and the idea is put to the store manager in her office during a performance review session. The offer is made using a verbal suggestion backed up by a simple cost-benefit sheet to suggest how the business could gain new custom from the idea.

Response

Once the offer has been received, the receiver will start to test meaning in the proposal by taking the words used and drawing some personal conclusion as to what they mean to them when compared with their schematic view of life. In this instance the manager considers the idea and starts to develop an opinion on what their reaction might be. Once a basic understanding is developed, as with the offer phase, a response in the form of a conceptual model is developed by the manager, building a yes/no answer with the appropriate rationale.

The manager then chooses a form by which the response can be given. This might be a verbal response, a written note or a written letter to formally thank the employee for the idea. Finally, as with the initial stage the response is given and the message is received by the original proposer.

Although this has a highly logical and linear feel, it can happen in a flash, without any real sense of structure or direction. It can happen instinctively without the person really thinking through the proposal and response in such a structured manner. In this case the deep subconscious kicks into automatic and develops arguments without any conscious reasoning. In the case of the socialisation process, this interaction will happen many times during the diffusion of an idea as it bounces around the organisation internal networks.

From the interaction shown above, the development of the shared understanding between the people has a degree of impact on the socialisation process. In transferring a message, the way in which a proposal is framed is equally as important as the content itself, since language is embedded in the frame in which it is presented (Fig. 12.9).

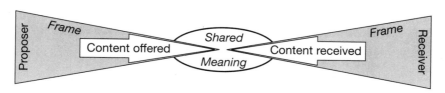

Fig. 12.9 Sharing meaning

As a simple example, consider the salesperson who is trying to land a big account. The final pitch to the board is made using a relaxed style, and includes a number of jokes. However, the salesperson's taste in humour veers towards the bawdy and sexist style of comedy. The jokes alienate the board so much that he losses the account. Even though the content of the sales pitch was fine, and would have been acceptable to the board, the way it was framed did not align with their view of the world.

On a practical level, the idea of developing a frame for the transmission of an idea is about understanding the world from the perspective of other people, to appreciate their schema, and to be able to take an idea and put it in that context, and in doing so construct a reality that makes sense to them. This is where the

167

use of metaphor and analogy become so important as a way in which to frame a complicated message.

Any individual who is keen to socialise an idea, needs to understand the notion of framing, to create the ability to draw on the various language tools that can help to frame a message for an audience. The list below indicates five methods by which an idea can be presented, so that it is incongruent with the receiver's view of the world:

Metaphors

These are used to help explain a particular idea in terms of another experience. The metaphor can be used in two ways. First, as an implied analogy, where comparison is drawn between two similar things (Ford and General Motors). Alternatively, it can be in the nature of a figurative analogy which draws a comparison between two seemingly different things (musician and manager).

Jargon and catch-phrases

These help to frame the idea in a set of words or context that help the recipient to feel comfortable. The danger is that gaining the attention of one group might alienate another who regard the jargon as confusing.

Contrast

Contrast is used to describe an idea in terms of its opposites, and so offers a polarised indication of what the idea is not. For example, try to frame an organisation in terms of an animal, first of all explain how it might be like a snail, slow and sluggish. Then turn it round to indicate how the business might need the qualities of a panther to survive for the next five years.

Spin

Takes an idea and deliberately offers it in a positive or negative light. This is used, sometimes over-zealously, by politicians as they try to angle a story so that it looks favourable to their party.

Stories

Often presenters will use a story to gently describe an underlying principle or key point that will be considered later. In doing this, the audience becomes engrossed in the story-line itself, and can forget that a common frame is constructed along which the content can be passed (Fairhurst and Starr, 1996).

Dangers in framing

The danger can be if an individual decides to focus more on the framing process than on the content of the message. This is often seen again in the political arena where politicians are invited to give a view on a hot topic of the day. However, the viewer will end up seeing 90 per cent framing skills, and only 10 per cent of the politician's actual view or understanding of the issue. This can be off-putting, dreary, and will in the end turn the audience off to such an extent that little or no content will be received.

In considering the idea of language as a socialisation enabler, the following points might be considered:

- Language has the ability to amplify or attenuate the progress of an idea through the social loop.
- It has the ability to generalise, distort, build, twist and filter meaning out of an idea, such that it can emerge as a totally different concept to how it started out.
- Used in a positive way, it can bring an idea of the knowledge element to life for another person.
- It should not be confined to facts and figures, but used to create parallel and alternative themes that support and build an idea.

In summary, where individuals come together as a group, the effective flow of knowledge and learning is entirely dependent on the ability of the people to use language in a positive and effective way.

Social class

Another key, but often unspoken factor in the socialisation of knowledge is that of organisational class. This is based upon the proposition that all organisations have a built-in, dynamic and unspoken class structure. This emerges because people have a need to create and hold some type of power in order to effect the necessary actions and changes. In the way that Marx believed that class struggle was the driving force for social change, so it can often be the driving force for change within organisations. As with children in the playground, there is always a pecking order, and someone's position in this league will affect their ability to generate and drive the socialisation of an idea.

The idea of class within an organisation can be seen in the way the formal and informal hierarchies are constructed. The primary structure is the traditional hierarchical system where the engineer reports to the supervisor, who reports to the manager, who reports to the department head and so on. This is an established model for organisations. However, there can be other forms of hierarchy within the business, but more often than not these are not published or recognised by the formal systems:

- **Gender** – In many organisations the unfortunate preponderance of men over women gives them the dominant edge in the management of the business. Stereotypical schemata kick in as women are regarded as secretaries and administrators but not as senior managers.
- **Age** – In recent years, the number of businesses that have downsized means that older people were the first to go. This almost created a sense that anyone over 40 was outside the business's desired age profile and would be leaving in a few years – so they might be perceived to be coasting and waiting to leave.
- **Race** – Again, the problems seen with race discrimination are commonplace, and still need to be addressed.
- **Product/project experience** – Often, as new technology comes into the business, the favoured people might be offered opportunities to attain the new skills. This creates a social barrier where those people with the new skill can operate on an assumption that they are more valued than other people.

Class difference of all forms will always exist and little action can be taken to eradicate them. However, for a business that wishes to enhance its learning capability, some attention needs to be given to understanding the class differences and how they impact on the learning process. Class suppression ultimately means that variety and diversity are being attenuated within the business. This type of behaviour can only result in the attenuation of the organisation's ability to be creative and innovative.

Knowledge bank

Well, everything in this building, everything in the criminal justice system in New York, operates on favours. Everybody does a favour for everybody else. Every chance they get, they make deposits in the Favour Bank.

Tom Wolfe, Bonfire of the Vanities

In the personality and psychotherapy theory of transactional analysis, there is an established idea called stroke theory. This suggests that human beings need to give and receive strokes of psychological stimulants that acts as a unit of recognition (Stewart and Jones, 1987). For example, if someone walks down the corridor and says 'hi' to someone, there is an expectation that the action will receive a positive response – if nothing is forthcoming, then a sense of hurt or emptiness can be felt by the giver. The result is that next time the same person is passed, there is a chance that the giver will ignore them, rather than risking another rejection. In addition to this, the perceived omission might well be remembered and stored in the 'stroke bank' for retaliation at a later date.

This same principle can be usefully applied to the socialisation of knowledge through an organisation. Imagine a new recruit who is motivated, focused and, most important, has a real talent for originating ideas. The first time the recruit comes up with an idea, it is discussed with a colleague and they decide to proceed and put the suggestion to the product review board. The next time, nothing might come back from the colleague. Then there is every chance that the recruit might feel a sense of unease – possibly that the knowledge bank is too biased in one direction. As a result, the individual might take ideas straight to the review board and bypass the other person.

If this happens, the socialisation process is in danger of breaking down as people start to act in an insular and selfish way. Hence, knowledge that might have available in a limitless supply is rationed and held in personal squirrel stores. There it is retained until the individual sees a chance to share with people who are prepared to reciprocate with ideas from their knowledge bank.

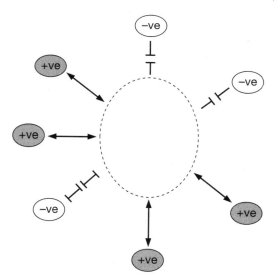

Fig. 12.10 Debit and credit in knowledge sharing

As a consequence, people may construct a tacitly held map of individuals who are in debit and credit with regard to knowledge sharing – as seen in Fig. 12.10. The net result is that invisible points of blockage can emerge in the social system, especially where people have a negative balance with more than one individual. If this happens, then these people can effectively be ostracised from the knowledge network. They don't offer knowledge and are not consulted about ideas as they flow through the business.

Although this idea might appear to be conceptual and somewhat inconsequential, it takes on a degree of importance when considered in relation to the use of internal computer networks. The installation of a new intranet system will rely heavily on the knowledge stroke maps that people build. If an individual believes that they are do all the contributing and other people are just extracting information, there is every chance that they might choose to socialise their knowledge using other, more traditional, processes. The end result is that a significant capital investment for the business can end up as a white elephant.

Memes

Genes exist in the human body to control the inheritance of specific physical characteristics and are made up of deoxyribo-nucleic acid, or DNA. In the same way, organisations can be viewed as having memes. These are the units of cultural transmission, or packets of ideas and knowledge that are used to spread information through the organisation and affect the behaviour of the host individual. This word was originated by the evolutionary biologist Richard Dawkins in his book *The Selfish Gene*. He suggests that memes are contagious information patterns that are copied inside the business. They are passed from mind to mind through human interaction, and shape the organisation's decision-making and socialisation process.

The key difference between an idea and a meme, is that an idea is passive, whereas a meme might be seen to have a life of its own. It will be seen almost as a living force that evolves and adapts as it spreads through an organisation. These can be commonly seen in the propagation of catch-phrases, pop tunes, inventions and fashions that develop in social systems. Importantly, one person's idea for a catch-phrase or song is not a meme. The meme only comes into being when it is repeated to someone else, and hence becomes transmitted knowledge or information. An example might be if the reader of this book goes to another person, and tells them about the idea of a meme, the theory of meme is then in itself a meme within that social system.

Memetic growth or evolution can take place over the course of a year, day, minute or seconds (especially with the Internet). For example, in 1997, the American on-line columnist Matt Drudge used the Internet to distribute stories about the president at great speed. The astounding speed with which a columnist could disseminate news and gossip accelerated a news cycle that had already reached warp speed with 24-hour satellite news (Goodwin, 1998). Drudge's reputation was such that his Web site could receive more than six million 'hits' a month. Whereas the ABC channel took 20 minutes to post a headline to the Web page, he did it in seconds. Thus the power he had to create memes across the world was phenomenal.

In many ways, a meme has the characteristic of a virus, but instead it is information or knowledge that is passed from one person to another, both con-

172

sciously and unconsciously. Once created, a virus of the mind gains a life independent of its creator, and evolves quickly to infect as many people as possible. A strong meme that is repeatedly shared can be found to spread quickly through an organisation. A weak meme does not gain acceptance and so rapidly dies.

An example of an organisational meme might be the rumour that a new director is about to be appointed. This will often take a life of its own, and can be dispersed around the organisation in days, or in some cases minutes. Now, at this stage, the thought has a life of its own. It might die out, as people realise that it is false information. Alternately, it might hang around in the people's subconscious, and start to influence and infect decisions they take. The characteristics of a meme can be described as:

- They generally contain a bait. This is the personal pay-back that the individual gets for receiving and passing on the information.
- Memes are stored in the belief space, and this can only accept so many. Once full, memes have to compete to hold on to the space.
- Contain a hook, which is the part of the idea that encourages replication.
- Can change as they are replicated and hence the ideas and stories can be seen to drift over time.

So, what does all this mean to the idea of socialisation? In essence, in the same way that organisations are critically aware of the damaging impact that software viruses can have on their operational performance, they must also be acutely aware of the impact of memes on the transference of knowledge.

People should be encouraged to be aware of the content of their belief space, and in particular the source of the beliefs. They should be able to differentiate between memes that are valid and of value, and those that are inaccurate or malicious. The organisation should also be aware of any dubious memes that are living within the business, and the damage that they might be doing to the knowledge creation process.

As an example, people can be encouraged to consider the key theories that are pertinent to their job and then consider where the idea came from, how valid it is, how they know it is true and who they shared the ideas with. If they are unable to answer these questions clearly, then how can the organisation be sure that they have not been infected with a meme that is false or counterfeit, and even more, to what extent they have acted as a host for the meme to replicate itself onto other people?

The value of memes comes from helping people to reflect upon their mental processes to differentiate what they understand to be hard fact, and what is simply knowledge that they have picked up somewhere along the way. Both knowledge elements are of value, but only when the person can differentiate between the two. When they can't, that is the making of cults, hero worship and guru adoration.

Conclusions

The following points emerge when considering how socialisation affects knowledge transference:

- Developing a shared sense of purpose can aid the socialisation process but only if the alignment is truthful. Simply telling people that they have a common goal can actually result in the transfer of knowledge being corrupted or attenuated.
- The imposition of rigid and prohibitive organisational boundaries can only result in the diffusion process being attenuated. Organisational barriers may need to be imposed for resource allocation and management systems, but when they go beyond this, they can become harmful.
- Without social connection between the individuals, there is limited chance that the socialisation process will be effective. However, it is likely that the most effective action will occur when the connection is self-driven and operates at a deep level.
- Although internal competition regularly occurs, it can affect the organisation's capability to generate and share knowledge internally.
- Decision-making is, and always will be, a dynamic affair. As such, it can never be predicated with any degree of accuracy. However, management of the socialisation process will be enhanced if people understand how decisions are typically taken.
- Language is core to the idea of socialisation as a key component in the knowledge system. Of all the factors associated with it, the ability to frame the knowledge content is critical in helping to create a socialisation process that can add to knowledge creation.
- As a human trait, class structure is well established and is likely to continue. As a business activity, it can be harmful to the knowledge creation process and organisations should always attempt to diminish its impact.
- Within a social group, knowledge can be traded as freely as people and plant. The only difference is that it might not be overtly regarded as something that is sold and purchased.
- Just because an idea is being transmitted across the social network, it does not mean that it will be of value to the business. Once an idea takes on the selfish form of a meme, it can wreak havoc with the content and structure of the knowledge system. Organisations must be alert to the flow of organisational ideas, and their contribution to the vale of the intellectual capital within the business.

The idea of a socialisation network within the knowledge system is critical to the idea of stimulating learning and creating knowledge within the organisation. The problem is that as an intangible, it can be ignored when decisions are taken on action that will bring about an improvement in the way that the business learns and shares knowledge.

Socialisation model dynamics

	How do we learn?	How do we share?	How do we use?	How can we improve?
Network (screen, embody, store and discard) The role that the socialisation network plays in managing knowledge is understood				
Purpose People have an open and shared sense of purpose				
Boundaries The impact of formal and informal perimeters upon the flow of knowledge is understood				
Connection The impact of cohesion on knowledge transfer is understood				

	How do we learn?	How do we share?	How do we use?	How can we improve?
Competition The positive and negative impact of internal competition is understood				
Language The process that takes ideas and schematic models from one person's mind and creates them in someone else's				
Decision-making The organisation understands how decisions are made as they pass through the socialisation process				

177

Socialisation model dynamics continued

	How do we learn?	How do we share?	How do we use?	How can we improve?
Social class There is an appreciation of the internal 'pecking order' and its impact upon the socialisation of knowledge				
Knowledge strokes The impact of internal knowledge strokes on the learning processes are understood				
Memes The flow of memes within the social system is understood				

Part 4

Infrastructure

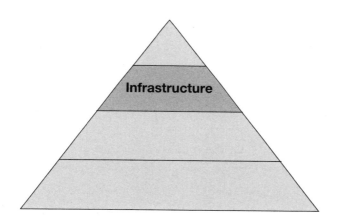

Chapter 13

....

Infrastructure

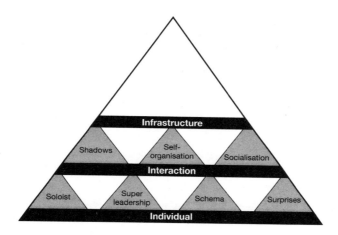

Fig. 13.1 Building a knowledge infrastructure

Within the Integrated Learning Model, this section on infrastructure attempts to describe the process of knowledge transfer across the organisation's internal communication streams. This has been considered in two areas: the knowledge structure that underpins the transfer; and the diffusion process that knowledge goes through when socialised across the business.

Structure

Knowledge has financial value, and this can be seen by simply taking a stroll round the local shops: stereo equipment that is 10 per cent packaging and 90 per cent intellectual expertise; the astounding number of magazines, all full of knowledge offered by an ever-increasing range of writers; or the Internet explosion, where the only capital traded is knowledge in exchange for symbolic money. The key thing organisations need to understand, is how to create a knowledge infrastructure that will enable the free flow of ideas around the business and following this, to ensure that processes are in place to embody the knowledge into the organisation's products and processes. The proposition is that within any organisation, knowledge might be processed through five different stages – discovery, diffusion, delivery, delay and disposal.

181

Sharing

The creation of organisational knowledge is about people, their interaction and the synthesis that arises from the sharing process. At the end of the day, creating the ability to share is about understanding the need for a new kind of learning; for the whole organisation to learn the ability to rapidly and effectively move the lessons learned from experience and experiments into the mainstream processes and products of the business.

The infrastructure used to transport and diffuse knowledge across the organisation can be seen as a key component within the learning process. The problem is that emphasis is often placed on the technical aspects, such as e-mail and intranet, rather than understanding the underlying social systems that really drive and support the diffusion process.

Karash (1995) makes the point that the focus should be on creating infrastructure that makes explicit knowledge more usable and valuable. The aim is to create an infrastructure that makes it easier to transform the tacit into the explicit; that makes explicit knowledge available to others more effectively and more easily; that supports the application of explicit knowledge by another person, thereby transforming it into new and enriched tacit knowledge. This is in essence the proposition behind the infrastructure chapters; without a clear and open path to each other, people will remain closed and insular, hence organisational learning will remain an aspirational dream.

Chapter 14

Structured knowledge system

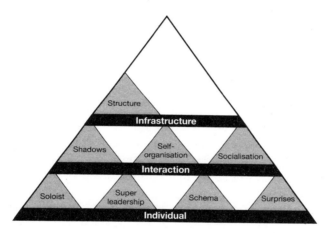

Fig. 14.1 Structure

*C*onsider a quiet beach. Three children decide to have a contest. They challenge each other to a game of skipping stones, trying to outdo each other in the goal of achieving the most skips, and reaching the furthest distance. John makes a double skip, that reaches three metres into the sea. Sara makes four skips, and manages to achieve a distance of five metres, Alison steams ahead and manages six skips, and reaches a distance of seven metres.

Defining exactly why Alison was able to win is likely to be difficult, but one key component will be the knowledge that she used in throwing the stone. Knowledge gained from watching other children play, from throwing stones in the garden, and maybe even knowledge gained from watching a film about the Dambusters.

Alison now has two choices. The first is to just carry on playing the game. The second is to trade her knowledge and, in return for some of their sweets, help the other children to develop a similar set of skills.

This chapter draws on many of the existing ideas about knowledge management, and offers a new framework that encapsulates, simplifies and builds upon these concepts. Two main subject areas are considered. First is the development of a 'working framework' for intellectual capital, and its component elements:

● data;
● information;
● knowledge;
● synthesis;
● intellectual capital.

Providing an overview of the five core attributes that are the backbone of a knowledge management system:

● discovery;
● delivery;
● delay;
● disposal;
● diffusion.

Even though books, articles and Internet sites abound on the topic of knowledge management, there is little agreement as to the nature of the word 'knowledge', let alone a clear definition of knowledge management. Much of the debate is grounded in the question of its origin, ownership and transferability. Is knowledge a tangible product that can be separated from its owner, and hence transferred from person to person? Alternatively, is it something that only exists in the eye of the beholder and is, in essence, a theory of subjective perception? On top of this, there is so often confusion over the relationship between data, information, knowledge and intellectual capital. This goes to make management learning and knowledge, an area that is desperately awaiting some clear definition.

Again, as with so many other topics in the field of management, there is a danger of veering into the realms of linguistic analysis or philosophical debate in order to arrive at a solid definition. It is probably impossible to come up with a structural definition that will satisfy all people, since the whole notion of knowledge and intellectual capital is in itself a subjective idea. As Stewart (1998, 69) suggests, the idea that knowledge can be slotted into a 'data-to-wisdom hierarchy is bogus, for the simple reason that one man's knowledge is another man's data'.

However, in offering a structural model of the management of knowledge, it might help to offer a temporary taxonomy of the meaning behind each of the key words and how they interrelate. The basic structure of the taxonomy is built around the idea of a knowledge ramp – as the extent of human interaction with the data increases, so it becomes possible to enhance its commercial value as seen in Fig. 14.2.

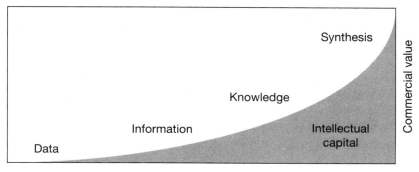

Fig. 14.2 Acknowledge ramp

Data is the raw and unprocessed material that arrives from the external world. It might be that human intervention has played a part in its delivery, but this is a mechanistic process and not (generally) a value-added one. Possibly, the test is that in considering the data, would anyone ever ask 'who prepared this data?'.

> **Example A** *Consider the receipt that one receives from a supermarket check-out desk. It simply transfers the price of the objects in the basket into a table of data. There is little sorting, categorisation or interpretation.*

Information is data that has been acted upon cognitively, codified and transformed into a framework to be used for specific purposes. It might include a variety of transformation processes including sorting, categorising, extraction, etc. At this stage it becomes possible to see the hand of a person involved in the transformation of the data into information. However, this human touch is still only there to rework the data, not to add a unique value that might be traced back to an individual or team. An example might be that of the software programmer who specifies that a particular routine should be used as part of the data processing process. Although some value is visible, there is little evidence of the human spirit in the formation and structure of the information.

> **Example B** *In many supermarkets there is an automatic process of discounting across linked product lines. This is often shown at the bottom of the shopping receipt as the total discount offered to the customer. At this stage the data has become of use to the customer, and some market value can be perceived.*

A favoured definition of knowledge is that offered by Nonaka and Takeuchi (1995, 58): 'Knowledge might be viewed as the first point in the transition process where the hand of human action is visible'. It is at this point that one might be able to see that a person has made a purposeful intervention in the process to give the data a specific purpose or meaning in life. This meaning might be driven by the goals and values of the company or the beliefs of the individual. Either way, the human touch will be apparent.

> **Example C** *At this stage, the shopping list would move from a mechanistic process that has limited human intervention to one where deliberate value is generated for the business and the customer. In making use of the data, the company can start to map purchasing histories and draw predictions to develop life-style profiles. The human hand will be clear at this stage because of the way in which the information is transformed.*

Relational synthesis is essential to the notion of facilitating learning and knowledge creation. It is rare that one could explicitly point to an idea that one person originated without help from another human being. All people are subject to influence in their creative process, be it positively or negatively. Knowledge will, in the majority of cases, be an effervescent process where one person's thought will trigger a memo by another that leads to a written proposal by someone else. The resulting synthesis that emerges following an interaction between people is where the real fruits of the future are embedded. Hence, it is the social construction of knowledge that is potentially most valuable in creating intellectual capital within the business.

> **Example D** *Once the supermarket has knowledge under its wing, it might develop other uses for the information that it holds. For example, the ability to manage financial transactions through the till offers them competencies and systems that are complementary to that of a high street bank. Hence, the resulting relationships that have recently been forged between the high street retailers and the banks.*

Intellectual capital is the 'measured' totality of the organisation's knowledge that has the potential to leverage revenue in the market. In particular, people's competencies, attitudes, intellectual capacity, ideas, feelings and relationships. It is inherently nebulous and transient, and, as such, will always be difficult to pin down and value.

> **Example E** *The final realisation of this knowledge into a capital asset is indicated by one of Tesco's promotional campaigns. Tesco used the purchasing data held on its customer base to target specific groups of customers with known buying habits. These people were invited to special cook-in promotional evenings with a famous chef. This both reinforced brand loyalty to the exclusion of other supermarket chains, and might encourage the customer to purchase the product used at the event.*

The process of knowledge creation is an incremental one with each component adding a further level of value as it is processed. As the degree of human interaction with the data is increased, so the area under the knowledge ramp curve increases, emphasising the growth in intellectual capital.

Where companies opt to work at a base data level without adding any potential from their people, they can be seen to operate in the commodity end of the market. At the other end of the continuum, developing the synthesis between raw data and the potential of the people will lock intellectual value into the company's products, services and systems.

The question is, what are the underlying systems that organisations can use to facilitate this generative process? How can data be converted into capital, where is it stored and what happens once the knowledge is redundant? The following model sets out a basic schematic outline. The aim is not to propose how it 'should' happen but simply to highlight some of the key areas that organisations need to consider when reviewing their knowledge management processes.

Knowledge management system

The creation of intellectual capital is based upon the successful discovery of new knowledge and its embodiment into the organisation's systems, processes and products. This process of embodiment is a topic that is widely discussed, analysed and procrastinated upon, but there is little agreement (and is unlikely to ever be) on its delivery.

The simplistic proposition is that within any organisation, knowledge might be processed through five stages:

- **Discovery** – This is where the knowledge is unearthed. This might be through a range of different processes, including personal invention, group socialisation or recruitment of external agents.
- **Delivery** – Once the knowledge has been discovered, it can become embodied within the organisation's product or processes. This might be as a new piece

of software code, an enhanced product design or a new customer service programme.

- **Delay** – Once the knowledge is discovered, it may not be practical to embed
  it immediately into the products or services. In this case the knowledge can be
  (intentionally or unintentionally), held in storage.
- **Disposal** – At some stage, the knowledge is likely to become redundant
  although it still might have some residual asset value to the business. Depending upon its half-life, this might be overnight, or it may be over a 100 years.
  The key is to ensure that the disposal process is controlled, and the financial
  gain for the organisation is maximised.
- **Diffusion** – The final component in the knowledge management system is the
  hub. This is a symbolic representation of the interface system that connects the
  four areas together.

In understanding how each of these five areas operate and the nature of the flow
between them, the company can effect greater control over the creation and use
of its intellectual assets.

Discovery

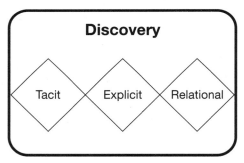

Fig. 14.3 Discovery components

At the root of the process is the idea of creating new knowledge. However, clarifying what 'new' means, can be perplexing. Some might say that nothing is new
and every idea is simply a regurgitation or synthesis of something that has happened in the past. Others might suggest that the recent changes in science, and the
world in general, prove that it is possible to create something that is totally new.

The stance taken in this chapter, is that new knowledge is something that the
organisation does not currently recognise as being part of its intellectual capital
base. In this sense it might be someone who offers a change of work practice in
the new idea's scheme; it might be a change in project design; or the employment

of a subject expert. The proposition is that however the knowledge is discovered, it will typically be realised through one of the following channels:

- **Tacit knowledge** is a deep, hidden form of knowledge that drives personal actions and behaviour.
- **Explicit knowledge** can be described and easily shared with others.
- **Relationship knowledge** is created as a result of the interaction between two or more people.

Tacit knowledge

Tacit knowledge might be described as the thoughts, feelings, dreams and intuition that go on in the background while people are performing a task. A succinct way of referring to it might be 'in the muscle learning', the natural acts that people perform without consciously thinking (Burns, 1998), like a natural baseball player, highly effective sales person or master carpenter might perform. This might be at an individual, team or organisational level. For the individual, it might be seen in the golfer who can line up, prepare and take a swing, while thinking about the people who are going to be involved in the next tournament. It might be the natural style that a successful sales manager adopts with customers. For a team, it may be the accepted norms that are followed when a group of people get together. One example is the deep experience contained in a group of footballers, or the way that one product group is able to constantly outperform another when evolving a new product design. At an organisational level, it might be characterised as routines, which are the rules, procedures, conventions, strategies and technologies that act as building blocks for the organisation (Levitt and March, 1996). It might also be regarded as the beliefs, frameworks and general cultural artefacts that make up the softer elements of the organisation.

Although the creation and exploitation of tacit knowledge is something that all people do, from a commercial viewpoint it does have a major drawback in that it can be difficult to transfer within the organisation. There are many reasons for this, but some of the key factors include:

- **Context dependent**, such as the case of the musician who is only able to shine when with a certain group of musicians.
- **Difficult to articulate**, as in the difficulties a chef will have describing what factors make the difference between a good and a great meal.
- **Hard to facilitate collaboration**. Since tacit knowledge is often thought of in terms of personal metaphors and symbols, a metaphor shared between two people might have a totally different connotation.
- **Requires presence**. Although it might be possible for a skilled pilot in a control tower to talk down a novice in a plane, it is probably very difficult. Some

skills and knowledge are not readily transferred without immediate and close visual contact.

- **Emotional barriers** may exist because some tacit knowledge has deep personal meaning for the expert. To readily share such knowledge may mean the expert has to trust the novice to respect his personal meaning, or for the novice to convince the expert that the knowledge will be used appropriately.
- **Emergent** knowledge is not always readily identifiable in a distinct form. It can be like a pot-pourri, and mixed up with other types of knowledge, experiences and feelings.

Although all of these factors can make it difficult to transfer, it should be understood that tacit knowledge is the fountain of wisdom. A large element of knowledge innovation will originate from a tacit level, and it grows in value as it is transferred from tacit to explicit level and from person to person.

Explicit knowledge

Explicit knowledge is something that can be easily talked about, shared and documented. It is a commodity that can be readily shared with other people, stored, retrieved and embodied in tangible products, service, or processes.

The distinction between tacit and explicit knowledge is difficult to pin down. However, the proposition is that knowledge becomes explicit when the individual is able to explain the actions they are taking. Examples of the type of things that display the attributes of explicit knowledge are:

- training manuals;
- newspapers;
- equipment user guides;
- college lectures.

While explicit knowledge has the benefit of being readily communicated, stored and retrieved, the downside is that it is easily lost to the competitor. It can be transferred over the Internet at the touch of a key stroke, overheard in a bar, or simply deduced by analysing the company's products. One common example of this can be seen in the automobile market. Companies will regularly purchase their competitors' products to rip them apart, in order to extract the embedded knowledge for application in their products.

Relational

The final suggestion is that knowledge can be created or discovered as a result of the interaction between two or more people. This point might be difficult to embrace, because it can be seen to give knowledge a life of its own – one that exists outside the mind of an individual. However, there are times when something inexplicable happens between two people – a manifestation that would not have happened to an individual.

This relational discovery process can take place in two forms, either at the tacit or explicit level. Tacit relational discovery might occur where people working together over a period of time will improve their working methods, but may not recognise or discuss the improvement. Examples might be musicians who work together for a long period, or comedians who intuitively grow their appreciation of each other's style and preferred methods of working. Alternatively, relational discovery can take place at the explicit level. Examples might be researchers writing a paper together, or a project team where people share ideas in building the project plans.

However, each of these three components is not exclusive or separate. The dynamic interaction that takes place between tacit, explicit and relational creates the flow of energy that is necessary to sustain the discovery process. The role that the organisation should take with respect to this model is in understanding how the transfer takes place among the domains, and what actions and behaviours help to stimulate the process. Examples of these interactions are offered in Table 14.1.

The key to knowledge discovery is not to try to codify, harness or control the process, but to create supportive processes that allow the free flow of information and knowledge within the business. In doing this, the organisation sends the appropriate signals to suggest that the discovery of knowledge is fundamental to the long-term growth of the business.

Table 14.1 Knowledge creation: types and examples

Individual tacit to individual explicit	Writing conference papers helps an individual to work through internal assumptions and models, and turn them into theories and models that others can apply
Individual tacit to relational tacit	Mentoring offers a process whereby subtle and private skills and experience can be offered to others. The mentor need not explicitly tell the other person what to do, but will subtly model the behaviours he or she has found to be effective
Relational tacit to individual tacit	Research projects can allow an individual to learn from other people's experiences. A research student, in undertaking an anthropological study of the relationship between a group of people, may well intuitively adopt many of the observed behaviours
Relational tacit to relational explicit	Brainstorming techniques offer a way in which people can expose hidden beliefs and ideas by working them through with a group
Relational explicit to individual explicit	Shadowing allows an individual to work with a group of people and to directly pick up the skills and behaviours that are being used in the team
Relational explicit to individual tacit	As people work in project teams, the sharing of explicit knowledge about planning techniques can help people to enhance their level of tacit knowledge, possibly their ability to manage their personal time more effectively
Relational explicit to relational tacit	Team meetings in the workplace allow groups of people to discuss interpersonal issues that affect the group. In doing so, this helps team members to agree on ways of working that make the team more effective
Individual explicit to individual tacit	New managers can often be nervous of giving a presentation to senior managers. However, once they are given the appropriate formal training, their competence will generally improve to the stage where they can give presentation in any context, without explicitly thinking about the techniques
Individual explicit to relational explicit	Teaching is the prime way in which one individual shares explicit knowledge with a group of people

Delivery

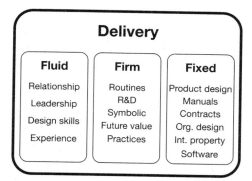

Fig. 14.4 Embodiment of knowledge

A high stock of intellectual capital is of little use if the company cannot realise its commercial value. Once created, knowledge should go through a process of review and filtration, to ensure it is of significance. If it is confirmed as having value, it should become embodied in the products and services that the business offers, or in the underlying systems that drive the organisation.

Asset forms

The embodiment process can be considered in three ways: fluid; fixed; and firm. Although this offers a slightly simplistic view of the asset categories, it helps to understand the structure and location of the knowledge when trying to facilitate learning across the organisation.

Fluid

The elements of knowledge that are contained within the hearts and minds of the people, and leave when they leave the business. It might be personal experience accumulated over a number of years in the business, or a long-term relationship cultivated with a customer. Sometimes it can be shared knowledge that has yet to be coded into the organisation's systems and processes. This might be an idea that a person has submitted but has been excluded or lost in the internal system. However, the bottom line is that if the person leaves, so does the knowledge.

Fixed

These are knowledge elements retained when an individual leaves. Once knowledge is locked in the system, processes or products, it can be seen as hard capital. It is available for anyone in the company to make use of, irrespective of the

193

originator's presence. Such examples might be coded software, product upgrades or business proposals.

Firm

These are the elements that are semi-permanent in that they only exist when the individual and firm are collaborating. This might be the unique sound that is produced from a musical genius playing a quality instrument. Individually each of the elements can perform to a satisfactory degree, but in bringing the two together, there is an added presence, a synergy, that enhances the levels of knowledge. Conversely, the knowledge might only be available when two separate elements are brought together, like the need for two opposing polarities to generate an electrical current. An example might be where an individual has independently created a database. Anyone else who attempts to use it will not be able to extract the information, because they do not have an intimate appreciation of the system's architecture.

So far, this chapter has considered the discovery of knowledge and its subsequent embodiment into the organisational systems and products. In some cases this might not be appropriate or feasible, and the knowledge may need to be stored until it can be used effectively.

Delay

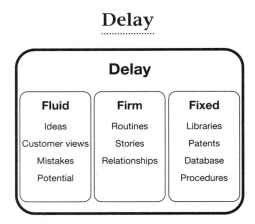

Fig. 14.5 Storage components

In many cases people will originate or discover new ideas and theories only to find that they cannot be immediately applied. This might arise because:

- the market is not ready for the idea;
- there are perceived or actual political barriers;
- existing technology is incompatible;

194

- there is a mismatch with existing products;
- base material costs are too high;
- competitive response may provoke a price war;
- the individual sees no advantage in sharing insights or ideas.

Any of these factors may result in the knowledge being held in storage. This might be a short-term action, such as overnight gathering of news material that awaits positive corroboration from a political source. It might be a medium-term process, like the problem with genetic re-engineering, where technically it is possible but there is a great deal of sensitivity around its use with food and animals. Finally, it may be a long-term storage process, along the lines of the knowledge that nuclear fusion is possible but the technology is not available to make it happen commercially.

For all of these factors, the key questions are, where is the knowledge to be stored? How is it stored? What is the retrieval process? If the organisation is unable to articulate clear answers to these questions, then it is in danger of losing control over the un-embedded knowledge. There needs to be a clear appreciation of the process by which knowledge that has yet to be capitalised upon is stored.

The storage mechanism might again be seen as fluid, fixed or firm. Each of these has its own access and retrieval methods and more importantly, has implications for the use of intellectual capital.

If an organisation wishes to use knowledge as an enhanced asset base, then it should have a clear appreciation of the storage mechanism. This does not mean an ability to reel off what databases are used and how many gigabytes of storage are available, but having a clear model of the storage processes for all three knowledge types (fluid, fixed and firm). In particular, it means understanding the benefits and problems associated with each storage mechanism.

For knowledge stored in fluid areas, i.e. people's minds, the retrieval process is likely to be flexible and easily transferable across the organisation. However, it also gives a problem in that the intellectual capital will walk if the person does. Hard-coded knowledge has the advantage of being locked in the organisation and does not have the volatility associated with the fluid storage. However, it can suffer from other problems. The fixed storage process can require mechanisms to hold the information, people to maintain the system, and resources to ensure that currency is maintained. This creates an overhead for the business, one that has to be set as a debit against the value of the intellectual capital. Lastly, storage in the firm area offers significant benefits in the uniqueness and synergy that can arise from the combination of two independent factors. The downside is in the dependence that is placed on the relationship as a storage medium. It implies that if either one fails to be in place, the benefit is lost for both areas.

In essence, for an organisation to effectively use its stored intellectual capital, the focus must be on understanding what storage mechanisms exist, their volatility, the degree of access and level of currency of the information.

Disposal

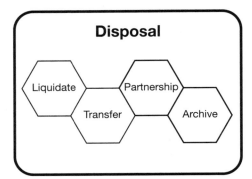

Fig. 14.6 Disposal components

At some stage, knowledge will become obsolete. This might be within a few seconds of discovery, as with an idea that is discarded in a brainstorming session. It might be after a day, as with the news carried by a newspaper. It might be after a year, as with much of the knowledge required to design and build microprocessors.

The key concept is how to maximise the disposal process and ensure that the intellectual capital will deliver the maximum amount of income as it leaves the organisation. The proposal is that there are at least four different strategies that an organisation might follow to enhance the disposal process.

Liquidate

The organisation recognises that a component of its knowledge base is no longer of value, and sells it. One example of this might be how software companies sell off their earlier programs at a reduced cost. Although the features that are on the older software are not as good as the more recent releases, there are people who are prepared to pay a lower charge for the reduced facilities.

Liquidation of the knowledge base can be a quick and effective way to realise income for the business. However, there is a danger that releasing the explicit knowledge to the open market will give the competition easier access to the organisation's knowledge base. It may be that in some cases, the safer option is to deliberately destroy the knowledge so that competitors are not able to draw upon the expertise that constructed the original intellectual capital.

Transfer

In some cases knowledge or skills that were once a core competence may have been superseded for a particular area, but might still be of use in another area. This happened in the UK when the mechanical telephony system was no longer required. The redundant equipment used in other countries where the elaborate features of the new electronic systems were not wanted. As a result, telephony companies were able to re-sell their maintenance skills overseas, as well as the equipment.

Partnership

One company might identify a particular knowledge set that is of diminishing value but recognise that some substance could be realised when partnered with a company with a different set of competencies. The turmoil in telecommunications highlights how companies are trying to create synergies by sharing their intellectual capital. Examples of this might be the computing firms joining with telecom companies, or geographically-scattered organisations coming together to share their knowledge about local markets.

Archive

In some cases it will be difficult to decide if knowledge is redundant. Decisions need to be made about future uses. The option is to archive the knowledge in a secure system so that it can be retrieved at a time when the market or technology will allow the value to be extracted. One example of this is the electric car. The technology to build it has been around for years but the problem rests with the battery technology. Once companies are able to build small, high-capacity batteries, all the archived knowledge will be resurrected to realise some commercial value.

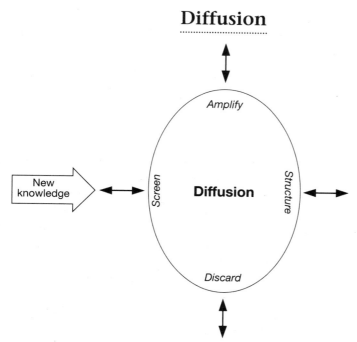

Fig. 14.7 Knowledge diffusion through the network

197

The final component in the knowledge management system is the socialisation network, as considered in Chapter 12. This is a symbolic representation of the interface system that connects the diffusion process. It is effectively the linchpin or hub that links the diffusion stages together to facilitate the free flow of knowledge.

The socialisation network plays a critical role in managing the knowledge as it circulates within the business. When a new idea or piece of knowledge enters the network, it can eventually take one of four paths as in Fig. 14.7. The four functions are described below and offer a view of how the socialisation process interacts with, and contributes to, knowledge sharing.

First, as knowledge is discovered or created within the organisation, a screening or filtering process will take place. Clearly it is not practical to allow every new idea to feed into the knowledge network, since this would result in overload and congestion. The idea is to have processes that allow the necessary freedom of expression to facilitate the generative process while at the same time filtering out those ideas that offer little value. Examples of this can be seen in new idea or schemes work. When a new idea is submitted, it might go before a panel of experts who determine its worth to the business. An alternative approach can be the internal market system; if a new product or project is proposed, the sponsor will generally need to gain support from the key stakeholders. Without the necessary political assistance, the idea is doomed to failure and will be discarded.

Once knowledge is accepted as having value, it needs to be amplified so it can gain respectability within the social organisation. The aim is to get the knowledge to a stage where it is accepted as being of value by all the primary stakeholders across the business. This amplification process might take many forms. It could be simply posting an idea on the noticeboard in the tea-room, writing an article for the internal house journal, or presenting a formal submission to the management board. Whatever processes are applied, the idea is to socialise and grow the circle of interest around the idea. In essence, to achieve as much political buy-in as required to ensure that the knowledge can become embodied in the appropriate area.

One common type of amplification for large organisations is the committee approval structure. Often new projects or products will have to submit a proposal to a range of committees to ensure that resources can be allocated. Although the espoused view is that this is to maintain commercial prudence, an added value is the amplification that takes place as the ideas are shared with new stakeholders.

Creating structure is another option in the screening process to recognise that an idea has value, but not in the present climate. In this case the knowledge should be structured and codified in such a way that it can be stored for later retrieval. The problem can be one of indexing and access. Consider knowledge that has been previously stockpiled. If the donating sponsor has lost interest, or moved to another company, it might sit in the system without anyone appreciating its hidden value. This is where an effective cataloguing system can help.

People need to be able to browse through the organisation's historic ideas, experiences and learning in the same way that one can browse the Internet for views and experiences. This is the practice that McKinsey and Co, the consulting firm, adopted to ensure that individual learning was shared across the organisation. The company maintains a central team of intelligent interrogators who manage a computerised database of knowledge and experiences. The library team can scour the library so that any questions from the field can be promptly answered, and thus facilitate the retrieval and disbursement of knowledge from across the organisation (Stewart, 1997, 125).

Finally, the filter system should allow for redundant data to be quickly and effectively discarded. Possibly, the easiest area to do this is with new knowledge, as it will have little political allegiance and only limited organisational resource allocated. The difficulty comes in trying to dispose of knowledge that is already embedded in a product, or locked into the storage system. It is not sufficient for companies simply to control the wisdom as it enters the network. There needs to be a continual process of internal reflection and appraisal in order to understand what intellectual capital is currently held, and of that, what needs to be discarded. Planning is needed for its controlled migration out of the business, rather than simply dropping the learning once it is deemed to have lost its value.

Conclusions

In offering the model outlined in Fig. 14.8, the idea is not to suggest that an organisation's knowledge process is linear or structured. The discovery, diffusion, delivery, delay and disposal of knowledge always will be complex and dynamic. The model simply seeks to overlay a temporary rational order so that managers can start to get to grips with many of the component parts.

In considering the topics covered in this chapter, a number of key points might be seen to emerge:

- Organisations need to move beyond offering superficial platitudes such as 'people are our asset'. They should move to a position where there is a real appreciation of the value of the intangible elements that people bring to work in their minds and experience.

- In understanding how knowledge is created, the key issue is around moving people beyond thinking that the only good knowledge is explicit knowledge. The value of tacit and relational learning needs to be appreciated and encouraged so it can be capitalised upon.

- At all levels in the organisation, there needs to be continual reappraisal of the half life of the asset base. How long will the organisation's knowledge have value and to what extent are individuals replenishing their knowledge stocks?

199

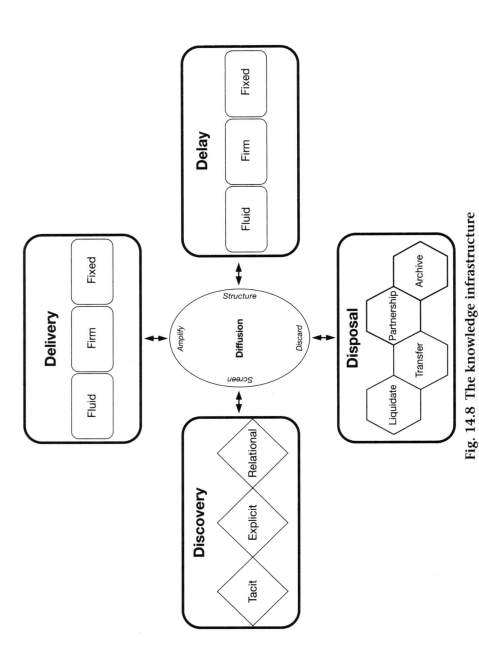

Fig. 14.8 The knowledge infrastructure

- Recognise that knowledge is not simple or static. It is multi-dimensional and the range of factors that affect its discovery, flow and delivery are all critical to effective use. People should be aware of the volatility level, the temporal nature of its value, and the fact that it can reside in many areas of the organisational network or structure.
- The installation of technology does not mean that the capability to learn and create knowledge has been accomplished. Technology, such as intranets, or video-conferencing, is often proposed as a panacea for business challenges. The truth is that it will achieve little if the human dimension is not understood.
- Any organisation that does not have a crystal-clear appreciation of the social network and its impact on the flow of knowledge may be seriously disadvantaged.
- Ultimately, it is the alignment between the formal data management systems and the social systems that will realise the creation of intellectual capital.

The structure of the knowledge system is simply a topographical map – a schematic model that offers a way for people to understand the flow of knowledge through the business. Its importance is in the spirit of knowledge mapping rather than its defined shape or form. If organisations wish to exploit their knowledge content and processes, then the first thing to do might be to construct their own schematic model, and hence create a map that is personal for the business. The paradox might be that in building such a knowledge map, it in itself becomes a piece of knowledge that holds value for the business within its intellectual capital base.

Structure model dynamics

	How do we learn?	How do we share?	How do we use?	How can we improve?
Knowledge ramp The organisation knowledge taxonomy is understood and mapped for all areas				
Discovery The balance between tacit, explicit and relational knowledge is understood and effectively utilised				
Delivery The process by which knowledge is embedded is understood at all levels				

	How do we learn?	How do we share?	How do we use?	How can we improve?
Delay The process for storing short-, medium- and long-term information is understood				
Disposal There is a clear disposal process which ensures that intellectual capital will deliver the maximum amount of income as it leaves the organisation				
Diffusion The hub that links the four knowledge areas together to facilitate the free flow of knowledge is mapped and effective				

Chapter 15

Sharing

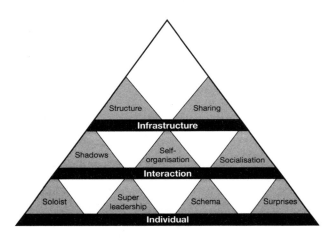

Fig. 15.1 Sharing in the Integrated Learning Model

In thinking about changes that have taken place over the past millenium, one of the most significant is the invention of the printing press in the fifteenth century. Before the invention of the press, credited to German goldsmith Johann Gutenburg, the ability to read and write had been confined mostly to tiny elites of nobles, priests and scribes. Once established, it brought about a radical change in societies around the world because is facilitated the sharing and transfer of knowledge to the masses. The use and knowledge of press technology spread so rapidly that by 1500, an estimated half a million printed books were in circulation.

It is this idea of sharing knowledge that became so pervasive in the fifteenth century that is at the core of the idea of organisational learning. Without knowledge exchange, individual learning cannot be transformed into organisational learning. Any organisation should be looking to understand its capacity to take a single parcel of knowledge and be able to spread this across the breadth and depth of the business. The aim is to offer everyone the chance to internalise other people's ideas and experiences and from this, bring about a change in the competitive nature of the business.

To help create this competence, there needs to be a robust appreciation of two areas that affect the organisation's ability to share knowledge:

- diffusion across the network;
- platforms that can be used to share the knowledge.

In developing an appreciation of these two areas, the organisation can ensure that its knowledge channels are able to effectively facilitate the sharing process.

Process of sharing

The introduction of knowledge into an organisation can be aligned directly to the idea of launching a new product. It is based upon developing a detailed understanding of the way in which the idea becomes socialised, accepted and desired by the people in the internal market. The company should be able to develop robust theories that describe how a new concept is accepted by a group of people who might have little interest in the product. In the previous chapter, the diffusion model outlined the various structural stages that a new idea or innovation can go through in shifting from discovery to delivery. However, there is also another view that can be taken when considering the flow of knowledge and that is the process by which knowledge is diffused within the social system.

The diffusion process might be considered as the social change that occurs as the idea is accepted within the organisation. Since the rate at which different people adopt a new idea will vary, it is possible to develop distinct categories that indicate the stages of diffusion. These types represent the degree to which people are innovative in themselves, in that they are prepared to accept and work with change and new ideas. This innovative nature is not just an attitudinal acceptance of the new idea, but a positive behavioural step change that indicates an individual's willingness to modify their schematic framework. The willingness to accept new ideas by individuals in the organisation can be mapped against time and the resulting profile can be constructed to indicate the total rate of diffusion across the business.

In doing this, five 'ideal' categories can be offered:

- innovators;
- early adopters;
- early majority;
- late majority;
- laggards.

These categories can be mapped against a standard deviation curve in order to understand the percentage of types that can be found in organisations (Fig. 15.2).

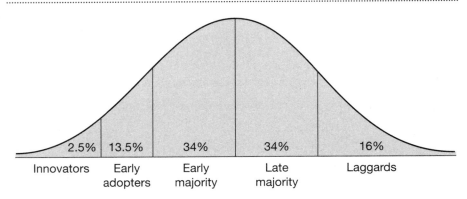

| 2.5% | 13.5% | 34% | 34% | 16% |
| Innovators | Early adopters | Early majority | Late majority | Laggards |

Fig. 15.2 People and innovation

Innovators

People who are venturesome in that they are happy to move beyond the ideas of their peer group to try new ideas and experiences. They have a tendency to do things that are rash and exciting, and have a disposition to act as the entry point, or for new ideas to enter into their social group.

Early adopters

These people act as a missionary for change, helping to lead the change and diffusion process through the organisation. They are adventurous enough to take risks, but have enough influence in the critical mass groups to help to facilitate change across the business.

Early majority

They welcome new ideas shortly before the average people in the organisation. They are in a position where they interact regularly with their peers but are not normally opinion formers within the business. They take their time before adopting a new framework, possibly because they take longer to actually make the decision to accept the change.

Late majority

This group accepts the idea after the average members in the organisation. They will be sceptical about new ideas and will possibly only accept the change after peer pressure forces them to accept the innovation.

Laggards

This is the last group in the organisation to accept a new idea or piece of knowledge. They will take decisions based on historic reasoning rather than consider what is right for today or tomorrow. It is important to understand that their resistance to new ideas is undertaken as a standpoint that is entirely rational from their viewpoint.

Although many conclusions might be drawn about this categorisation, a key one is that the essence of effective knowledge diffusion is driven by peer imitation. In deciding whether to internalise a new idea, people will be heavily influenced by their companions, and especially those who are in the higher adoption category. Hence, this might indicate the power that dominant opinion leaders can have upon the acceptance of a new idea within the organisation. As such any change agent should have an appreciation of this power if they are to be effective. Conversely, the organisation should be acutely aware of the location of these opinion formers and understand the potential that they have to amplify or attenuate ideas and knowledge. Consider the implication of a person who falls into the late majority or laggard category and sits in a gatekeeper position within the business (Fig. 15.3).

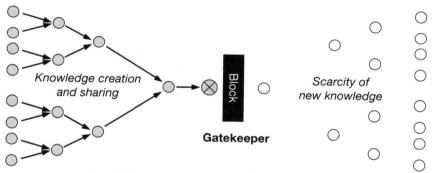

Fig. 15.3 Gatekeeper as knowledge block

This might be the chairperson of a financial approval committee, or the administration manager for a new ideas scheme. Wherever they sit, their criteria and rationale for taking decisions are likely to be based on past events, playing safe, and taking a more traditional view of life. What happens then if the organisation decides to invest time and money into a programme that facilitates the learning processes? In effect, the entire programme can be slowed down or stalled because a few people are able to block initiatives. This scenario gets worse the more senior the individual is within the organisation. In the worst case, the board might consist or two of three late majority types who are able to slow down the whole process of change and knowledge creation.

One of the ways in which the blockage presented by a passive gatekeeper can be overcome is through the generation of sufficient critical mass. The critical mass is the point where enough people have accepted the new idea that further adoption becomes self-sustaining. Like a ball bouncing in a room full of mouse traps, there reaches a stage where the released mouse traps start to bounce around and end up setting off further traps. At this stage the room is into the idea of positive feedback, and the process will continue irrespective of any impact the ball is making. Taking the idea outlined in Chapter 12 on socialisation, it is possible to become a meme engineer, someone who deliberately sets out to give a piece of knowledge a life of its own so that it can bypass the entrenched gate-keepers.

An example of the impact of critical mass can be seen in the diffusion process that the Internet has followed. One of the first forms of the Internet system originated in 1981, with the interlinking of two US colleges (New York and Yale). They were using their own network a great deal, and so decided to interlink their systems with a dial-up telephone line. At the end of 1981, four additional universities joined the network that was called Bitnet (Because It's Time Network). These first adopters can be put into the innovator or early adopter range of the diffusion model. In 1982, a long-line link was set up to enable the University of California to join the network, thus the west coast of America became involved in the idea of sharing knowledge. Suddenly the rate started to increase, and by the end of 1983, 19 universities had joined. Between 1984 and 1985, Bitnet doubled in size every six months. The point of critical mass occurred when the assumption was made that people would automatically have a connection to the Bitnet, and those that did not were disadvantaged. Bitnet then joined in with the US Department of Defense network called Arpanet, which was created in 1986, to allow contractors to share computer services.

This growth of the Internet might not have turned out to be the same if the point of critical mass had not been achieved in the early days. If for example, the government had acted as a gatekeeper and stepped in to regulate the deployment of the networks, there is every likelihood that the Internet would now be a totally different and more attenuated system.

The crucial idea in sharing knowledge across the organisation is to identify those nodes or people whose adoption will most rapidly influence other people to join in the sharing process. For the growth of Bitnet and the Internet, the point when the west coast of America joined, triggered the shift towards critical. The next trigger point was when Bitnet joined with the other computer network and created a sense of reciprocal interdependence (Rogers, 1995, 317). Rogers suggests some possible strategies that might be used to develop critical mass around an idea that is being shared:

- Target senior managers for the initial adoption of the idea. Adoption by this group will send the appropriate signal to people that the idea is desirable.
- Create a positive aura around the idea by implying that the end result is inevitable and that it will be accepted across the organisation.
- Introduce the idea to groups where there is a good chance that the members

are likely to adopt the idea at once. Taking a whole group at one time increases the ability to reach critical mass early on in the diffusion process.

- Provide incentives for the early adoption of the idea until critical mass is achieved.

Although creating critical mass is important in the diffusion of knowledge or ideas, in overly focusing on this, there is a danger that the sharing process can shift from a collaborative and open style to one that is manipulative and hidden. This will ultimately be counter-productive to the underlying principles that drive the desire to create a learning environment. The goal is to understand the idea of critical mass and how it affects diffusion; it is not to encourage the entire population to play games to get resources for their ideas.

Platforms

In understanding the nature of organisational sharing, four primary areas can be considered that describe the process:

Human interaction

Where the intercourse can take place directly between two people and no direct technological support is necessary. In this type of communication, there is a level of intimacy and contact that allows the individual to be fully aware of the presence of the other person. By using all of the senses, it becomes possible to really experience an idea as the other person shares it with the individual or group.

Technology link

A process that is driven primarily by electronic systems and offers the necessary freedom and flexibility for people and teams to break the constraining bounds of time and space. The individual does not have to be present at the same time as the other people, similar to the change that the invention of the postal system facilitated. Space, because it eliminates the physical gap, in the same way the telephone changed how people worked together, and now the intranet has changed how organisations work.

Instant

In this case, instant refers to the speed at which the sender receives a signal or acknowledgement from the recipient. There will be an indication that the process of sharing has been accepted and understood. Instant can be a precise word for an imprecise action, but it might be regarded as receiving feedback at a speed that feels comfortable for the originator.

Delayed

Although the offered transaction might be instant, it may be some time before the information is received by the other parties. This means that a storage or buffering process is being used in the communication pathway. This might be because the other person is not available, or that some type of processing is taking place in order to modify and deliver the knowledge.

The combination of these four factors produces a model that can indicate the profile of the mechanisms in the sharing process. It might be thought of as a conduit by which knowledge is being pumped around the organisation with the different types of communication producing a 'sharing profile' that indicates the various advantages and disadvantages (Fig. 15.4).

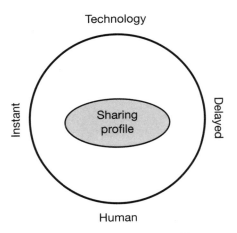

Fig. 15.4 Sharing profile

Using this simple form, five different sharing profiles have been considered. These profiles are not offered as the definitive taxonomy, they are simply indicative of the different profiles that might be found within an organisation. Ultimately, to understand how the sharing process operates, businesses will need to undertake a profile analysis to understand and determine the most effective way to diffuse knowledge.

Meetings

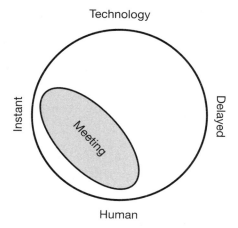

Fig. 15.5 Sharing profile: meetings

At a simple level, the organisational meeting, workshop or seminar, might be considered as one of the most common that organisation use to share knowledge. Whatever the purpose of the meeting, the primary focus will be around people meeting people, and giving and receiving immediate feedback.

Meetings must be one of the oldest forms of sharing and learning. However, it can be seriously abused (both knowingly and un-knowingly). Often the moment a problem surfaces, a meeting or workshop will be convened. The anticipation is that any decision taken at the event will be mutually shared and consensus will be developed. The danger in this is to assume that human interaction operates on a rational level, and that all of the people in the group are prepared to both listen to others, and offer valid contributions. This is at odds with the way in which many meetings are conducted. As outlined in Chapter 10, there will be countless shadow issues, both for the individual and for the organisation. These issues will be routed in politics, power struggles, selfishness and the formation of temporary coalitions.

These underlying factors underpin human nature, but an organisation can put them to positive use by making the undiscussable discussable. In considering the diagnostic model offered by the shadow bar, every time this is dropped by a millimetre, so the level of dialogue and openness will increase, as will the capability of the organisation to share knowledge.

Electronic messaging systems

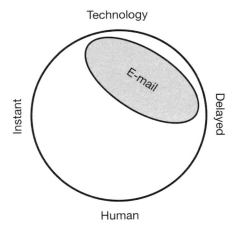

Fig. 15.6 Sharing profile: e-mail

The emergence of e-mail within and between organisations has brought about an amazing transformation in the knowledge diffusion process. E-mail addresses are standard on business cards, and the thought of sending someone something by mail can seem almost prehistoric. Interestingly, in one UK company (Hewlett Packard), paper mail is sometimes used to indicate that the message is of some importance, since e-mail has become so commonplace, that it has lost its sense of importance and urgency.

What e-mail provides in itself is nothing new, in that it just replicates the postal system. The difference is in the speed with which it transmits the information, the distances that can be covered, and the relative ease with which the knowledge can be copied to other people.

As a sharing tool, e-mail is a powerful and effective way in which to share knowledge. However, there are a few factors that can be overlooked when considering its potential for sharing knowledge:

Transitory in nature

It is a wonderful process for originating and managing conversations 'in the moment', but to support the continuing, evolving conversations of the learning organisation, it can become a barrier. As the growth in messages continues, so people become overloaded with data, and there can be a tendency to have the ritual clear out of the e-mail 'in-box'. The danger with this is that every time the delete key is pressed, there is a potential to lose a piece of knowledge and its associated history within the business. One major organisation recently underwent a process development review, where it wanted to gain a greater appreciation of the way in which processes operated in the business. However, it turned out that much of the activity had been undertaken by e-mail and the end result was that the organisation's history of the project had been destroyed as people regularly cleared out their e-mail.

Unfriendly

The ease with which e-mail can be originated and received can lead to artificial social barriers. In one case, a manager thought that he was interacting with his people in a normal way: he felt he knew what they were doing, the problems they were experiencing, and that he was helping them out where necessary. However, when speaking to his team, it became apparent they felt ignored, and left out in the wilderness. His reliance on e-mail meant that he rarely went to chat over social issues with them. Sharing can be managed electronically but human nature being what it is, there is often the need to socially interact and connect with people on a sensual level. Often the only way to really understand what it is that someone is trying to share is by using all of the senses. Relying on the use of language that is passed through a cold medium is not enough.

One of the key problems that seems to be emerging with e-mail, is the tendency to switch off the brain before answering the message. Because so many messages can arrive in one hour, there is often a tendency to simply type a response without giving it considered thought. Once sent, the person then panics that it might have been better to have taken more time before sending a final response.

Canteen conversations

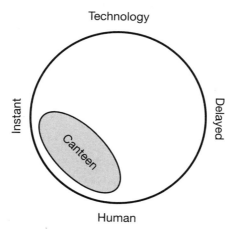

Fig. 15.7 **Sharing profile: canteen conversations**

Imagine a busy office at a photocopier repair centre. As the engineering field supervisor walks out of her office, she notices a few people hanging around the canteen talking. Often the reaction to this might be to tell them to get along and do their work, or in some cases to take disciplinary action. Although it might well be that these people were wasting time, it might also be that they were sharing valuable knowledge among themselves – discussing some of the irritating problems that seem to be cropping up but they have been unable to resolve individually. In this case knowledge is being shared but in a way that the senior managers do not get sight of and have little control over.

The canteen conversations are those things that people might believe are of minimal significance, so they will just chat to people when they happen to meet with them. This might be at the water cooler, in the corridor or over lunch. The conversations are generally spontaneous, instant, happen on a personal level, and are closely allied to the connectivity between the individuals.

On one level, these interactions are powerful and can in many cases drive the development of corporate strategy. The possible downside is twofold: first is that knowledge is hidden at the level where it is being applied, and cannot be exploited; second, it is highly linked to the personality of the individuals. As in the social class section in the earlier chapter, the peer groups will generally associate and share knowledge with those people who are seen as equals in the organisation. This can result in the sharing process becoming insular and sterile, and not necessarily used in those parts of the business where it could be put to good use.

In both examples, is knowledge is an asset that is not being exploited. Keeping ideas within a locked social group limits the organisation's ability to grow and cultivate its knowledge base. The effective organisation will understand this and take steps on two levels. The first level would be to ensure that the canteen conversations are given space to take place so that ideas and discoveries can be developed within the group. The second level would be to capture the ideas and market them internally, so that all groups can share in the new experiences and inspiration. This process by which ideas will be shared depends on the nature of the company. However, options include in-house magazines, team meetings, teach-ins or developing home pages on the intranet.

Communities of interest

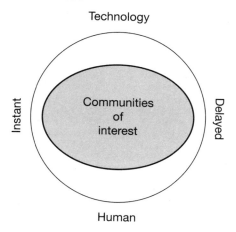

Fig. 15.8 Sharing profile: communities

Communities of interest are generally groups of people who meet informally to share ideas or learn from one another. They consist of people who carry out similar roles, share similar competencies or have a shared outcome. The sales people that meet together every morning for coffee so that they can talk about the areas they are covering, or the football supporters that follow the same team. It may be that they have little in common but for this one key thing: they share an interest that they are keen to talk about.

The community's main process for learning is through the sharing of stories and personal anecdotes. To an outsider, this approach might appear to be of little value. However, it can actually be more powerful than the traditional forms of teaching. People recount stories not just because the performance is enjoyable, but in order to influence other people's understanding of events and so illustrate their personal knowledge. They will often contain elements of humour, realism and words appropriate to the setting. This facilitates the general shifting of knowledge from one group to another without any work on the recipient's part.

One area where the storytelling process can take on a new form is in the generation and synthesis of new knowledge. In the case where different people recount their stories from opposite perspectives, they are able to develop a shared schema of the situation, and so enlarge their understanding and the collective knowledge of the organisation. Once this shared collective story is understood by the various members, so it becomes explicit knowledge that they can take away and enact within their own circle of influence.

As a sharing tool, one point to be wary of is distortion. First of all, the subjective element of the story means that some degree of distortion will occur in the general message and meaning that is offered. Second, as a sharing tool, language is open to misunderstanding and misinterpretation, so that distortion might occur in the translation process. However, as long as the basic underlying message remains core to the story, any misinterpretation should be of an incidental nature.

Groupware/intranet

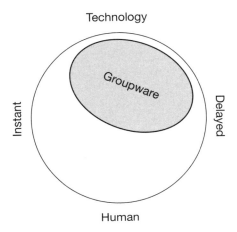

Fig. 15.9 Sharing profile: groupware

Consider the way organisations create, transfer and share their knowledge. The common approach might be to use classrooms, printed material, telephones, word of mouth, facsimile, etc. However, these methods can cause problems if the organisation operates in an environment that crosses time boundaries, has a high churn of staff, or has only limited facilities to bring people together. Additionally, these processes can often be slow, have limited access, and are not always reliable.

The need to increase the access and speed of knowledge transfer across diverse and separated industries resulted in the rapid emergence in the use of 'groupware or intranet sites'. This technology can foster new collaborative links and eliminate many of the barriers that have hindered productive communication in the past.

Groupware tends to be an all-encompassing name that includes a range of subsystems, including electronic mail, calendaring and scheduling, group document handling, workgroup development tools, group decision systems and meeting support, information sharing and conferencing products. When put together into a single package, the idea is that these systems can aid efficient distribution of information and in particular, help to create new knowledge in a collaborative way. It might be viewed as technology that helps to transfer the knowledge that is in the employee's head into a system that is accessible to the whole organisation.

However good the idea is, it may not be a panacea. Consider the following issues:

- Unless people change how they behave, there is little benefit in installing the systems. People should be willing to donate and withdraw data, as without this, little sharing and learning is likely to take place. Groupware simply disseminates information, it cannot do the sharing and learning for the individuals. In the same way that building a library in a school does not mean that the students will use it.

- Companies often treat learning as the static transfer of information from experts to non-experts rather than a dynamic, collaborative effort to add new value and create new knowledge. The installation of a distributive computer system can in many ways reinforce this false notion.

- The greatest benefits come from not only the knowledge and experience of people who work there, but from the interactions and relationships within the business. By introducing a computer, it is possible that some of the generative dynamics will be lost.

- Groupware implementation is not just a systems project, it involves deep cultural change. If approached without this understanding, the organisation might well encounter resistance, inertia, and even subterfuge.

- There is a limit to the amount of knowledge that can be loaded on a system. Much of what happens within a business is not suitable for handling by a computer network, since it is non-standard and difficult for computers to manipulate. Hence, there might be a limit to using a computer system.

As a platform for sharing knowledge, groupware or similar systems can be a powerful tool. However, the danger is when the organisation places its faith in the system as the mechanism that will deliver organisational learning. It can never do this because ultimately learning is a human activity, and so will always need human involvement and ownership.

Conclusions

Sharing is the final operational link in the idea of building the organisation's capability to learn. The creation of organisational knowledge is about people, connectivity and the interaction and synthesis that arises from the sharing process. Bearing this in mind, there are a number of key points that organisations need to understand about the sharing process:

- Like the Gutenburg printing machine, the mechanism of sharing is complicated. It needs to be understood, mapped and enhanced in order to aid the free flow of knowledge.

- The social structure of any organisation will be made up of people who fit into the five categories of innovator, early adopter, early majority, late majority and laggard. Each of the types has a key role to play in the sharing process. The trick is to understand that role and how it operates in the context under consideration.
- The idea of peer pressure and peer watching is a key factor in the sharing process and its ability to enhance the diffusion process.
- Be aware of gatekeepers and, where possible, understand which category they fit into.
- If an idea is worth pursuing, then reaching critical mass as soon as possible is an important factor in making the sharing process work and helping the idea to stick.
- Mapping the organisation's sharing strategies onto the technology, human, instant and delayed model, can help to determine some of the problems that might be encountered.

Without the ability to share knowledge across the business, many of the other topics covered in the book will be sharply attenuated and restricted. If this happens the organisation's ability to enhance its knowledge base might well be curtailed.

Socialisation model dynamics

	How do we learn?	How do we share?	How do we use?	How can we improve?
Diffusion process There is a clear appreciation of the way that ideas become socialised, accepted and desired by the people in the internal market				
Organisational platforms The business platforms for knowledge sharing are understood				

Part 5

Intent

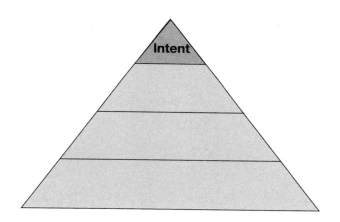

Chapter 16

Intent: purpose and direction

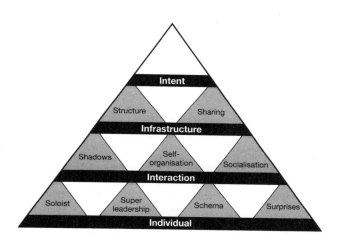

Fig. 16.1 Intent in the Integrated Learning Model

In the Integrated Learning Model, intent might be described as the purpose and direction that an organisation takes to improve its ability to enhance the learning processes. For example, in writing this book, there was a clear intent to produce something new and original about the field of organisational learning and knowledge management.

In theory, fulfilling the intent is quite easy: just sit down and write a chapter every month, and out pops the finished book. However, nothing is quite so simple. Along the way different things occur that both slow the process down, and cause energy to be diverted from writing the book and transferred into other areas. The children's homework, family problems, boredom, etc., all conspire to drag the author away from the original plan.

In the same way, organisations might define goals to enhance the ability of their people to create knowledge, but along the way, things occur that cause a deviation from this activity. The suggestion is that the greatest cause of intent corruption can often be the organisation itself. That in many cases, the weight of the structure and bureaucracy that is built around a change process can take energy away from the overall intent behind the transformation.

Consider the sole trader. Within reason, everything that the individual does contributes to the declared goal. There is a straight line that connects the energy of the individual to the customer, and the intent is clear and understood as seen in Fig. 16.2.

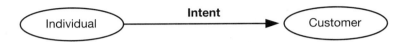

Fig. 16.2 Intent is clear

Once a business starts to grow, people will be recruited and the birth of a new organisation might be seen. However, at this point it is possible to see activities taking place that are not directly related to delivering customer service, such as the occasional meeting to discuss missing stock, forms to fill out to satisfy the Inland Revenue, and agreeing the arrangements for cover when people are ill. The intent is still in place, but the energy is being drained from the intent, causing it to be attenuated (see Fig. 16.3).

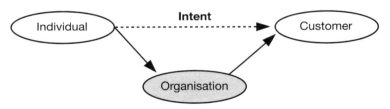

Fig. 16.3 Growth damages intent

After a year or two, a full-blown organisation might be in place with a hundred people, and all of the associated trappings that go with this scale of organisation. It is now possible to see the effect of organisational gravity acting upon the planned intent. The weight of business systems makes it harder for the intent to be delivered. The business has people whose sole responsibility is to deal with internal matters – half-day meetings on budget preparation, two-day workshops on setting the vision, and resolving problems that the organisation created for itself. It is at this stage that the weight created by the organisational gravity can stop the change process from taking place.

At this stage, Fig. 16.4 shows how the energy is focused more upon the needs of the organisation, than that of the intended outcome. This can be seen in many of the change programmes that have taken place. Consider the supporting bureaucracy that was often built up around total quality and the cumbersome systems that

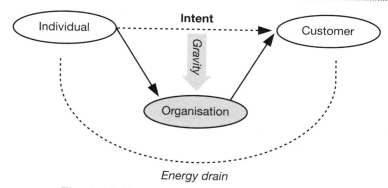

Fig. 16.4 **Energy is drained from intent**

are regularly built to achieve ISO 9000 registration. Even now companies can go for overkill in the way that they are attempting to achieve the Investors in People certification. These outcomes might be likened to the author whose intent is to produce an 80,000 word book but ends up becoming enticed and enthralled by the new wordprocessor. The fun of the grammar check and system crashes conspire together to drag the author away from the desired outcome as they can act as a gravitational field that slows or diverts the change.

If an organisation makes the choice that learning and knowledge creation are important, then the strategy they choose to deliver it is critical (see Fig. 16.5). Simply dictating what people should do, building systems, and constructing elaborate measures will not achieve the desired outcome.

Hence, the strategic options outlined in the next chapter indicate the approach that might be used and what the component elements could be. In building the strategy around this type of structure, the proposition is that the gravity drain is likely to be diminished, as the organisation attempts to support rather than drive the change process. The end result is that the organisation seeks to support the learning process rather than building a bureaucracy and acting in a way that drains the energy process.

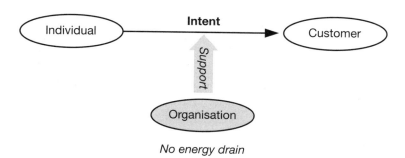

Fig. 16.5 **Building support from the organisation**

225

Chapter 17

Strategy

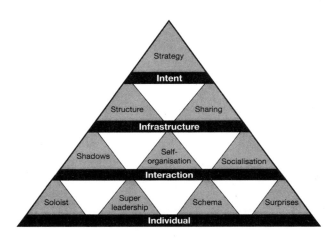

Fig. 17.1 Strategy: topping out the Integrated Learning Model

Often strategy at a corporate or senior level can refer to the act of planning, and creation of predetermined and premeditated actions for the business – to effectively analyse the future market, decide what the end goal is, and then build an action plan to achieve the desired outcome. However, in taking this approach, it is possible to become sucked into the idea that the future can be pre-determined, and that a linear plan will succeed in a non-linear world. It can also become a process that operates in a way that is distant from the people and away from the real activities of the organisation. In essence, it can become easy to adopt the mechanistic model discussed in Chapter 11.

If any of the Integrated Learning Model core principles are accepted, then it might behove the organisation to rethink how it enhances its learning capability. It might need to move away from the traditional model of milestones, project plans and fixed outcomes, since they might not be appropriate for transforming learning processes. Enhancement of the learning capability within an organisation is not a project or programme, it is a schematic orientation. New equipment can be installed, skills can be taught, systems can be implemented, but the desire to learn needs to be ingrained as part of the organisation's cultural system. It will not be developed from the introduction of superficial programmes and products that try to impose a new way of working from outside.

If this idea is accepted, what does a strategy look like that can engage the learning processes within an organisation? It cannot be one of imposition, direction and driving, since this can negate many of the concepts ingrained in the idea of generative learning. The proposition is that a learning strategy should be based on core principles:

- An inside-out approach where the change is focused on realising internal capability, not just importing external ideas.
- Emergent style, so that an adaptive approach can be undertaken.
- Interpretive rather than predictive where alert foresight is used to ensure that timely adjustment can be made as shifts in the environment are observed.
- Predicative processes are used, not to guess the end results, but to anticipate what patterns are likely to occur as the change unfolds.
- Qualitative measures to be used as much as quantitative measures.
- Grounded in the organisation's own belief system.
- Understand that now and the future are not separate; they are interrelated through many different relationships. As such, people's existing action, expectations and anticipation form how the future is constructed, so planned outcome is affected by the anticipatory process.
- Use internal resources to drive change, and external agents to help energise the transformation.

In accepting these principles, a strategic framework can be developed to help the organisation undertake a shift in its learning style. In developing a strategic framework, the more traditional approach has been discarded in favour of the emergent model of change. It proposes a more holistic approach where the proposition is that certain activities might need to be undertaken but the time and delivery mechanism entirely depends on the organisation's context.

Holistic model

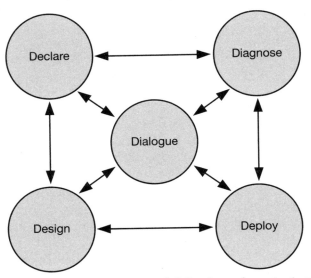

Fig. 17.2 A holistic model for learning strategy

The holistic strategy model is built around five key themes shown in Fig. 17.2, where the point of entry can be taken at any stage. No one theme has greater importance or prominence because they all drive, and are driven by, each other.

Declare

This is an individual's, team's or organisation's affirmation that they intend to increase their focus on improving the capability to learn. This might be a director announcing his or her intent to improve the company's ability to acquire knowledge; a team member suggesting that knowledge management should play a greater role in managing the team; a lone individual deciding that they need to develop a lifelong approach to learning in order to improve their career options. Whatever the situation, the suggestion is that a voluntary choice needs to be made rather than simply drifting into the change process. In making the choice, the option is to then declare the decision. This declaration might be to others, or it may be that the declaration is intrinsic, and that the choice is a private one.

Diagnose

Often, the common approach to managing change is to separate diagnosis and action. Many change models use the approach where investigation precedes action, and the two are separated by a natural boundary. However, in many ways this approach takes a linear view of the world, assuming that any investigative action will remain current and valid over the life cycle of the change process. The approach taken with this model is that diagnosis is a constant state rather than a one-off event, and might be regarded as a state of mind rather than a set of tools.

Dialogue

This word derives from two roots: 'dia' meaning 'through', and 'logos' meaning 'the word'. The benefit gained from allowing people the time and space to simply 'talk' is staggering. Creating an environment where people can meet to reflect and talk about 'life' is already realising benefits. The idea of having meetings without fixed agendas, rules or a chairperson, really allows individuals to expose beliefs, thoughts and ideas. Most important is the idea of a meeting of equals where rank and power do not influence either the process or the outcome. It is through this type of meeting that people can really experience the power and energy of reflective and adaptive thinking. The challenge is to turn this approach into a personal and commercial advantage.

Design

This term has many implied connotations. It can often intimate that a mechanistic model is being considered where the outcome is determined; that cause and effect are understood; and that things will go according to the pre-defined parameters. Now, if a child sets out to build a sword from three pieces of wood, barring any major problems, there is a degree of certainty that he or she will achieve it. However, there is little certainty in the idea that a parent can persuade three children to jointly build a wooden sword, since they have the benefit of free will and an independent spirit. So, if this is difficult, what chance is there that the change process for 100, 1000 or 10,000 people can be 'designed'? In the context of a learning style of behaviour, the idea of design is one that thinks in terms of creating an operating framework, rather than a detailed blueprint.

Deploy

This focuses on the idea of moving from concept to action. The dilemma is that in traditional management, this might imply formality, control and defined outcomes. The assumption of this book however is that people cannot be made to learn or create knowledge. Hence, the deployment process should be based on arranging a context that can ease learning and deliver an environment that welcomes individualism and creativity. In particular it has the sensitivity to understand the nature and benefits of feedback, and possibly most difficult of all, to create measurement systems that use both qualitative and quantitative methods.

If it is accepted that the organisation can be seen as a living organism rather than a machine, then the process by which learning and change are managed needs to be thought through carefully. It must be viewed as a whole and not just a conglomeration of bits and pieces. It must be accepted that there is a living and interconnected flow of ideas and knowledge that runs through the business, and change and learning in one part may well have dramatic effect on other areas. It is this core principle that underlies the approach offered in this chapter with the five interconnecting strands of the model offered as guides and thought-provokers rather than rules and practices. No suggestion is made that these five areas will be right for all organisations, or even one organisation. What they should do is stimulate the reader to consider and ask questions about their current change strategies, and how they might be improved if a more holistic and open-ended approach was taken.

In accepting this, the rest of the chapter considers each of the five areas and in particular teases out some of the sub-elements.

Declare

Many strategic change programmes follow the mechanistic idea that transformation is a linear and controllable process, that it can only happen if senior managers say so. This might be the case where capital investment or organisational scale are involved, but this is a fallacy for learning, since this is something that is constant within an organisation. The proposition in this book is that one person, team or unit should always have the freedom to make the simple declaration that they wish to place greater focus on creating their capacity to learn. It might be just one person making a commitment to go back to college, a team deciding to undergo a review of their personal and shared assumptions, or a manager taking time out to coach a team on learning skills.

This is a very distinct shift from the idea that tends to pervade many organisational cultures – primarily where the person at the top says what people should do, and how they should do it. The 'declare' theme can be considered in the context of four elements: behaviour, voluntary, principles and no delegation.

Behaviour

In using the declaration approach to bring about a change in the organisation, the risk is that people's positive stated intentions can be lost or forgotten once the pressure of work increases. Making a private or public declaration of the importance of learning is a significant thing. However, even more significant is the delivery of a tangible behavioural change.

All too often organisations experience the situation where managers make grandiose public statements about supporting a new change programme, only to find there is little change in their personal behaviour. There is often a kind of 'emperor's new clothes' performance seen in organisations, where everyone is prepared to suspend judgement about the supposed changes. During this phase, people can get away with murder, quite literally advocating one set of behaviours, while choosing not to actually make a personal change. However, this only lasts for so long. Eventually reality bites and people realise that the words used in the declaration process are empty and meaningless. At this point, the declaration process is doing more harm than good, as people realise how large the gap is between the espoused statement of intent and the behaviour adopted.

If the declaration process is to be of any use, the person who makes the assertion must really consider what impact it will have on their life, habits and behaviours; clearly chart what it is they will have to do differently; and understand the implications, for both themselves and others. If an individual or team is not able or willing to reflect on the necessary long-term personal changes, it is better not to make the declaration in the first place.

However, when the behaviour does match the language, powerful transformation can be seen across the organisation. The senior manager that walks the talk can be a commanding figure, and one that is able to really influence learning across the business. The organisation that then takes the time to positively recognise this alignment, can make a significant shift in stimulating and encouraging people to change their behaviour.

Voluntary

There can be a real dilemma for organisations that seek to enhance the businesses learning capability. The senior team might have made a public declaration that the organisation needs to be more adaptive, but how can they deliver this without resorting to a coercive approach? Unlike programmes that deliver a new product, procedure or fixed asset, a desire to build a learning culture does not really result in anything that is physically different. The only thing that has to change is people, and their desire to operate in a different way.

The mistake companies can make is to believe that they can force people to adopt a learning attitude and create knowledge for the business. This is not really a good decision, as eventually problems will surface. When people are forced into a new way of behaving, a short-term change might be delivered. However in many cases, this is a pseudo transformation which depends upon the manager being around to make sure it is sustained. Like the parent that tells the children not to play with the paint, and then stands there watching to make sure they do not. The moment the parent walks away, the dependency disappears and there is every chance that they will play with the paint. In an organisational setting, the business can enforce a change but it can shift and return to the natural state once attention is focused elsewhere.

However, if the organisation can accept that creating a learning culture is about long-term orientation there is more scope to let people adapt to the idea naturally. As the diffusion model suggests in Chapter 12, the rate at which people will accept a new idea will vary across at least five different types. If the organisation can work with this, the superior strategy is to focus just on those people who are ready and able to change, and to leave the rest to come along as the critical mass starts to grow. In allowing people to adapt and respond in a voluntary structure, they will be more committed, and the change is more likely to be effective and sustained.

Principles

In declaring a desire to enhance the capability to learn, one danger is that people will start to look at the products and tools that enhance learning, rather than understanding the underlying principles. There must be a clear distinction between these two areas, since products will always have a life cycle while the underlying principles will be relatively timeless.

For example, a project team decides to improve their ability to review and learn from the mistakes made in a project. To do this, they call in a trainer to run a review workshop. However, during the workshop, two things happen that make them doubt the validity of their original idea: first, the trainer uses the workshop to try to sell additional projects and techniques; second, the trainer's espoused words of openness and honesty do not match the in-use behaviours. The end result is that the project team decides that the pay-back for the time spent on the workshop is poor. They in turn advise their colleagues that the idea of incorporating learning reviews into the project cycle is of little value.

The problem is that the team has confused the product with the principle. As an underlying idea, the notion of learning reviews can be fundamental to improving the project team and business performance. The thing that let them down was the product and its ability to support the outcomes offered by the principle. This has been seen over and over again where people criticise programmes like total quality without realising that these are just the tools to achieve the end goal of quality improvement.

The end suggestion is that the declaration process should focus on the baseline principle and not on the product or practices used to achieve them. So, a valid declaration might be 'to improve the capability to maintain lifelong learning' and the product-based declaration might be to 'take a new college course every year'. The first one is clear and focuses in what is to be achieved, the second, is simply the delivery process and one of many options that might be used to achieve the primary goal.

No delegation

Imagine a single water droplet running down a dry pane of glass. It seems to go on and on, but eventually the large drop has shrunk to a tiny globule of water. The same can be seen if people try to delegate the responsibility for enhancing the organisation's learning processes. Consider the managing director who makes a declaration that knowledge management is the key thing for the business. Once the declaration is published, the task is delegated to a director, who then passes it down the chain to the middle manager who is given the task of delivering a learning organisation. Each time the idea is delegated, it becomes diluted, distorted and drained of energy.

The idea and principle of self-enacted learning cannot be passed to someone else to achieve. The only way progression can happen down and across the company is through a process of socialised diffusion, where people interact on a common level and come to understand the personal benefits they will gain from taking a more open and adaptive approach to managing their work.

In pulling together the four ideas of behaviours, voluntary, principles and no delegation, it might be seen that the process of declaration cannot be treated as a light-hearted decision. For an individual or a team to deal with each of these ideas seriously takes time, energy and deep commitment. This is not something that can always be counted on when simply implementing a project plan. Declaration is about taking a personal decision and accepting deep down that a choice has been made. Hence, this is not a responsibility that can be passed on for someone else to deal with. However, in taking this approach, any resulting change will be honest, long lasting, and is more likely to gain the respect and support of colleagues.

Diagnosis

The diagnosis area is concerned with raising people's awareness of the system and the environment under consideration. Although the subject areas being considered in the diagnostic review will depend upon the context, the basic assumption is that, as well as 'intent', the other nine areas outlined in the Integrated Learning Model might offer a reasonable starting point. Hence, the areas that might be questioned include:

- To what extent do people feel that they have the personal motivation and ability to enhance the learning processes within the work domain?
- In what way are people's values considered as important to business performance?
- Do people take the time to listen to each other, or is it a case of just putting forward their own ideas?

- What encouragement is there to innovate and create new ideas?
- To what extent do hidden issues drive the business?
- How are decisions made regarding new ideas?
- Are the routes by which the knowledge is transported across the business, mapped and understood?

As diagnostic questions, these are entirely valid and would offer a reasonable insight into the state of the organisation. However, it is important that data is not taken purely at face value, since a number of underlying dynamics need to be considered when interpreting the data. An idea of the various dynamics that affect the diagnostic information – open systems, attractors, shadows and intrinsic inquiry – are considered below.

Open systems

In attempting to diagnose an open system, the problem is that life as it is today is not how it will be tomorrow. New structures will constantly emerge to replace old structures, and connections with the outside world will be changing all the time. It is impossible to derive a map of the organisation that will stay constant for more than a limited period of time. This brings into question the approach that the traditional diagnostic model takes in developing a change strategy. The standard model assumes that in understanding the system as it looks today, a change process can be developed that will be applicable the following month. The diagnostic model for an open system has to move away from this approach and take on a more dynamic style.

In the same way that the open system interacts and adapts to the outside environment, so the individual or team undertaking the diagnostic exercise should maintain a close interaction with the system so it can adapt to changes. Consider a product team that is about to undergo a review process to enhance the product range. Historically, they have brainstormed as a team and come up with design variations that have been put to the engineering production team for development. They realise that in operating this way, they have worked primarily from their schemata, and not taken the customer's viewpoint into account. To correct this, they decide to undertake a joint focus group with their customers and the engineering team. The event goes well and they pull together a number of valuable learning opportunities that can be fed back into the product review process. However, two days later the engineering division is reorganised, and the support team is changed. The dilemma now is that the new group of engineers has not been exposed to the same experience as the product group, and so may not buy-in to the product changes. At this point there might be a natural tendency to become frustrated with the whole idea of the shared experience, and cancel the process.

234

The alternative view might be to accept that the diagnostic process may have been diverted but it is not over. The key idea in this situation, is not to see the world in black and white but to view it in terms of incremental variation. The engineering change has created an incremental shift, not a radical change. Accepting the view that the system has been modified, the question to ask is, what has been learned from the experience, and how can this knowledge be used to the team's advantage? If the situation is viewed from an open systems perspective, then the idea is one of a building process, rather than a radical rewrite.

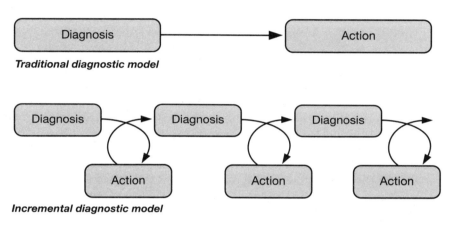

Fig. 17.3 Diagnostic stages

From the first diagnostic stage shown in Fig. 17.3 emerges a picture of an incremental diagnostic model. Diagnosis is followed by and almost parallel with an action phase, that is aligned with another diagnosis phase. The important point behind this approach is that at no stage in the development process is the view taken that there is a true, current and stable view of the world. The diagnostic exercise simply draws a picture of the open system as it is, but does not attempt to predict or assume how it will look in the future.

Attractors

One of the key things about open systems is the tendency to toggle between different states or conditions. As discussed in Chapter 11, systems can have a number of preferred states or points of attraction:

- Point attractor;
- Limit cycle attractor;
- Torus attractor;
- Strange attractor.

If this is the case, when undertaking a diagnostic review, great care should be taken in interpreting the data. It might be that the picture being presented offers a view of the system at one particular state of rest, and this might be very different to how it will look when attracted to another state. Consider the various states of attraction that a limit cycle system can be pulled between:

- centralisation to decentralisation;
- cost reduction to cost increase;
- profit focus to revenue focus;
- redundancy to recruitment.

Hence, imagine a change exercise that indicates how training people in certain skills and competencies will enhance the creation of new knowledge. This might be supported by the organisation and people might be actively encouraged to volunteer for the training. However, it may be that the diagnostic exercise took place when the organisation was in a state of high spend and low redundancy. Imagine what will happen if shortly after there is a sudden change, and the training has to be cancelled because of the introduction of a cost reduction programme as in Fig. 17.4.

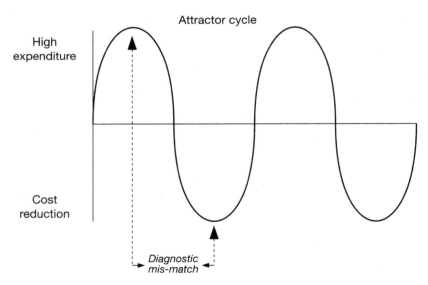

Fig. 17.4 Cycles can disrupt diagnosis

Knowledge of the theory of attractor states cannot prevent this type of problem. However, if the individual or team undertaking the diagnostic exercise had understood the potential attractor states for the organisation, it might have suggested that other options could be used in the event of a change occurring in the attractor position.

Shadows

In undertaking any diagnostic exercise, the idea is to gather data by which decisions can be taken to effect a change in the system. In achieving this, it is important to ensure that an equitable balance is obtained between the shadow and open aspects of the organisation. The problem is that people and the business are generally happy to talk about those issues that are in the overt part of the shadow diagnostic's box. The problem comes in trying to expose some of the issues that lie beneath the surface.

Unless the diagnostic process climbs inside these concealed areas, any action taken to enhance the learning process is likely to be resisted by the shadow network. Like an immune system, the shadow aspect has amazing capabilities to resist any external invader. It does this by issuing its own antibodies – actions and behaviours that fiercely resist any external agent trying to change its equilibrium. These behaviours might be industrial action, adherence to senseless company rules, increased tribalism, or budget games.

Once the immune system kicks in, an amazing amount of effort has to be expended to overcome people's fears and defensive actions. Hence, the diagnostic process should really attempt to understand the immune system before it can do any real harm to the change process. Often the only way to achieve this is through a deep process of dialogue, so that people really start to understand each other's schematic viewpoint.

Intrinsic inquiry

One of the unspoken shadow issues that can affect the diagnostic process, comes from the feelings and ideas of the individual or team undertaking the exercise. Often when considering any organisational investigation, there can be an unspoken pressure on the individual to be objective, and to present a 'true' view of the situation as it really is. This approach is based upon the assumption that:

- reality is tangible and can be fragmented into discrete units;
- the investigator and the situation under investigation are independent;
- time and context-free generalisations are possible;
- there are real and independent causes which are directly observable;
- inquiry is a value-free activity.

However, pure objectivity is unattainable (Lincoln and Guba, 1985). It could be achievable only if there were a single reality 'out there' to be observed and touched. This is not so, because reality is a construction of the people who have played a part in its development and delivery. Everyone distils what they are seeing and hearing, thinking and what they are willing to share with others through their own schematic models. This drives reality as perceived by different members of a group.

Hence, it is reasonable to assume that any individual or team undertaking a diagnostic exercise will also be filtering and labelling experiences. The normal tendency might be to ignore these feelings or average them out to offer a composite and normative picture of the shared experience. However, in either ignoring or watering down their views, the danger is that distinct and unique data will be lost. Therefore, the diagnostic team can do two things. The first is to develop a clear understanding of their personal biases, values and assumptions before undertaking the exercise. In unfolding these, the diagnostic group can then view any resulting data with fresh eyes and, if appropriate, rebalance the data taking their filters into account. The second thing is to include their personal views and feelings in any final report, since it offers valuable intuitive data that will give the reader a sense of 'being there'.

When considering learning as an organisational process, the only device that can give a real feel for potential action is the human instrument. The rationale is that only the human instrument is capable of grasping the variety of realities that exist in a complex situation. The innate ability to draw on deep intuition, thoughts and feelings, makes the human being a powerful data-gathering tool. This is not to negate the intellectual capability that diagnostic work requires, but social and emotional attributes can contribute in a significant way to the diagnostic process.

Design

Design is essentially about creating the framework for action, not specifying the action that will take place. The aim is to set the boundaries and basic operating rules, but leave action and detail up to the agents involved in the change process. Consider the idea of designing a backpacking trip round the world. It is possible to know where the end stop is likely to be and what the broad pattern of the journey will be. However, accurately predicating what stops will be taken at any time would be risky to say the least. The best thing is to ensure that a flexible and emergent plan is developed – one that can allow the people to respond to any changes or variation without incurring any undue problems.

Design will here be considered under four headings: non-linear, context, participation and artifacts.

Non-linear

Although it might be seen as heresy, there are probably training and consulting companies that are quite happy to enter into an organisation with a pre-prepared model for implementing a learning programme. It will have built-in assumptions, outcomes and logical, structured steps along the way. The reality is that in a non-linear world this cannot be done. In a linear system, the interconnection between the component elements is one way and predictable, and hence a standard plan or approach can be dropped into the organisation. In a non-linear system the relationship between the system elements are multi-directional and complex, and therefore need an adaptive and emergent structure.

The design process should create a set of strong outer boundaries that can accommodate the change process while giving it space to unfold and develop its own set of patterns and processes. In the linear model, the strength is contained in the pre-determined structure of the tasks and relationships. In the non-linear mode, the strength comes from the clear boundary that is defined at the outset of the change process.

Context

This section of the chapter can be nicely summed up by a quotation from Stewart (1997, xvii), when he suggests that:

> Too many business people – bad business people – want someone to give them plug and play answers. Too many business books – bad business books – indulge them.

In the same way that there is no standard way to discipline a naughty child, paint a masterpiece, or play the perfect guitar solo, there is no one way to develop a learning culture. The difference between these three things is the people involved and the context in which the situation is taking place. Like the gardener trying to transport a plant from one part of the garden to another, the slightest variation in the acidity, dampness or composition of the soil can prevent the plant from taking root. So, trying to transplant a management idea from one business into another is fraught with problems.

The solution is to work on the inner strengths of the organisation, and not to try to import too many alien ideas or projects. For example, imagine that Super Sponge Ltd has successfully achieved a market position by building quality management into its corporate ethos system. What often happens is that the Natural Sponge Company sees this, and decides to follow suit. However, they try to achieve it by using the same tools, models or consultants that Super Sponge used, and often at a faster rate so that they can catch up on the competition. Now, all that the people in Natural Sponge might see are their senior managers importing a range of ideas and tools that are not aligned to their whole ethos and infrastructure. This can cause a negative reaction because people do not have a chance to buy into the idea emotionally. In addition to this, they might believe that they also have ideas and practices that are just as valid but have been ignored.

Instead, what Natural Sponge could do is to make a positive declaration that developing a quality ethos is a valid and commercial proposition, and one they wish to pursue. Once this is declared, they can look internally and try to understand what action can be taken to develop the idea as a dominant value and ethos. So, before even looking at the tools and projects, it should try to understand its own cultural context and determine how quality can be achieved from an inside-out process.

Participation

As part of the design process, arranging opportunities for people to participate is important, not to define who, what, where, when and how people become involved, but to ensure that opportunities exist for people to take part in learning activities. However, the idea of participation is not always one that people in an organisation easily and readily accept. The following points should be considered when trying to design a strategy for involving people in the learning process:

- In many cases, much of the underlying rationale for the organisation's structure and power base might be enshrined in the idea of secrecy and non-involvement, so participation might be a counter-intuitive process.
- Often social barriers can exist that prevent people from becoming involved. Factors such as organisational class, race and gender discrimination can play a big part in preventing engagement.
- Participation has to be something that people are happy to do with their minds and not just their bodies.
- People might feel that they don't have the necessary skills and social abilities to be able to interact in an effective way.
- It is important to ensure that people are made aware of the opportunities to become involved. If the communication process is pushed down through the organisation, often the messages become blocked or delayed so that people do not have the time to join in.
- Participation takes time, so the organisation needs to legitimise the idea that people will be allowed time out to become involved.
- Do not assume that managers have the capabilities to help and support people in the participation process. Skills such as listening, questioning and coaching are not always well established or practised.

Positive learning happens as a result of the connectivity between members within the social system. If the idea of creating knowledge is significant for the business, it is important to stress its dependency on the level and quality of interaction among the people.

Artifacts

The organisation's artefacts are all the things that people see, hear and touch in relation to the business. This can be its architecture, language, technology, projects or visible behaviour (Schein, 1992). However, in trying to stimulate change, many companies will create a false layer of transformation artifacts that are supposed to help and develop the new cultural ethos. Witness the proliferation of mugs, posters and ties that can accompany a new change programme. These may be worthwhile from a visibility angle, but potentially quite destructive from the point of view of long-term cultural change.

The moment someone in the organisation sees a mug proclaiming 'we are a learning company', there will be a subliminal association with the idea of learning as a finite product. It separates the ethos and the product but unfortunately places a greater emphasis on the product side. The artifacts on which an organisation might try to focus are common behaviours, shadow behaviours, leadership style and reward systems. People will associate these things with the deeper issue of the business, and not the superficial promotional aspects.

Dialogue

Although the strategy model is not built upon a linear foundation, the idea of dialogue is quite deliberately at the centre. All of the other four propositions (declare, diagnosis, design and deployment) are driven by the idea that sharing ideas is at the heart of the creation of a learning culture.

Its use in this context is about trying to go behind the normal level of conversation that people follow, and to unearth what people really mean: to shine a light on some of the shadow issues that drive people's thoughts and actions and to encourage people to explore the individual and collective suppositions, thoughts, beliefs and feelings that can quietly dominate their interactions. Hence when people start to understand other people's schematic model, shared meaning emerges where people find that they are neither opposing one another, nor are they simply interacting.

Increasing trust between members of the group, and trust in the process itself, leads to the expression of the sorts of thoughts and feelings that are usually kept in the shadow area. This can take place without any rules or directions it is simply a desire to understand the other person and what motivates them. Dialogue is in itself a learning activity, not as a means of examining or criticising a particular theory or programme, but rather as part of an unfolding process of creative participation between peers (Bohm, 1995).

In trying to achieve this type of interaction, the following section offers four factors that can contribute to an effective dialogue process. They are not meant to offer a definitive set of rules but they should be seen as important in developing a deeper level of discussion.

Invitation

In what can only be a case of clear common sense, there is little chance of getting to a deeper level of interaction with someone who is not willing to be involved. To this end, people should be invited to be involved in the dialogue process and not mandated. This invitation should be value-free, non-judgemental and with the understanding that people are free to leave at any time.

Suspension

The suspension of belief, impulses, opinion, etc., is at the heart of the dialogue process. The unspoken base instincts that people take for granted can drive both their open and shadow behaviours. So asking people to put aside their judgements is like asking someone not to put up their arms if they are about to be hit in the face by a ball.

However, when people are able to suspend their assumptions and judgements, so their reactions, impulses, feelings and opinions become exposed to others. In doing this, it allows the individual to unfold and understand how they view the world, and so appreciate what schemata they inadvertently apply on to others.

Once an individual is able to go through this process, there is a greater chance that the group will be able to suspend its judgements. If this happens, many of the deep underlying processes that drive the shadow issues will be exposed and may start to make sense. This shared deep understanding can then develop what Bohm calls a 'collective intelligence'. As the group becomes used to operating at this level, the proposition is that it will pervade the normal workplace relationship and help it to be more open and effective.

Creativity

Since by its very nature dialogue is a non-linear and exploratory process, it is impossible to set out any rules or a direct framework to give it structure. It is about the individual understanding the potential within themselves, their interaction with others, and how the meaning flows between them. In this case, one thing the participants should attempt to do is let their creative spirit run free. An individual or group might have two options when entering a level of dialogue. They can play safe and let things out that feel dependable and comfortable and follow predictable processes that the group like. Alternatively, they can take risks and experiment by saying different things in different ways, to reach different ends. In doing this, they can both test themselves and understand how other people react to a change in their 'supposed' character.

Dialectic

If dialogue is used as a tool to aid the learning process, then it can help to uncover many of the deep underlying issues that create blockages. In entering into a deliberation with another person, and with both parties being prepared to both share their assumptions and listen to the other person, a dialectic approach emerges. The outcome can be that a new and invigorating synthesis emerges that offers a creative solution for both parties.

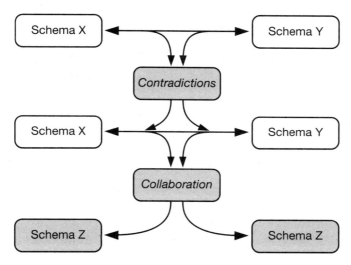

Fig. 17.5 Interpretations in a dialectic approach

As seen in Fig. 17.5, the dialectic approach has many different interpretations, but in this instance it is about recognising that all arguments have two sides. In accepting this, it can really benefit both parties to explore and understand each other. In many cases this might mean that deliberate contradiction and barriers are raised just so that each person can see and feel life from the other person's schema. Hence, by going through a process of thesis and antitheses, eventually a shared synthesis emerges that makes sense to all the people involved.

It is important to note that dialogue is not being advocated as panacea, nor as a method or technique designed to succeed all other forms of social interaction. It is just another type of social communication – but possibly a special one that can help create opportunities to climb inside many of the deeper issues than can ultimately corrupt the learning process.

Deploy

One desired outcome is likely to be a desire to enhance the capability to learn across the organisation. This is on the assumption that people cannot be made to learn, but they can be encouraged and supported in the learning process. Deployment is about understanding what action can be taken that will actually help people to make the shift to a knowledge and learning based culture.

Outcome

Although the focus in the book has been about emergent strategies, non-linear systems and non-equilibrium approaches, this does not mean that the organisation cannot make a choice about its desired future. The difference is that in choosing where it wants to be, it does not then lock itself into a mind of 'and this is where we will be in x years'. This difference is in having a positive affirmation about the future rather than a naïve belief.

In defining the outcome, it is important to ensure a number of things:

- That it is not linked to an assumed future environment.
- That it is an outcome that all people can understand, and not a vague long-term goal that means little to the individual.
- It is focused upon creating the future, not having a future stage dictated by something else.
- The outcome should not describe the process by which it is to be achieved.

In deploying a strategy to facilitate an organisation's ability to learn, people will want to know why, what the benefit is for the business, and how it will help them. The outcome should be clear enough that it makes sense to people why a change is necessary, and what they will gain from it personally.

Flow

Often, in developing a change strategy, there can be a tendency to ignore the fundamental principles that are being introduced within the change process itself. How often are quality programmes implemented without any process controls; management development programmes by untrained facilitators, and cost-cutting exercises by expensive consultants? In the same way, it is important that whoever takes the journey towards enhancing their ability to learn and create knowledge can use this living experience to understand how they learn.

Consider the team manager who decides to run workshops that will help to enhance a team's ability to learn. What steps might be gone through to design and run the event? There will be a need to:

- Find out if anyone is interested, and work out how to respond to those people who do not want to attend.
- Talk with people to understand their goals, and do this by understanding their schematic view of the world.
- Build a trusting relationship, so that people will not feel that there might be some dark, hidden purpose behind the workshop.
- Ensure that the dynamics of the workshop are such that people do not feel constrained by a fixed agenda, and so on ...

All these activities are covered in the Integrated Learning Model, so the journey turns in on itself. The goal is the learning journey, not the final outcome. Now consider the difference if the manager had employed a consultant to run the event. It might be presented professionally, and look good, but what learning would have taken place?

This aspect is key to the whole process because the focus should be on valuing the journey as a learning experience in itself. It is not simply a project to 'install or implement' the new approach. Improving the capability to learn is grounded in the process of giving people the opportunity to experiment and the change journey is the prime opportunity for this to take place.

Feedback

In building a change and learning strategy, one of the common aspects will be the installation of feedback systems to monitor progress. The potential problem with this approach is that people can be too sensitive to the signals that the system offers. Often the linear mindset will tend to dominate the change strategy. When this happens, as the feedback systems indicate that a deviation has occurred, interventions will be made to dampen them down, so as to put the change process back onto the right track. This can go against most of the underlying principles discussed in Chapter 11. Just because there is a deviation from the expected norm does not mean that it is wrong or that an intervention needs to be made.

Consider two examples. The first is the team that goes away to reflect on its learning style and to develop new and improved ways of working. It comes back totally dispirited and torn apart because of the negative interaction between the members. Now, a typical response from the senior managers behind the team might be to try and put a fix in place, to pacify people's feelings and to resolve the issues. However, doing this can destroy any opportunity the people have of actually getting below the surface and pulling out some of the shadow issues that are driving the group behaviours. A second example might be the team that has a great idea of a new product but is advised not to bother because another part of the business has the situation in hand. Rather than squashing the ideas, it might have been better to let them amplify it, and so take the team and the project into new and uncharted regions.

Feedback is the life-blood of any open system, and needs to be carefully nurtured and understood. In creating a learning culture, people need to be aware of the principles of feedback and how a mis-timed intervention can actually make a long-term and significant difference to how the business operates.

Measurement

With any change process, be it learning, quality, re-engineering, etc., the questions will always come back to: how do we know how we are doing and how do we know when we have got there?

Within the strategy measurement process there are primarily two things to consider and two methodologies that can be applied. There is the extent to which measurement is qualitative or quantitative. The second concern is where the measurement is on the process being used to effect the change, or on the actual outcome of the change process. In pulling these two dimensions together, the matrix in Fig. 17.6 can be constructed.

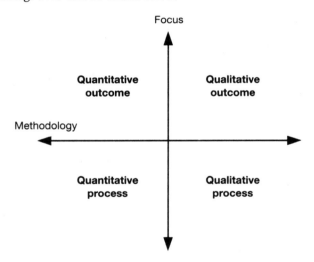

Fig. 17.6 Measurement matrix

From this, four types of measurement might be developed to track the progress.

Quantitative outcomes

Against this, it would be practical to set many of the factors that may have contributed to the approval for investment in the strategic change process. For example, the number of people undertaking external training programmes, cost of internal workshops, increase in intellectual capital, etc. However, this is a really dangerous measure, and one that can be abused. The use of quantitative measures can drive a mindset where people try to achieve the measures, rather than trying to change the culture. It can also create a false sense of end goals, such as 'well we meet the 75 per cent criteria so we can back off now'. Finally, any manager with a degree of common sense can meet the targets, either by prudent modification of the internal states, or the gentle shifting of resources. At the end of the day, measurement of quantitative outcomes can result in the escalation of shadow behaviours, and this can be counter-intuitive to the goal that the organisation is attempting to achieve.

Quantitative process

This would include many of the standard project management measures that are commonly used: milestones, completed tasks, cost overrun, etc. As a tangible measure, it is very effective for keeping the minds focused on the process of change, and ensuring that resources are carefully managed. This is fine if the organisation is installing a new computer system or building a new extension, but people are not plant or equipment. The whole idea espoused in the Integrated Learning Model, is that people are unpredictable, hence social change is uncertain. The idea of hard measures for the process is entirely correct, but there has to be a degree of care. If the measures become more important than the desired outcome, they tend to take the focus away from the end goal and act as an attenuator that restricts the change and learning process. Although the old adage is that 'what gets measured gets done', often the reality is that 'what gets measured gets bluffed'.

Qualitative process

This approach will be concerned with understanding how people feel about the change process that is taking place. It is driven by the style of measurement that is based upon understanding how people perceive the change at an intuitive and emotional level. The difficulty is that there is nothing that the accountant can really get a handle on to produce a cost benefit chart, and little for the whole business to get a hold of to get a feel for the change. The only way that people can really get a feel for progress is by becoming a part of the change itself. In doing this they will also derive an intuitive appreciation of the progress made and where the change is heading. Although this style aligns closely with some of the underlying ideas associated with the principle of self-organisation, it has many danger points. The key point is that companies are not run for pleasure – they are run to maximise the profitability of the shareholders' investment. If these people cannot be satisfied that the investment is worthwhile, there is always a chance that any resources allocated to the change process will be withdrawn.

247

Qualitative outcomes

This section is virtually the same as the qualitative process, except that it is concerned with the change in daily life as perceived by people in the business. These measures might be drawn from interviews with people after they have been through some experiential parts of the change initiative, and will help to understand how the deeper issues around the culture are transformed. One approach might be to map people's perception of the changes in the cultural artefacts within the business, and the extent to which a learning culture can be perceived as becoming the norm.

The measurement process is a minefield and is fraught with danger. However, one thing that should always be understood is that measurements exist to gauge progress, not to drive the change process. The push should come from people's desire to make the change, and the pull should be driven by an agreed outcome, not the numbers on a spreadsheet or project plan.

Conclusions

Strategy, as considered in relation to developing a learning style, is concerned with developing an action-based framework that can help to deliver the outcomes and behaviours that the organisation desires. In achieving this, the strategy component considers the following:

- In committing to encouraging a learning ethos, a private or public declaration can stimulate support and encouragement.
- Diagnostics are concerned with raising people's awareness of the organisational system and the environment in which it exists.
- Designing a process to facilitate knowledge creation is about fashioning a framework for action, not specifying the actions that will take place.
- Dialogue is about trying to go behind the superficial level of conversation, and to unearth what people really mean.
- Deployment is about developing a pragmatic action strategy that will encourage a learning ethos.

The ILM strategy process offers a number of points that can help the organisation to create a degree of structure around its learning initiatives. It is not offered in any way as a paradigm for success. Organisations should determine their own recipe for prosperity, and cannot just adopt a strategy template that someone else has developed.

Strategy model dynamics

	How do we learn?	How do we share?	How do we use?	How can we improve?
Declare Individuals, teams or organisations have the freedom to affirm their intent to increase their focus on improving the capability to learn				
Behaviour A declared change in intent is matched by a change in behaviour				
Voluntary People are allowed to adapt and respond in a voluntary structure				
Principle Change processes focus on the underlying principle and not on the practices used to achieve them				

Strategy model dynamics continued

	How do we learn?	How do we share?	How do we use?	How can we improve?
No delegation The idea and principle of self-enacted learning is not mandated or handed over for someone else to achieve				
Diagnose Diagnosis is seen as a constant state rather than a one-off event				
Open system The world in not seen in terms of black or white but as a series of incremental variations				
Attractors The various states of attraction that a system can be pulled between are understood				

	How do we learn?	How do we share?	How do we use?	How can we improve?
Shadows The diagnostic process considers the shadow as well as the open side of the organisation				
Intrinsic inquiry People are able to talk about change as they perceive it rather than offering a normative view				
Dialogue Individuals are encouraged to expose their beliefs, thoughts and ideas to consider previously unexplored issues and ideas				
Invitation People are invited to be involved in the dialogue process and not mandated				

Strategy model dynamics continued

	How do we learn?	How do we share?	How do we use?	How can we improve?
Suspension People are invited to put aside their judgements and schematic biases in order to understand each other				
Dialectic People try to recognise that all arguments have two sides, and use the power of this difference to create a third way forward				
Creativity People are encouraged to take risks and experiment by saying different things in different ways				

	How do we learn?	How do we share?	How do we use?	How can we improve?
Design Design uses an open but bounded framework, rather than a detailed blueprint for action				
Non-linear The use of adaptive and emergent viewpoints are encouraged				
Context Change builds on the inner strengths of the organisation, and does not try to import too many alien ideas or projects				
Participation The organisation ensures that opportunities exist for people to take part in many learning activities				

253

Strategy model dynamics continued

	How do we learn?	How do we share?	How do we use?	How can we improve?
Artifacts The focus is on deep and relevant artifacts rather than short-term superficial items				
Deployment The organisation understands what action can be taken that will actually help people to make the shift to a knowledge and learning based culture				
Outcome Change and goals are focused on building a positive affirmation about the future rather than a naïve belief				

	How do we learn?	How do we share?	How do we use?	How can we improve?
Flow People are encouraged to use the experience of change to understand how the learning process works				
Feedback Slight deviations from the expected do not result in major interventions				
Measurement Motivation is driven by inspiration and desire, not by the numbers on a spreadsheet or project plan				

Chapter 18

··

Theory into action:
possibility space

In the preface to this book, a relatively confident (some might say audacious) statement is made regarding the idea of creating the possibility searching company – one where people with rich and diversified individual knowledge bases can create new wisdom. If the Integrated Learning Model is to help facilitate such a change, two final aspects might be considered that can help the transformation:

- The role that technology plays in gearing up the organisation's flow of knowledge.
- How the business can identify the unique learning possibilities that exist within the organisation.

It is in these two areas that so many organisations seem to have difficulty in corporate transformation. First of all the almost blind devotion to the false god of technology can so often result in companies spending large chunks of their capital budget without seeing any significant change in the learning or knowledge management processes. An Internet link for all schools might open the door of learning, but it doesn't mean that children will walk through. The delicate balance between opportunity and motivation needs to be clearly understood if technology is to help organisations to move into the new and uncharted waters of its own possibility space.

Second, the way that businesses seem to repeatedly fall into the trap of trying to 'install' change processes that are alien to the culture is a trend that needs to be reversed. Companies need to understand that the key to their future lies in the untapped and latent potential that exists in their unseen possibility space and not in publications by new and audacious authors. At best, books, consultants and academics should energise and educate businesses on the change process; at worst they should implement and instruct them. The ILM framework attempts to overcome this by offering a simple process by which people and organisations can start to look at their own regions of possibility, rather than slavishly following the component model outlined during the book.

Yet again, the notion in this chapter is not to provide 'the answer'; the goal is to indicate that these two areas might need to be included in the change dialogue.

In allowing people to discuss such issues, so the undiscussable becomes discussable, and there is less chance that phantoms from the shadow world will step in to corrupt or defeat the idea of organisational change.

Technology gear

Realistically, with organisations stretching across global sites, time boundaries and cultures, helping individual leaning to migrate to an organisational setting might only be facilitated through the positive application of technology. This is effectively the linking gear that can pull the various elements into a coupled whole as seen in Fig. 18.1.

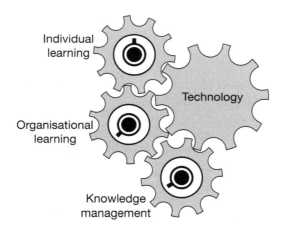

Fig. 18.1 Technology as a linking gear

As stated at the outset, this book does not aspire to focus on the technology aspects of learning and knowledge management, simply because that will take another book in its own right. However, it may benefit the reader to see how the Integrated Learning Model can be useful tool in helping to understand the implications that technology might have on the desire to enhance the learning processes. To do this each of the ten components in the Integrated Learning Model have been funnelled through the technology sieve.

Soloist component and technology

Often, two core issues drive people's ability to take on a soloist role within an organisation. First is the balance of power. Does the organisation control or dictate how individuals behave, or do people have the necessary freedom to deal with issues as they feel appropriate? Second, is the notion of connectivity: to what extent do people have the opportunity to increase their span of interconnection? The introduction of network technology has the possibility to erode both these issues from the landscape because cyberspace transcends locality – it involves nothing less than the instantaneous and unbounded sharing of data (Rees-Mogg and Davidson, 1997, 178). This freedom offers people the opportunity to work privately on many of the traits outlined in the soloist chapter – using the network to enlarge their learning circle, build powerful allies and use its connectivity to ease the change process.

However, change that diminishes the power of the monarchs or senior managers can be unsettling, and this covert shift in authority may well cause a kickback against the freedom of the individual. It might be that over time the corporation's ethos will reassert itself to subtly gain greater control over the scope the individual has to use interaction across the networks.

Super leadership and technology

The leader needs to appreciate how the increased use of networks will affect relations between people. Historically, the leader could to a great extent control how people collaborated and interacted with each other; now, collaboration is no longer limited by the social rules and arbitrary boundaries that the leader defines. Software and networks have established a new set of rules such that traditional constraints are eliminated. Through the network people operating independently can co-operate with more people, more remotely, and in more asynchronously ways than ever before (Quinn *et al.*, 1997).

However, to what extent can confidence be developed over a technological link? Can the five attributes of trust (truthful, responsive, uniform, safe and trained) really be cultivated via a relatively cold medium? For example, as the growth in organisational intranets increases, so the potential for rich and varied data becomes possible. However, to what extent will someone believe information when they do not have personal contact with the originator? What guarantee is there that the data is timely, rigorous and complete?

Schema and technology

One of the key themes behind the schema component is the need to encourage people to both share their schematic models and also understand other people's frame of reference. Technology plays a significant part in this process by allowing conflict-free opportunities to present ideas and innovations to the world. The Lotus Notes and intranet platforms offer a great way to instigate discussion groups, publishing forums and virtual coffee rooms, all processes by which schemata can be opened and shared. One particular process by which schemata can be expanded is the application of hypertext links: the powerful way that intranet documents can have embedded pointers to other sources of information. This creates a tool that introduces a semi-random element into the scanning process, such that people are introduced to new and different areas of knowledge that they might not have considered before.

However, knowledge is intrinsically linked with power, so people might perceive that giving information away on a discussion group is tantamount to giving away authority and prestige. If this way of thinking is dominant within the culture, then little schema modification or learning will take place – whatever new systems are installed.

Surprises and technology

Technology can play a significant role in organisational innovation, including research models, needs analysis, prototyping, product design, virtual skunk works and remote collaboration (Quinn *et al.*, 1997). In all areas of the surprise component (intuition, experience, scanning, serendipity and relations), one of the core aspects is the need to offer people increased access to other people and events. Clearly, technology helps to achieve this by overcoming the boundaries of time and space.

One of the key ways that technology is now changing the surprise process is through the use of search tools on the Internet. These offer a powerful way in which to scan knowledge repositories from across the world, picking up new ideas and information almost seconds after the innovator might have placed them on the Web or intranet.

However, organisations should be aware of the reliance that can be built into the design of the software. Search engines will hunt according to algorithms set by the programmers, and so will have a significant impact on the type of data that is returned, and may limit or redirect a search process.

Shadows and technology

The basic premise behind the idea of the shadow organisation is the difference between the espoused and in-use behaviours. Some might suggest that technology will increase the level of connectivity and the flow of knowledge with a resulting reduction in shadow activities. However, it might be that the company wishes to use the new technology to increase the levels of regulation, enlarge the number of processes and import a range of new measures, thus potentially causing people to respond in an underhand way to the increased levels of control.

Increasing the opportunity for connectivity might reduce the negative factors associated with the shadow side, but only if the intent behind the technology comes from the open side and is not driven by shadow issues.

Self organisation and technology

The nature of self-organisation might be seen as the apparent disorder and randomness that exists within organisations. Interestingly, consider the Internet and how it can look to an outsider, it has all the makings of order emerging from randomness, with individual freedom to add or manipulate content at will, while offering a powerful tool for knowledge creation and exchange.

For an organisation, the use of an intranet can offer the similar experience of an interconnecting network that allows people to add and delete knowledge at will, so infusing the business with an innovative energy. The flexible approach means that fluid knowledge has greater chance to be shared across the network. However, it is in the construction and maintenance of intranets that problems can occur. The tension that exists between the mechanistic and complex aspects of the business can be seen in people's desire to control, structure and moderate the intranet. Organisations can balk at the apparent freedom and openness that the intranet offers, and might want to put a degree of discipline into use by limiting what people can say and how they say it. It is this limitation that can result in the effectiveness of the network being reduced, in the same way that regulation and mechanistic control of the Internet could eventually see it turn into one large interconnecting set of intranets, with the freedom of the individual to become involved being limited or cut out entirely.

Socialisation and technology

Socialisation is about the social interaction between groups of people. It promotes a richness of connectivity that enhances the nuances and human traits that occur with face-to-face contact. Knowledge emerges from the rich, subtle and unspoken interactions that take place between people. So to what extent can technology support this type of behaviour? Clearly desktop video conferencing, multimedia, and all the rich technologies are helping this to occur, but can they actually replace the face-to-face meeting?

The proposition is that once people have met socially for the first time, then subsequent interactions can be held using the technology links. Interestingly, research indicates that commitments and promises are honoured more when the relationship is made using face-to-face technology (video, etc.) rather than on the phone or mail systems (Davenport and Prusak, 1998, 22).

Structure and technology

The knowledge infrastructure exists to transport wisdom from its point of origination to the most relevant area within the business. This might be from discovery to embodiment, from storage to embodiment, or from embodiment to disposal. The question is, what can technology offer to ease this process?

One of the ways it might help is in the construction of company knowledge maps. These are software systems that can refer to storage points in the organisation, highlighting where knowledge is stored or emerging. This might be by pointing where certain files or documents are stored, or the development of capability management systems that hold knowledge about people's competencies.

While this is clearly a valuable tool, as with any data management system, there is always an overhead, be it system costs or administrative resources. As the use of the map grows, so it behoves the company to allocate more time on its maintenance to ensure that it is current since the only thing worse than no map, is one that offers obsolete data.

Sharing and technology

One area where technology helps the process of sharing is with the dispersion of knowledge across the business. Whereas the traditional diffusion process depends on mail or meetings, the networking explosion has cleared away many of the conventional barriers to the transmission of knowledge. If people have the will to share knowledge, there are numerous tools that can help the process, such as the Internet, intranet, Lotus Notes, video conferencing, etc. There is little practical reason now why virtual team cannot operate on a global scale, pulling together diverse mixes of international, inter-function and inter-skilled teams. However, as mentioned before, this may offer the means, but is does not create the desire!

Strategy and technology

The core proposition within the strategy component is built around the idea of people and their freedom to interact in an open and fertile way. The elements of declare, diagnose, design, dialogue and deploy are based upon a paradigm that considers transformation as an ever-changing set of patterns, not just a bank of pre-determined tasks and milestones.

As such, any role that technology plays in this will emerge as the strategy itself emerges, and hence it is difficult to predict what role it might take. However, one key area where it can play a part is in opening up channels of communication. The root element in this component is the idea of dialogue – people talking and sharing ideas and thoughts that are not constrained by personal assumptions and bias. To achieve this, people do not have to be in the same room, building or country. Open discussion can take place between people on separate continents, and the network is the tool that makes this possible.

Technology is only a pipeline and storage system for knowledge exchange. It does not create knowledge and cannot guarantee knowledge generation in a culture that does not favour those activities (Davenport and Prusak, 1998, 18). Investment in a new intranet does not mean that people will share more, desktop videos cannot guarantee that socialisation improves, and IT-based training systems will not secure enhanced learning. They might offer the capability for these changes, but they do not create the will or desire.

Possibility space

If there is sufficient interest in the concepts outlined in the Integrated Learning Model, the question is, what practical action can be taken? One answer might be to replicate the approach used at the end of each chapter: to ask 'how do we learn', 'how do we share', 'how do we use the knowledge' and finally, 'can we build on these existing processes?'.

However, in going through this approach, the possibility is that organisations might take each of the component parts of the model and consider them in turn against their organisation's existing operating methods. In doing this, there is a danger that a model which advocates a non-linear and unconfined approach to learning is actually being used in an unbending way that becomes self-limiting. The design of the Integrated Learning Model is such that this problem can be simply avoided. Clearly a theme running through the book has been the metaphor that compares individuals and learning to the idea of musicians and a band. In this respect, consider what differentiates one band from another. It is this intangible ether, the space between the musicians, the notes they play, and the way they feel that give every piece of music its unique sense of individuality. In the same way, it is the possibility space between the components in the Integrated Learning Model that allows it the freedom to be unique for a specific organisation.

Possibility space is the place where new and original ideas come to the fore – a metaphor that describes the areas that people can go to, but normally prefer to avoid (Battram, 1996, 104). Often when exploring new ways of working or thinking, arbitrary self-imposed constraints exist that prevent people and organisations from tackling normal problems in new and innovative ways. There can be a tendency to stick with the knitting, play safe and stay inside the comfort zone. Even worse might be the desire to keep other people in their comfort zone as well, as in the 'possum box' (Fig. 18.2). In the possum quadrant, people will be happy to copy ideas, will not take risks and will effectively follow a cloning strategy.

Even when stepping outside the possum box, there might be a tendency to stay in control and push other people into areas where they are less comfortable, to effectively possess them. Alternatively, people allow themselves to be pushed into areas of discomfort while their colleagues might stay safely in their comfort area, thus making the individual feel possessed.

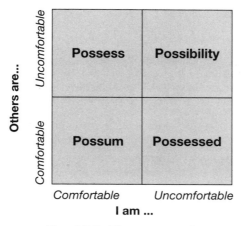

Fig. 18.2 The possum box

However, when all individuals in a group can be encouraged to step outside their comfort zone, and into an area where they are less than comfortable, then possibilities can open up for new ideas and ways of working. In discarding the real and imaginary constraints and barriers, the learning processes can be examined in ways that were hitherto considered too difficult or risky. The aim is to adopt an approach that ignores the linear, closed and structured style of investigation, and move to an open-ended, and spontaneous way of thinking.

In using this ethos, the ILM framework has been constructed in such a way as to leave space between each of the component areas – effectively creating open spaces where new possibilities can be unearthed. This might help people to consider the model not as a normalised framework that might be 'implemented', but rather as a tool that the organisation can use to enhance its understanding about existing learning styles.

So as in Fig. 18.3, each of the component areas can be seen to interact with the other areas across the possibility space, and in doing this demonstrates the holistic view that needs to be taken with learning and knowledge management.

In Fig. 18.4, Super Sponge Ltd is using the ILM to try to understand the effectiveness of current learning and knowledge management systems. As it positions itself in the possibility space, so it can use a process of synthesis to build a unique map of its own learning processes. So for example, by sitting in the possibility space between soloist, super-leader and shadows, the organisation can create a set of questions that relate to these three areas. In doing this, the organisation will arrive at questions that are different and unique from those that any other might arrive at.

So, 'Super Sponge' would first of all develop its interpretation of the dynamics that are appropriate for the three areas of soloist, super-leader and shadows, as in Table 18.1.

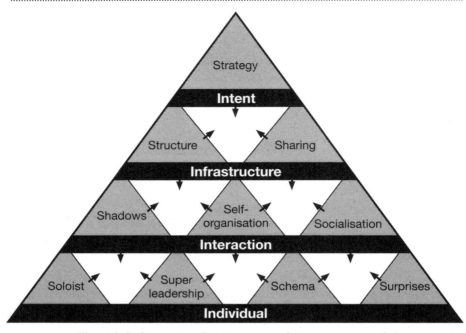

Fig. 18.3 Space in the Integrated Learning Model

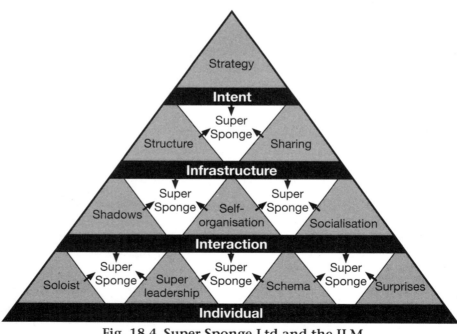

Fig. 18.4 Super Sponge Ltd and the ILM

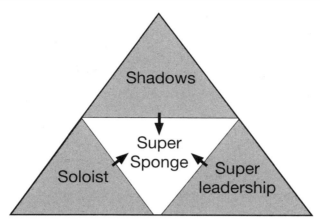

Fig. 18.5 Unique questions for a company

Table 18.1 Interpreting the dynamics

Soloist	Super leadership	Shadows
1. Compelling future	1. **Trust**	1. Open and shadow individual
2. Change mastery	2. Trustworthy	2. **Open and shadow organisation**
3. U-loop	3. **Thin and thick trust**	3. Shadow bar
4. Change agent	4. **Trust index**	4. Shadow models (A–F)
5. **Generative learning**	5. Knowledge flow	5. Johari window
6. **Challenging ethos**	6. Relationships	6. Espoused against theories in use
7. Continual learning	7. Neuro-logical model	7. **Defensive routines**
8. Contract alignment	8. Value mapping	8. Positics
9. Caring	9. Value matching	9. Terrain mapping

Once the dynamics for each area have been defined, the organisation can go through a synthesis process, whereby questions are assembled using material from two or more of the three areas. For example, it might develop a set of questions along the lines of:

- If the idea of generative learning is applicable for our company, to what extent do people trust the management team to operate in the open rather than shadow area?
- To what extent does the development of a challenging ethos depend on people's need to operate in thick trust relationships?
- If the business decides to use the trust index, how can it be sure that the defensive routines won't come into play?

PART 5 · INTENT

• If the business wants to stimulate the creation of a challenging ethos, how can it be sure that people are not doing it from a shadow perspective?

None of these questions will offer 'the answer', or help to direct the organisation towards the holy grail. However, they will help to start the process of reflective diagnosis, so helping people to understand first of all what learning is about, and then starting the journey to focus into the possibility space.

This use of the possibility space with any of the ten components within the model offers a powerful way to generate new ways of thinking about the learning style within an organisation. The combination of the sub-elements produces more combinations and questions than a formal diagnostic process could ever wish for, in many ways bypassing much of the work that a consultancy might undertake. All an organisation needs is to take a random selection of components, and build up a series of diagnostic maps. By using each of the maps in Fig. 18.6, a host of variable and complex diagnostic questions can be developed that will help any organisation to understand its own learning and knowledge management processes.

In summary, for an organisation to enhance and develop its capability to learn and leverage the resulting knowledge, it must first look inside at its own deep culture and systems to discuss the un-discussable. Then it needs to make real many of the customs and practices that are forgotten or conveniently overlooked every day. By using the idea of possibility space with the ILM, the intention is that organisations can unearth these hidden practices, and start to think in new ways. By this method, the organisation can enhance its learning capability. In doing this, it can shift towards the notion of becoming a 'possibility searching company' – one where individuals are able to continually learn and create knowledge that can respond to and shape the market (Nonaka and Takeuchi, 1995, 115).

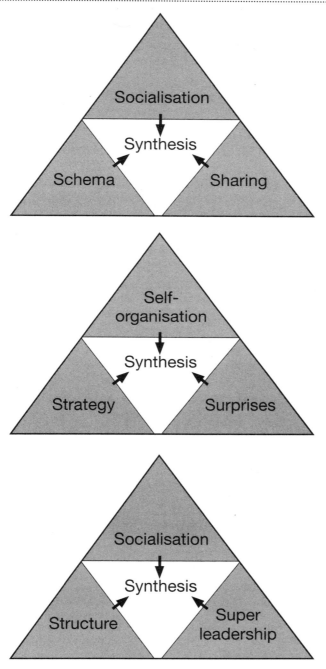

Fig. 18.6 Diagnostic maps

Epilogue

In reflecting on the book, and in particular the summary components set out at the back of each chapter, there is a sudden anxiety that the sheer number of elements will conspire against the original goal, and result in offering a model that is perceived to be deterministic, predictive and normative.

If anyone is in doubt, let me reiterate the core proposition – learning is something that is natural, personal and difficult. No model offered by a remote and alien author can ever hope to provide a simple solution that an organisation can install overnight. In the same way that it took me years to learn to play the guitar, pass my exams, or understand how to spell phenomiological, organisations that aspire to enhance their learning and knowledge systems must be in it for the long haul.

My hope is that this book will help people to clarify what organisational learning and knowledge management means for them and their business. If this can be achieved, then it has all been worthwhile, if not, then thank you for taking the time to stick with it until the end.

References

Preface

Covey, S. (1992) *The Seven Habits of Highly Effective People*. London: Simon & Schuster.
Davenport, H. and Prusak, L. (1998) *Working Knowledge*. Cambridge, Massachusetts: Harvard Business School Press.
Nonaka, I. and Takeuchi, T. (1995) *The Knowledge Creating Company*, New York: Oxford University Press.
Rees-Mogg, W. and Davidson, J. (1997) *The Sovereign Individual*. London: Macmillan.

Chapter 1

Percival, E. (1997) Workshop discussion on Stephen Covey 'seven habits' programme.

Chapter 2

Davenport, H. and Prusak, L. (1998) *Working Knowledge*. Cambridge, Massachusetts: Harvard Business School Press.
Stewart, T. (1997) *Intellectual Capital*. London: Nicholas Brealey.

Chapter 3

Nonaka, I. and Takeuchi, T. (1995) *The Knowledge Creating Company*. New York: Oxford University Press.

Chapter 4

Ghoshal, S. and Bartlett, C. (1998) *The Individualised Corporation*. London: Heinemann.
Senge, P. (1990) *The Fifth Discipline*. London: Century Business.

Chapter 5

Argyris, C. and Schon, D. (1996) *Organisational Learning II*. USA: Addison Wesley.
Buchanan, D. and Body, D. (1992) *The Expertise of the Change Agent*. London: Prentice Hall.
Carnall, C. (1995) *Managing Change for Organisations*. 2nd edn. London: Prentice Hall.
Covey, S. (1992) *The Seven Habits of Highly Effective People*. London: Simon and Schuster.
Ghoshal, S. and Bartlett, C. (1998) *The Individualised Corporation*. London: Heinemann.
Gioia, D. (1995) 'Contrasts and convergencies in creativity' in Ford, C. and Gioia, D. (eds) *Creative Action in Organisations*. USA: Sage.
James, T. and Woodsmall, W. (1988) *Time Line Therapy and the Basis of Personality*. USA: Meta.
Kanter, R. (1984) *The Change Masters*. London: Unwin.
Schein, E. (1994) MIT Internet paper Http://learning.mit.edu/res/wp/10002.html
Senge, P. (1990) *The Fifth Discipline*. London: Century Business.

Chapter 6

Argyris, C. (1990) *Overcoming Organisational Defences*. USA: Allyn and Bacon.
Covey, S. (1992) *The Seven Habits of Highly Effective People*. London: Simon and Schuster.
Dilts, R. (1994) *Effective Presentation Skills*. USA: Meta.
Espejo, R., Schumann, W., Schwaninger, M. and Bilello, U. (1996) *Organisational Transformation and Learning*. New York: Wiley.
Ghoshal, S. and Bartlett, C. (1998) *The Individualised Corporation*. London: Heinemann.
Jacques, E. and Clement, S. (1991) *Executive Leadership*. USA: Blackwell Business.
Meyerson, D., Weick, K. and Kramer, R. (1996) 'Trust and temporary groups' in Kramer, R. and Tyler, T. (eds) *Trust in Organisations*. USA: Sage.
Peran, M., Roderick, C., Mulroney, C. (1995) *Learning Organisation in Practice*. Maidenhead: McGraw-Hill.
Senge, P. (1990) *The Fifth Discipline*. London: Century Business.
Senge, P. (1996) 'The Leaders: New Work' in Starkey, K. *How Organisations Learn*. London: International Thomson Business Press.
Senge, P., Kleiner, A., Roberts, C., Ross, R. and Smith, B. (1994) *The Fifth Discipline Fieldbook*. London: Nicholas Brealey.
Shapiro, E. (1996) *Fad Surfing in the Board Room*. UK: Capstone.
Sims, H. and Lorenzi, P. (1992) The New Leadership Paradigm. USA: Sage.
Tushman, M. and Nadler, D. (1996) 'Organising for innovation' in Starkey, K. *How Organisations Learn*. London: International Thomson Business Press.

Chapter 7

Bolman, L. and Deal, T. (1991) *Reframing Organisations*. San Francisco: Jossey Bass.
Bransford, J. and Johnson, M. (1972) 'Contextual prerequisites for understanding: Some investigations of comprehension and recall', *Journal of Verbal Learning and Verbal Behaviour*, 11, 717–726.
Harris, S. (1994) 'Organisation culture and individual sense making', *Organisation Science*, 5 (3).
Kuhn, T. (1970) *The Structure of Scientific Revolutions*. Chicago: University of Chicago Press.

Chapter 8

de Bono, E. (1967) *The Use of Lateral Thinking*. Harmondsworth: Penguin.
Cooper, K. and Sawaf, A. (1997) *Executive EQ*. USA: Orion Business Books.
Nonaka, I. and Takeuchi, T. (1995) *The Knowledge Creating Company*. New York: Oxford University Press.
Senge, P. (1990) *The Fifth Discipline*. London: Century Business.
Shapiro, E. (1996) *Fad Surfing in the Board Room*. UK: Capstone.

Chapter 10

Argyris, C. (1996) 'Skilled incompetence' in Starkey, K. *How Organisations Learn*. London: International Thomson Business Press.
Argyris, C. (1992) *On Organisational Learning*. UK: Blackwell Business.
Argyris, C. and Schon, D. (1996) *Organisational Learning II*. USA: Addison Wesley.
Egan, G. (1994) *Working the Shadow Side*. San Francisco: Jossey Bass.
Litwin, G., Bray, J. and Brooke, K. (1996) *Mobilising the Organisation: Bringing strategy*

to life. London: Prentice Hall.
Luft, J. and Ingham, H. (1955) *The Johari Window: a graphic model for interpersonal relations*. California: University of California, Western Training Laboratory.

Chapter 11

Capra, F. (1997) *The Web of Life*. London: HarperCollins.
Goldstein, J. (1994) *The Unshackled Organisation*. Portland, Oregon: Productivity Press.
Kauffman, S. (1995) *Order for Free*. London: Penguin.
Mintzberg, H. (1994) *The Rise and Fall of Strategic Planning*. London: Prentice Hall.
Stacey, R. (1992) *Managing Chaos*. London: Kogan Page.
Wheatley, M. (1994) *Leadership and the New Science*. USA: Berrett-Koehler.

Chapter 12

Fairhurst, G. and Starr, R. (1996) *The Art of Framing*. San Franciso: Jossey Bass.
Goodwin, C. (1998) 'Is he a man or mouse?', *The Sunday Times*, 10 May.
Honderich, T. (1995) *The Oxford Introduction to Philosophy*. New York: Oxford University Press.
Janis, I. and Mann, L. (1985) *Decision Making: a psychological analysis of conflict, choice and commitment*. New York: Free Press.
Morgan, G. (1986) *Images of Organisations*. London: Sage.
Schein, E. (1998) *Organisational Psychology*. USA: Prentice Hall.
Simon, H. (1960) *The New Science of Management Decision*. New York: Harper.
Stewart, I. and Jones, V. (1987) *TA Today*. UK: Lifespace.

Chapter 13

Karash, R. (1995) *Groupware and Organizational Learning*,
http://world.std.com/~rkarash/GW-OL/

Chapter 14

Burns, P. (1998) Conversation at BT.
Levitt, B. and March, G. (1996) 'Organisational Learning', in Cohen, M. and Sproull, L. *Organisational Learning*. USA: Sage.
Nonaka, I. and Takeuchi, T. (1995) *The Knowledge Creating Company*. New York: Oxford University Press.
Stewart, T. (1998) *Intellectual Capital*. London: Nicholas Brealey.

Chapter 15

Rogers, E. (1995) *Diffusion of Innovations*. 4th edn. New York: Free Press.

Chapter 17

Bohm, D. (1995) *Dialogue: a proposal*. http://world.std.com/~lo/bohm/0001.html
Lincoln, Y. and Guba, E. (1985) *Naturalistic Inquiry*. New York: Sage.
Schein, E. (1992) *Organisational Culture and Leadership*. New York: Jossey Bass.
Stewart, T. (1997) *Intellectual Capital*. London: Nicholas Brealey.

Chapter 18

Battram, A. (1996) *Navigating Complexity*. London: The Industrial Society.

Davenport, H. and Prusak, L. (1998) *Working Knowledge*. Cambridge, Massachusetts: Harvard Business School Press.

Nonaka, I. and Takeuchi, T. (1995) *The Knowledge Creating Company*. New York: Oxford University Press.

Quinn, J., Baruch, J. and Zien, K. (1997) *Innovation Explosion*. New York: Free Press.

Rees-Mogg, W. and Davidson, J. (1997) *The Sovereign Individual*. London: Macmillan.

Index

contract violation 35–6
new open contracts 34–5
and value 146
control 31, 136
Cooper, K. 88, 89
Covey, S. xi, 8, 22, 46
creative failures 31–2
creativity 31, 85, 242
see also surprises
curiosity 89

data 185
Davenport, H. xvi, 8, 260, 262
Davidson, J. 258
Dawkins, Richard 172
Deal, T. 80
decision making 137, 162–5
defensive routines 24, 121–3
deflected schema interaction 76
delayed sharing 210
delivery of knowledge 95–6, 193
delta factors 97–8
denial of change 23
deployment
    feedback 245–6
    measurement matrix 246–8
    and outcomes 244
design 238–41
    artefacts 241
    context 239–40
    non-linear 238–9
    participation 240
diagnostic model of shadow
        behaviour 110–11
diagnostic stages 233–8
    attractors 235–6
    intrinsic inquiry 237–8
    open systems 234–5
    shadows 237
dialogue 241–3
    creativity 242
    dialectic approach 243

invitations 242
suspension of beliefs 242
diaries 132–3
diffusion process 80, 94, 96–7,
    197–9, 205–9
Dilts neuro-logical model 54–6
discarding change 24
discovery of knowledge 95, 188–90,
    191–2
disposal of knowledge 196–7
double loop learning 27–30
Drudge, Matt 172

e-mail 212–13
Egan 108, 121, 126
electronic messaging systems 212–13
embarrassment 123
embodiment of knowledge 193–4
emergence in social systems 143, 148
empowerment 33
entrepreneurial hostages 37
Espejo, R. 56
espoused behaviours 117
experience 90, 170
experimentation 31
explicit knowledge 190
extrinsic inert schemata displacement
    73
extrinsic organic schemata
        displacement 73
extrinsic realisation schemata
        displacement 74
extrinsic regulation 140
extrinsic revelation schemata
        displacement 74

facades 114
factual decision-making 164
failures 31–2
Fairhurst, G. 168
feedback systems 136, 245–6
feelings 137–8

276